THE ABUSES OF PUNISHMENT

Forsyth Library
Fort Hays State University

Also by Robert Adams

PRISON RIOTS IN BRITAIN AND THE USA

PROBLEM-SOLVING WITH SELF-HELP GROUPS (*co-author*)

PROTESTS BY PUPILS: Empowerment, Schooling and the State

QUALITY SOCIAL WORK

SELF-HELP, SOCIAL WORK AND EMPOWERMENT

SKILLED WORK WITH PEOPLE

SOCIAL WORK AND EMPOWERMENT

THE PERSONAL SOCIAL SERVICES: Clients, Consumers or Citizens?

The Abuses of Punishment

Robert Adams
Professor of Human Services Development
University of Lincolnshire and Humberside

Consultant Editor: Jo Campling

St. Martin's Press
New York

THE ABUSES OF PUNISHMENT
Copyright © 1998 by Robert Adams
All rights reserved. No part of this book may be used or reproduced
in any manner whatsoever without written permission except in the
case of brief quotations embodied in critical articles or reviews.
For information, address:

St. Martin's Press, Scholarly and Reference Division,
175 Fifth Avenue, New York, N.Y. 10010

First published in the United States of America in 1998

This book is printed on paper suitable for recycling and
made from fully managed and sustained forest sources.

Printed in Hong Kong

ISBN 0–312–17614–7 cloth
ISBN 0–312–17617–1 paperback

Library of Congress Cataloging-in-Publication Data
Adams, Robert, 1944–
The abuses of punishment / Robert Adams ; consulting editor, Jo
Campling.
p.   cm.
Includes bibliographical references (p.   ) and index.
ISBN 0–312–17614–7 (cloth). — ISBN 0–312–17617–1 (pbk.)
1. Punishment.   2. Offenses against the person.   3. Criminal
justice, Administration of.   I. Title.
HV8665.A33 1997
364.6—dc21   97–13512
                                                              CIP

To Charlotte, Kirsty, Jade and George

> I have heard the key
> Turn in the door once and turn once only
> We think of the key, each in his prison
> Thinking of the key, each confirms a prison
>
> (T. S. Eliot, *The Waste Land*, ll. 412–15)

Contents

Acknowledgements

I should like to acknowledge the contribution made to this book by many people with whom I have worked and shared experiences, over the past quarter-century – school pupils, children and young people in local authority care, prisoners, trainees in young offender institutions, and students at Leeds, York and Hull. I should like to thank many colleagues for their help, particularly Stanley Cohen, Kelvin Jones and Philip Jenkins. I am grateful also to Peter Newell for sending me a quantity of material from STOPP. I must make it clear that, except as indicated in the text, none of the above-named should be associated with any statements, mistakes and omissions in this book, for which I alone am responsible.

Introduction

This book argues that punishment is a pervasive feature of society, not restricted to the criminal justice system, which is predominantly abusive in its applications. But academic discussion of punishment has tended to remain with penologists and to focus on criminal justice. This book takes as its focus the view expressed by Sylvester in 1977 (Sylvester, 1977, p. 9), that punishment and criminal justice need dislodging from the behavioural scientists and penal administrators who monopolise them.

The area of punishment needs to occupy the forefront of debates about the treatment of children, young people and adults, not only in criminal justice, but also in schooling, work, hospital, day care, residential care and domestic settings.

Some commentators focus on the moral aspects of punishment, others on the technical aspects of penological devices, others yet again on the urgency, to them, of developing sufficient punitive power to curb in-discipline, wherever they perceive it – in the home, the street, the school, the young offenders' institution, the prison. As this book is being written, in the autumn of 1996, the Government has announced its intention to introduce a Crime Bill which includes tougher sentences for offenders, and an Education Bill to strengthen disciplinary sanctions in schools.

The intention of this book is to undertake an examination of punishment which does not ignore these concerns, takes account of the political and social context of punishment, but which concentrates on the abuses of punishment. However, this is not to detach punishment from the histories of the key participants in its staging, or to neglect the power behind the punishers and the punitive systems and institutions. But it is to acknowledge the centrality of these different components of both acts of punishment and the structures which punish.

The book argues that the formal, criminal justice mechanisms for dispensing punishment are of a piece with informal mechanisms and processes. The prison, the whip, the execution chamber, are different manifestations of punitive features common to different aspects of any given society. Further, the more closely punishment is examined, the more its abuses – the use of spanking at home, corporal punishment in schools, physical restraint in the behavioural regime of the mental hospital or other treatment setting – come to the fore. That is, the abuses of punishment, rather than any intrinsic merits or disadvantages, are the main arguments

1

against it. For example, in certain circumstances punishment may have a deterrent function. The question is whether this can be guaranteed and appplied in particular circumstances with predictable effectiveness.

In addressing the *abuses* of punishment, this book visits the role of punishment in society, but its purpose is not to provide an exhaustive catalogue of all the *uses* of punishment. It is not a comprehensive analysis of perspectives on punishment; it would be inconceivable in any case to consider duplicating, let alone competing with, David Garland's outstanding, authoritative sociological study of theoretical perspectives on punishment: *Punishment and Modern Society* (1995). Garland's concern is with penality, penal institutions and with legal, formal punishments; the present book also deals with informal punishments including those which are not legally sanctioned. This book does not aim to provide a detailed history and contemporary analysis of the applications of punishment throughout the world. It does not claim to be a history, though in parts it draws on historical material. Neither does it claim to be comprehensive in its coverage of punishments throughout the world, in Western countries, or even in the UK. To the extent that Western countries – notably Britain and the USA – have felt the impact of events in other countries, it refers to them, though selectively. The purpose is to provide a critical review rather than an encyclopaedia of punishments past and present. However, this should not be taken as an implication that other places and happenings are less significant or engaging than those selected for comment. On the contrary, it simply reflects the fact that very often the influence of Britain has been experienced elsewhere in the world, rather than the reverse. Additionally, some aspects of punishment have been omitted, partly because of lack of space, and partly because further treatment of them within the space available will not contribute significantly to the argument.

The moral, political, social, economic, rational, emotional and judicial arguments for and against punishment are complex. This book focuses on areas of widespread abuse, in which ultimately the arguments against punishment prevail. It provides an exposition of the prominent features of punishment, as well as a critical commentary on perspectives from which its theories and practices, histories, character and effectiveness may be viewed, concepts of punishment, different approaches to histories of punishment, different forms of punishment including more detailed examination of the following: punishment by deprivation, punishment by restraint or constraint, corporal punishment and capital punishment. It appraises research and debates about the effectiveness of punishment and concludes with a prospective view of the future of punishment.

1 Concepts of Punishment

a change in our attitude toward every instance of punishment ... demands that we never view a punishment as something which is the obviously fitting, appropriate or deserved reaction to an offense: that we see it as, at best, a needed but nonetheless lamentable form of societal control.

(Wasserstrom, 1972, p. 341)

INTRODUCTION

This chapter aims to show how the predominance of penology in discussions of what constitutes punishment has militated against the wider consideration of other forms of punishment, outside criminal justice. To this end, it identifies the main forms of punishment; it examines the nature of punishment; it comments on the centrality of punishment, and the spread of new forms of punishment – such as punishment in the community – particularly in Western societies such as the UK and the USA; it acknowledges the need to challenge the dominance of physically and psychologically violent forms of punishment in keeping with the muscular and macho conceptualisations of crime and responses to crime which dominate criminology; it deconstructs the act of punishment and assesses the arguments for and against the use of punishment. Finally, it introduces the argument of the whole book, that whilst some punishments in theory may be justified, many are corrupted and employed abusively. Thus, while justifications may be found in principle for certain minor forms of punishment, they remain all too often flawed in practice.

WHAT IS PUNISHMENT?

The concept of punishment is as problematic as its uses and abuses are controversial. At the outset, it may be helpful to identify a theme which forms a substratum to this chapter and is a core argument of the book, but may not be obviously so at this early stage. The entire territory of punishment – its knowledge base, the disciplines informing penal codes and practices, the institutions of criminal justice and penal systems, as well as mechanisms for formal and informal punishments and the workforce implementing them – is imbued with a particular brand of *machismo*, often

3

violent, even brutal, which accords with the gender imbalances within many settings where punishments are carried out. Whilst punishment – notably, the informal physical sanctioning of children in the home – is not exclusively a male preserve, there is little doubt of the generality of the equation between punisher and *macho* masculine person; it is likely that, in societies where there are oppressing and oppressed groups, personnel responsible for punishment will be overly drawn from the former group and victims from the latter.

Punishment may be described simplistically as the infliction of pain on a person as a penalty for a violation, fault or offence. In reality, punishment cannot be defined in simple, unambiguous, unidimensional terms. It is not, as is sometimes implied, an aspect of the social contract between punisher and punished, in whatever setting – prison, school, household. In some senses, the involuntariness of the person punished may be underestimated. As Grace notes of the analysis of patterns of slavery in Africa, it is wrong to regard the person made slave as more or less cooperating in some kind of process with the agents of society, to eventual mutual benefit (Grace, 1975, p. 3). By analogy, when the boy being caned is told 'it's for your own good', this is fundamentally to bolster the position of the punisher rather than the punished.

The scope of the definition of punishment used in this book extends also to the authorities and providers of residential, day and community services and members of society at large. Although there may be consensus that certain core penological activities such as capital punishment constitute punishments, it is more difficult to specify the boundaries between punishment and neighbouring concepts such as social control. Social control may be viewed as the more global concept and punishment one – penological – aspect of it. There is no finality about such distinctions, but without any prospect of it being a final statement, it is acknowledged at the outset that while this book is about *more* than penality alone (à la Garland, 1995), it concerns far *less* than social control (à la Cohen, 1985). Further, it may be difficult to specify the relationship between punishment and therapy in such areas as behavioural work (see Chapter 3). The more closely the question 'what is punishment?' is addressed, the more amorphous it becomes. As Cohen notes of social control, it 'starts dissolving into much wider issues: political ideologies, the crisis in welfare liberalism, the nature of professional power, conceptions of human nature' (Cohen, 1985, p. 197). For Wilson, punishment has a moral and educational component, whereas control is an aspect of management (see below).

The concept of punishment is not restricted to one interpretation. It changes constantly through time and from place to place. Moreover, since various forms of punishment – notably corporal and capital punishment – evoke powerful images and emotions, objective description and critical appraisal of them are made very difficult. As Garland puts it, 'the phenomenon which we refer to, too simply, as "punishment", is in fact a complex set of interlinked processes and institutions, rather than a uniform object or event.' (Garland, 1995, p. 16) Judgements about the moral justification for punishment or its technical efficacy are not restricted by limited awareness of the lack of consensus over the definition of punishment and its role in society. Not only are the nature of penological and criminological knowledge contested, but also the range of perspectives from which to view them. The study of different punishments is made more problematic by the lack of free access to data concerning their uses. The incidence and significance of corporal punishment in informal settings such as public schools, for example, remains a basis for dispute.

Whilst there is little doubt of the contemporary pervasiveness of punishment, in developed and developing countries alike, there is less consensus about the actual concept of punishment than might appear at first sight. This lack of agreement concerns the nature of punishment involved in a particular action or situation, and also the punitive character of the act itself. What one person regards as punitive may not be regarded as punitive at all by somone else. Thus, behaviour therapy, such as aversive techniques, may be viewed by professionals as legitimate 'helping' activity, whereas its subjects, or critical commentators, may view it not only as unpleasant but also as punitive. Again, the degree of punishment accorded to a particular activity may generate disagreement. Thus one person may rank verbal disapproval, which may be relatively open-ended, as more punitive than a smack. Also, as a corollary it is difficult to establish the precise boundaries between related concepts, such as punishment and social control.

It is acknowledged by one of the eighteenth-century authors from whom Foucault's analysis of penality develops that the concept of punishment is inextricably linked with that of control: 'A stupid despot may constrain his slaves with iron chains: but a true politician binds them even more strongly by the chain of their own ideas' (Foucault, 1982, pp. 102–3). It is a moot point whether power relations, for example between the offender and the agent of the state, are exercised with punitive intent, or with the aim of social control. The fact that these concepts are mutually permeable reinforces their respective impact.

The frame of reference of commentators shapes their definition of what constitutes punishment. A minimalist definition of punishment is widely applied in a behavioural context. 'Punishment occurs when a consequence is applied to a behaviour that reduces the probability of the behaviour recurring' (Carey, 1994, p. 1006). However, as Carey admits, this statement is somewhat tautologous, since there is an inherent assumption that, for a behavioural consequence to be regarded as a punishment, the behaviour must decrease; if it does not, then the consequence cannot be regarded as a punishment (Carey, 1994, p. 1006). In these terms, punishment may consist of removing something pleasant from a situation, such as by timeout (see Chapter 3) – or removal – from reinforcement, or adding something unpleasant or aversive. However, Carey's view is that punishment is not necessarily painful, the only criterion being that an undesirable behaviour is reduced (Carey, 1994, p. 1006).

Garland (1995) only considers the territory of formal punishment within the criminal justice system. Others regard punishment as embedded in wider activities. For Azrin and Holz seem to imply, somewhat questionably, that these wider activities are, in effect, the field of behaviour therapy. Azrin and Holz define punishment differently from their behavioural predecessors, who view punishment procedurally, as delivering an aversive stimulus following a response (Dinsmoor, 1954; Keller and Schoenfeld, 1950; Skinner 1953). Azrin and Holz, however, define punishment as occurring when the punitive act produces a response reduction (1966, p. 382). Punishment differs from conditioned suppression, in that whereas with punishment the direction of aversive stimuli changes according to the response, with conditioned suppression, the aversive stimulus has no fixed relationship to those responses, but simply relates to a previously neutral stimulus (Azrin and Holz, 1966, p. 430). Punishment and conditioned suppression are different ways of reducing undesired behavioural responses. In some programmes, desired behaviour may be rewarded and undesired punished. Reward-based programmes use learning theory as their basis and simply reward desired behaviour, whilst not responding at all to undesired behaviour. Thus, in these terms, punishment and reward are mutually antagonistic concepts. The most common forms of punishment in behaviourally-based programmes involve the use of noise, electric shocks, timeout and various kinds of tokens of approval and disapproval.

The true existence of punishments throughout the world, formally in institutions as well as informally (Lindesmith, 1968) can only be guessed at. Benthall concludes his anthropological discussion of the deep-rooted incidence of corporal punishment in the British public-school system:

Physical abuse of children came into the news in Britain in the 1960s, and sexual abuse of children in the 1980s. The British ruling classes were subjected to a nice combination of the two over a long period, allied with the tradition of noble values, 'muscular Christianity', and devotion to the nation which made up the ideology of public schools .... If such practices were normal at educational establishments which were otherwise, for their time, liberal and enlightened, it is very possible that comparable 'rituals of authority' have developed in the many residential institutions for children which exist in Third World countries, such as orphanages, children's homes, and penal homes, many of them originally modelled on now outdated European practice.

(Benthall, 1991, p. 387)

The dominance of particularly macho forms of punishment for many years in the education system and in the field of criminal justice meshes with similarly masculine theories, research concerns and commentaries in criminology (Newburn and Stanko, 1994). Hence, it is predictable that the appropriateness to this book of those aspects of punishment addressed in Chapters 3, 4 and 5 will be more controversial than those in Chapters 6 and 7. However, the need to redress the imbalance in the knowledges to which they relate makes their inclusion necessary.

Any examination of punishment needs to acknowledge the centrality of its institutions in relation to other major societal institutions, and the inadvisability of attempting to disentangle it from an understanding of how social order in society is constructed and maintained. More than this, punishment – like religion and politics – touches other aspects of personal and social life. For example, as examination of hunger strikers' resistance to punishment (Chapter 9), or the use of the guillotine in the French Revolution (Chapter 7) demonstrate, imagery associated with its nature and issues resonate throughout societies. Punishment occupies a central place in societies partly because of the symbolic, and literal, scope and depth of the meanings associated with it. The evidence of this is woven into the history of major institutions such as the Church (see Flagellants in Chapter 6 and the Inquisition in Chapter 2), the military (see Chapter 6), and schooling and the family (see Chapter 6). Sociologists and anthropologists have studied the archetypal location of punishment in societies. Garland (1995, p. 274) notes that 'sociologists such Georges Gurvitch or Mary Douglas might attribute this symbolizing power to punishment's status as an arena of social tension and social conflict' (Garland's references to Gurvitch, 1945; Douglas, 1966).

It is, after all, the site at which law and deviance are brought most visibly together, where social anomalies and contradictions are directly addressed, the point at which purity and danger dramatically intersect. Penal institutions deal with human and moral problems of a profound and intractable kind – with the fragility of social relations, the limits of socialization, the persistence of human evil, and the insecurity of social life. And as anthropologists have shown, the intractable problems of social and human existence provide a rich soil for the development of myths, rites, and symbols and cultures strive to control and make sense of these difficult areas of experience. Punishment 'figures prominently in some of the most important cultural artefacts of Wetern society, including classical drama, traditional cosmologies, religions such as Christianity, and heresies such as psychoanalysis'.

(Garland, 1995, p. 274)

Further, as Garland observes (1995, p. 274),

the institutions of punishment connect directly into other major social realms and institutions, linking up with the circuits of power, exchange, morality, and sensibility which hold society together. In this sense punishment has some of the qualities of what Marcel Mauss described as a 'total social fact'. It is an area of social life which spills over into other areas and which takes its social meaning as much from these connections as from itself, thus accumulating a symbolic depth and richness which go beyond its immediate functioning.

(Garland's reference to Mauss, 1967)

An adequate understanding of punishment needs to be located outside the frame of reference of its functions and purposes; a great variety of forms of punishment occur independently of legal punishments in criminal justice, while in contrast, the former have received relatively marginal attention from criminologists. This is an obvious feature of the demarcation of the territory of criminology itself. It also reflects the compartmentalisation of knowledges contradicted by the ubiquity of punishment in all its forms and settings.

Whilst punishment plays a significant part in social settings and institutions outside the legal system, on the whole, the penological literature is not concerned with these. The occurrence of a range of formal and informal punishments in such settings as schools, families, workplaces, religious institutions and military organisations, has fallen outside the scope of most criminological literature. Although Garland accepts the multifaceted nature of punishment, he restricts his focus in the book *The Sociology of Punishment* to 'the legal punishment of criminal law offenders' (Garland, 1995, p. 17). Thus, he regards the term 'penality' as a more appropriate synonym for the wider meanings of punishment (Garland, 1995, p. 17).

Garland excludes from consideration forms of punishment lying outside the criminal justice system and those which, though routine, are non-legal – for example, 'the informal rituals of humiliation involved in some police work or the implicit penalties involved in the prosecution process' (Garland, 1995, p. 18). Whilst this approach has the merit of achieving a sharper focus on the admittedly still complex domain of legal punishment in criminal justice, it creates an ironic contrast with the appreciation that punishment is merely 'a legally approved method designed to facilitate the task of crime control' (Garland, 1995, p. 18). However, Garland observes that whilst commentators such as Mead, Rusche and Kirchheimer and Foucault have recognised the weaknesses of understanding punishment in functional terms, as an instrument of crime control, they have not transcended the conceptual difficulties, since their perspective still relies on the purposive or teleological assumption that punishment acts as a means to an end 'if not now the end of "crime control" then some alternative telos, such as social solidarity (Durkheim) or political domination (Foucault)' (Garland, 1995, p. 19). Garland stands outside this restricted conceptualisation, in his assertion that

> institutions are never fully explicable purely in terms of their 'purposes'. Institutions like the prison, or the fine, or the guillotine, are social artefacts, embodying and regenerating wider cultural categories as well as being means to serve particular penological ends. Punishment is not wholly explicable in terms of its purposes because no social artefact can be explained in this way. Like architecture or diet or clothing or table manners, punishment has an instrumental purpose, but also a cultural style and an historical tradition.
>
> (Garland, 1995, p. 19)

Crime control and punishment, therefore, serve as self-justifying slogans for good order in societies where change and conflict make disorder inevitable and, in these terms, undesirable.

TRENDS IN THE USES OF PUNISHMENT

Have punishments become more abusive, either intrinsically, or as a consequence of their increasing incidence? There is evidence of both. The incidence of formal punishments has increased in Western countries such as the USA and the UK, through two main means: the increased use of existing methods, such as penal custody, epitomised by prison; and the intensification of punishment. Through both, the stigma of criminality becomes pervasive and persistent. The eponymous 'hero' of Ibsen's play, John Gabriel Borgman, never escapes the influence of his crime and imprisonment. To those about him, he becomes a dead man. His fate symbolises that of entire generations of those labelled as offenders.

There have been many predictions about the increasing likelihood of social disorder, and the decreasing effectiveness of measures of social control. These tend to increase towards the end of each century, and no doubt will do so as the millennium approaches. Jack London portrayed in his quasi-*Nineteen-Eighty-Four* novel of 1907 his vision of society in collapse (London, 1957). H. G. Wells wrote in the novel *The Shape of Things to Come* in the early 1930s (Wells, 1933) of the prospect of increasing disorder and social anarchy as economic prosperity collapsed. There is an increased use of punitive institutions. Some criminal justice systems – the USA and the UK are noteworthy in this respect – are in the process of extending and intensifying their punitive sanctions. Thus, more people are being subjected to more severe penalties. Statistics concerning the increasing size of the penal system serve to confirm the thesis that society is becoming more lawless, rather than pointing to the over-use of penal facilities. In 1996, it was estimated that one person in 176 in the USA (1.6 millian at the time of writing) will spend time in a custodial institution. In the USA, there are two dimensions to this enhanced severity; it signifies both a greater willingness to turn to capital punishment and the increased use of longer prison sentences, ultimately to ensure the offender stays incarcerated for the remainder of his or her natural life. More than 5 million people are now locked up in prisons in the USA; the number incarcerated in Britain by October 1996 exceeded 57 000, is expected to exceed 60 000 during 1997 and, on the present trajectory of the Government's boosted prison-building programme, could double within the next 20 years. This is in a period when the proportion of the population of an age when most offences are committed – between, say, 12 and 30, is set to fall to an unprecedented low, in the post-industrial period at any rate.

The intensification of punitive sanctions becomes evident in a review of the continuum of punishment in Chapters 3 to 7. For example, there is a deployment of harsher penal sanctions such as chains and shackles for those imprisoned (Chapter 4) and the imposition of greater injury on the offender through such penalties as corporal and capital punishment (Chapters 6 and 7).

Informally, whether in the household, on the street, or elsewhere in the community, or institution, the practice of punishment continues – sustained by the myths – or at least, problematic assertions – of its acceptability, utility and long-term benefits to all involved.

The Changing Nature of Punishment

The character of punishment is not immutable, but continuously subject to change. Changes may affect punishment in several ways. Its context may change, in the sense that public attitudes affect the law and bring about legislation which either introduces new and stricter penalties for offences, or, as in the late 1960s in the case of the abortion law reforms and changes in the laws affecting homosexuality, ameliorates their harshness. In the eighteenth century, for example, there was a discernible shift towards an extension of the criminal law to new offences, and increasingly harsh penalties for existing offences, such as poaching and trespassing on common land subjected to enclosure. Some forms of punishment, such as fines, may in strict financial terms be repaid, if later found to be mistaken because the offender is found innocent. However, the social stigma, and the personal, psychological impact of such a sanction are not so easily reversible. The psychological and physical traumas of corporal punishment, for example, may not be erased in retrospect and capital punishment is, by definition, irreversible.

One of the most publicly debated issues in the mass media concerns whether life sentences awarded to murderers should be subject to political, judicial or public opinion, or a combination of these. In the case of the two boys sentenced for killing James Bulger in 1993, the Home Secretary intervened in the judicial process, affecting the decision about the minimum sentence they should serve. There is a question about whether it is acceptable for a person serving a life sentence for murder, such as Myra Hindley, along with Ian Brady, the so-called Moors murderer, to be informed that she will never be released. In effect, the Home Secretary is advising her, over and above the sentence of the Court. Is this an unacceptable interference by a politician, or an action to be applauded by those who abhor the crimes for which she was found guilty? Public attitudes towards the murders committed by Ian Brady and Myra Hindley, and other prisoners serving life sentences, still affect debates about the release of Myra Hindley several decades after the court case. Senior judges, in 1995 and 1996, expressed reservations about the constitutional appropriateness of such political intervention in the decisions made by the judiciary (see Chapter 7).

The question as to whether punishment can be cancelled retrospectively, many years later, may be less dramatic, since the public reactions at the time of the trial and sentence may have abated, but nevertheless is as problematic. Clearly, prisoners can appeal to have their sentences reduced. But once time has elapsed, in literal terms it cannot be retraced to the point before it was taken away from a prisoner serving a sentence. In more extreme circumstances, one of the arguments against capital punishment is buttressed by examples of convicted murderers executed and subsequently found, or claimed to be, innocent. The law is not static; neither is its application unproblematic. New evidence may come to light; public sensibilities may change over a period of time. An attempt made to rehabilitate Oscar Wilde in February 1995, 100 years after his play *The Importance of Being Earnest* was performed for the first time, days before his trial and imprisonment for offences of gross indecency, by unveiling a plaque in Poets' Corner, Westminster Abbey, was called into question by his grandson; he observed that Wilde himself would have squirmed to have had this response from the society he satirised.

Denials and Distortions

The relative prominence, and expensiveness, of the apparatus of penality in contemporary societies makes it unsurprising that the key interests tussle over who controls information in and around it – notably statistics about prisoners. One of the most notorious controversies in modern history concerns the numbers of Jews who were imprisoned and killed in the Holocaust. The many manifestations of denial by some officials and members of the public in Germany and elsewhere of the realities of the extermination of Jews in the Holocaust are well documented (see for instance Levi, 1985, pp. 220–1). An enormous weight of evidence, however, attests to the fact that in the ghettos of Europe, as in concentration camps, the threat of 'severe punishment' usually preceded mutilation and death (see, for example, the documents from the Lodz ghetto assembled by Adelson and Lapides, and see Adelson and Lapides, 1989, p. 410). The horrors of other prison systems have from time to time been exposed to independent critical scrutiny. In the wake of Solzhenitsyn's exposé of Stalin's labour camps (1963, 1984), Rossi documented in great detail the nature of the system of Soviet prisons or Gulags (Rossi, 1989), in which hundreds of thousands of political and civil prisoners were contained alongside criminals.

Stanley Cohen's illuminating analysis of torture in Israel distinguishes three responses by the authorities: 'nothing is happening', 'what is happening is really something else' and 'what is happening is completely justified' (Cohen, 1985, p. 21). He asks

> how does one claim that 'nothing is happening' while simultaneously maintaining that 'what is happening is justified'? I came to realize that the puzzle only exists if you see these elements as separate and logically contradictory. In fact, they are politically dependent on each other. There is a fixed official discourse of torture (and other gross violations of human rights); these three elements always complement each other.
>
> (Cohen, 1985, p. 22)

Superimposed on this, of course, the liberal defence can always deflect accusations by asserting that ' "It's worse elsewhere" (and, in the case of torture, this is true; the Israeli methods are indeed "moderate"); "Everyone is picking on us" (which is also sometimes true)' (Cohen, 1985, p. 24).

Studies of protests by pupils (Adams, 1991) and riots by prisoners (Adams, 1994) – some of which are responses to perceived over-punitive or inappropriately punitive acts by the authorities – show up some of the strategies of denial in relation to the phenomena of collective protests, which may be adopted by the authorities. Perhaps it is more accurate to respond to the simultaneous reality of the authorities playing down and playing up the existence of rioting, by suggesting that these responses are only contradictory if one perceives them as separate.

The restriction of the definition of punishment constrains discussion of its pervasiveness and, necessarily, may lead to denial of its harmful impact on many groups of people, in many circumstances. Thus, outside the criminal justice system – the traditional focus for discussions of punishment – its abuses may arise in the street, in the home, in the workplace and in many non-penal settings where people are subjected to block treatment. For example, Wolf Wolfensberger's analysis (1994) of the historical shifts in the treatment of people with learning disabilities highlights the segregation in institutions and ghettos of groups such as Indians, Black people, older people, and children who are deaf and blind, as one aspect of blame of the individual for the blemish which is how their situation all too often is represented. The deviant,

> being perceived as unpleasant, offensive or frightening, can be segregated from the mainstream of society and placed at its periphery ... . Deviance can be seen to be someone's fault or perhaps a sign that the deviant's parents had sinned and were being punished by the God. The belief that a blemish in the offspring is the result of punishment for

parental wrongdoing appears to be deeply engrained in the unconscious of the people. Often, this belief is overtly repressed.

(Wolfensberger, 1972, p. 63)

Discrimination in the criminal justice system, against Black people and people from ethnic minorities, reflects aspects of discrimination in wider society (NACRO Race Issues Advisory Committee, 1986, p. 37).

Formal and Informal Punishments

Informal punishments are not to be confused with those aspects of radical anti-discrimination strategies lying beyond diversion, in what Cohen calls delegalisation and informalism:

> calling for justice 'outside the law' or 'without the law'. This was not just an operational criticism of the legal system, but also an explicit attempt to transfer power from the state to the 'people' (victims, disputants, the local community), or even (at its most radical) to remove the coercive, constraining and dehumanizing features of the legal order.
>
> (Cohen, 1985, pp. 34–5)

The ubiquitous nature of punishment is expressed in the fact that formal sanctions with punitive intent may be employed by nurses, health care assistants, care managers, care assistants, educational psychologists, doctors, careers officers, housing officers, youth workers, hostel wardens working both for the statutory services and in the voluntary and private sectors, teachers, probation officers, priests and social workers. Informal sanctions may be employed by parents and other relatives, neighbours and colleagues. The vast range of settings where punishment may take place includes not only penal establishments, hospitals and schools, but also old people's homes, day centres, nurseries, playgroups, households and families.

Different manifestations of informal punishments occur, depending on a variety of social, economic, political and policy conditions. The range of applications of punishment illustrate its differing definitions. Whilst the narrower definition of punishment may involve the infliction of formal, deliberate and avoidable physical or mental suffering, the above discussion points to the need to conceptualise it so as to encompass deprivations, for example of life or liberty, or the kind of lifestyle which the punished person desires (Honderich, 1976, p. 11). Informal punishment may occur in a range of domains, such as the household, and settings where children and older people are looked after. Some commentators, such as Grupp (Grupp, 1971) exclude informal and interpersonal punishments from consideration of punishment of the adjudicated criminal through the formal system of criminal justice. According to this view, punishments are measures of retribution and deterrence imposed through the due process of law. Others are prepared to acknowledge the range of such punishments, whilst still not treating them commensurately with their significance (Howe, 1994).

Punishment used informally in the household, on the street, in the factory, tends to attract less interest from criminologists and criminal justice professionals and more from campaigners for anti-oppressiveness, justice and equality. Arguments about whether punishment in the home is justified, for example, may excite debates involving feminists about structural, gender imbalances of power and *macho* and sexist socialisation processes.

At the formal end of the continuum, punishment has been used very widely to bolster the political stability of governments. The corollary of this is that the ways punishment has been conceptualised have been circumscribed by the concern with meting out the sentence on the offender, to the exclusion of the wider process, from apprehension, through remand, trial, to judgement, during which defendants, whether innocent or guilty, are subjected to similar processes of stigmatisation, control or deprivation. At the informal end, the person may experience a variety of sanctions or exclusions, whose consideration is beyond the scope of conventional criminology. It is in the interests of those meting out informal punishments – parents, employers, those running institutions, residential, day-care or community facilities – for them not to be made accountable to any due process by the state.

The conceptual segregation of formal from informal mechanisms for dispensing punishment is accurate but has the consequence of discouraging the inclusive consideration of different punitive activities, within different domains of society. It constrains the development of a critical understanding of changes which occur. For example, during the past century and a half, in the USA, the Thirteenth and Fourteenth Amendments to the Constitution 1865 and the Civil Rights Act 1871 contributed to the outlawing of slavery and involuntary servitude. But this exempted circumstances where the person had been convicted of a crime. This allowed the former states of the Confederacy to use prisoners as labour in prison institutions which came to resemble plantations. Thus, in Texas, these prisons

> were located on large sections of land in East Texas. Inmates were used
> to raise cotton and corn, to tend livestock, and to maintain such public

accommodations as roads and waterworks. Order within prison was maintained much as it had been under the old system of slavery. Physical domination was paramount. Whippings were permitted and dog packs chased down escapees. Prison units were segregated; Black inmates were more likely than their white counterparts to be found in the fields picking cotton. These prison plantations would remain very much in evidence a full century later.

(Marquart, Ekland-Olson and Sorensen, 1994, p. 2)

Much of the literature is preoccupied, perhaps understandably, with the formal mechanisms for punishing people, through criminal justice and penal systems. However, in the second half of the twentieth century, research, and campaigns by reformers, increasingly have opened up hitherto less accessible, but no less real, areas where punishment takes place, notably in the home and in the community. The classic example of informal punishment is Northern Ireland, where the campaigns of republican and loyalist groups have delivered sectarian punishments on the streets, in the form of individual or collective reprisals, such as shooting in the kneecap or killing.

Rachel Hodgkin notes that little research traditionally was carried out into the incidence of smacking children by parents (Hodgkin, 1986, p. 48). Hodgkin records that exceptionally, the study by John and Elizabeth Newson indicated that 62 per cent of parents hit their one-year-old children, 93 per cent hit their four-year-olds and 'by the age of seven eight per cent are being hit at least once a day and a further one third not less than once a week; 22 per cent of this age group (being) ... hit with some implement', overall trends being high in all social classes (Newson and Newson, 1970, referred to in Hodgkin, 1986, p. 48).

Components of Punishment

Punishment involves four components: the intention to inflict hurt as a means to an end – whether described in deterrent, reformative or educative terms, an act of punishment, a punishing person, one or more persons punished and a punishing system. If the punishment is formal, it will be associated necessarily with a group, institution or state. Acts of punishment, whether formal or informal, may be ritualised. The treatment of Tess of the D'Urbervilles in Hardy's novel relates to a history of 'rough music' referred to by E. P. Thompson (1971); a more extreme and violent example is that of the lynch mob (see Chapter 7). Such rituals may contribute to the achievement of punishments, particularly those which involve the infliction of physical hurt or even death. This may be achieved through staging punishment as a public drama, the script of which reinforces the justification: that is, the morality of the act and the badness of the offenders. This helps to overcome two potential threats to the accomplishment of punishment: the infliction of hurt by one person on another; and the management of the paradox that the offender momentarily ceased to play the perpetrator and has replaced the original victim as the victim of punishment. Rituals of public punishment overcome the dangers of inversion of the values of this event and reversal of the direction of the act of punishment. Sometimes these rituals solemnify and accentuate the violence, as before the twentieth century, when public execution functioned partly as a demonstration of the state's power to match the awfulness of the crime with an equivalent measure of retribution.

The siting of punishment may facilitate the accomplishment of rituals of carrying it out. The location may link with institutional structures to enable what is, in effect, a cold-blooded act by one person of inflicting hurt on another, to be accomplished. For example, whipping and flagellation have been employed for centuries as forms or punishment or penance. The prominence of whipping as a penance is indicated by the fact that the term 'disciplines', originally used to refer to the different ways of doing penance, came to mean solely *disciplina flagelli*, the discipline of the whip (Cooper, 1869, p. 18). Flagellation forms part of a lengthy history of informal, sado-masochistic practices, the incidence of which, as Storr notes in a brief review from the obsessions of the novelist Proust to Swinburne the poet, is difficult to estimate (Storr, 1991, p. 79). The boundary between so-called 'legitimate' punishment and punishments which afford the executioner some perverse satisfaction is impossible to discern. Often, perpetrators of acts which inflict harm on other beings, whether animal or human, are drawn to situations where they can practise their perversions under the cloak of legitimacy. Even philosophers as diverse as Arthur Schopenhauer and Jeremy Bentham, who abhor the imposition of violence on animals in general, find means to justify killing animals when it suits their argument (Singer, 1991, p. 210).

Punishment invariably involves violence, whether real or symbolic, individual or social. In acts of punishment, as in other acts of violence, the victim loses control of his or her situation or body. Though this loss of control may be short-lived, some aspects of it may persist. The victim may be encouraged by the perpetrator to believe that the punishment is appropriate and deserved (Taylor and Chandler, 1995, p. 19). The success of this tactic by the perpetrator may lead to the confirmation of the identity of the victim, whereas denial of its attempted justification may be disconfirming. The perpetrator may manipulate the context, so that it confirms the 'naturalness' and 'fairness' of the punishment and undermines the victim's ability to develop a contrary understanding of the experience. Reference may be made back to some alleged offence of the victim, thus redefining the victim as a perpetrator, and justifying the punishment with reference to the wrong done to another assumed victim. Punishment of this kind achieves a one-sided legitimacy, in favour of the current perpertrator. Ironically, the punishment may mirror aspects of the original crime – which may have been an abusive act, that is, it is an inherently abusive act of domination over the victim.

One feature of the term punishment noted above is its wide span of applications, from the sanctions applied informally in the household to a minor misdemeanour by a child, which may attract a telling-off, to the exemplary public execution of an offender. Another feature of punishment is the juxtaposition of the concept against other concepts such as treatment. Thus, Professor Sanford Fox of the Boston Law School was quoted in relation to the controversial implementation of the Children and Young Persons Act 1969, as advocating the child's right to punishment rather than treatment: 'I think that there are a number of advantages to viewing the problem of what to do with juvenile offenders as a matter of their right to punishment rather than a right to treatment' (Taylor, Morris and Downes, 1977, p. 39). But this use of the word punishment was intended as an alternative to the child's loss of rights, privacy and control over release dates from custody, which were dependent on staff assessments of 'response to treatment'. Fox actually described what Giller and Morris (1983) and others termed a justice approach, based on dealing with the child according to the seriousness of the offence.

Concepts such as treatment which seem to be antithetical to punishment are, in fact, closer than might be imagined. Care and control share a common value base in social care and social work, from the mid-nineteenth century to the present day (Adams, Allard, Baldwin and Thomas, 1981, pp. 10–11). In some professions such as nursing and social work, this tension may be managed by a gender-based division between carers and controllers; in others, notably in the relationship between nursing and medicine, 'the male/masculine control is exercised by another occupation' (Hugman, 1991, p. 49). Behavioural therapy may, in effect, be masculine – though not necessarily men's – work, that is, punitive in character. Howard Jones notes that 'certain kinds of psychological technique of a "brainwashing" variety are also not to be tolerated' (Jones, 1967, p. 89). He suggested (1967, p. 82) that 'the idea that a wrongful act should always be followed by some kind of punishment is deeply ingrained in our natures … . The idea of having "paid for", or expiated one's guilt after punishment is strong in all of us.' He points out that organised religion supports such retributive views. William Temple, as Archbishop of York, wrote: 'It is, I believe, the first moral duty of the community, and of the State on its behalf, to reassert the broken moral law against the offender who has broken it.' Lord Longford, a Roman Catholic, asserted of punishment that 'its medicinal, its restorative, its healing function, makes it an essential element in salvation' (quoted in Jones, 1967, pp. 82–3).

Punishment is located on a continuum of oppressive acts by one person, group or institution over one or more persons. The boundary between punitive and non-punitive violence may be difficult to draw. Research into the rape of women by women contributes insights into the links between interpersonal male violence against women, including the rape of women by men, and social circumstances where collective violence occurs. Notably, sexual violence by men 'is one of the most effective means of control. It has long been used as a weapon in war, though the emphasis here is on demoralising the male members of the enemy and, by implication, the enemy nation' (Taylor and Chandler, 1995, p. 18).

Finally, there is what was referred to above as the punitive system. This is more than a set of procedures, or even institutions, even if we do not adopt Cohen's somewhat pessimistic, global vision of a carceral system, widened, diversified and transported from the institution into the community through the major strategies of expansion, dispersal, invisibility and penetration (Cohen, 1985, p. 85).

The Punishment Industry

Punishment is one of the most traditional means by which compliance is enforced in society. Past societies have amassed a vast and terrifying array of punishments, which it is not within the remit of this book to examine. The vast expansion in the apparatus for formal, state-sanctioned punishment since the late eighteenth century has necessitated a proliferation of professions in the workforce of the human services concerned with interventive work with people (Hobsbawm, 1995, p. 201) and in the punishment industry (Cohen, 1985, p. 162). The policy of 'three strikes and you're out' (three convictions and you receive a long prison sentence) plus the end of parole have increased the use of prison custody in the USA. Similar measures were proposed by the UK Conservative government in the Criminal Justice Bill presented to Parliament on 26 October 1996. Prisons, whether goverment-funded or private, are an expanding business and the building of a prison brings similar prosperity to a depressed area as the arrival of a moderate-sized industrial plant. In the USA, 123 new federal and state prisons were opened or under construction in 1996. One new prison due to open in February 1997 was anticipated to bring 250 jobs to the area and increase the size of the town by 1000 people (Lamb, 1996, p. 14). The expansion of what Cohen calls the business of social control (Cohen, 1985, p. 231) overlaps significantly with the proliferation since the nineteenth century of that segment of society which delivers punishment to those deemed deserving. Often, punishment is subsumed in a wider span of activities performed by a person. The techniques for punishing people, and their linked technologies, have expanded accordingly. The reality is still more complex and paradoxical. As the power of formal punishment has become concentrated in, and symbolised by, the institution of the prison (Foucault, 1982), so punishment which blurs into 'projects of docility' (Cohen, 1985, p. 85) is dispersed throughout society.

The manufacture and export of instruments for physical restraint (Chapter 3) contributes to the global availability of a range of methods of punishment and, in extreme circumstances, torture.

A variety of occupations contribute also to the implementation of particular forms of punishment. Professionals, semi-professionals and sub-professionals (sometimes known as vocational staff) have proliferated in the workforce of the human services concerned with custodial work with people (Hobsbawm, 1995, p. 201) and in the punishment industry (Cohen 1985, p. 162). Much of this expansion has been at the lower end of the occupational hierarchy. Managers 'command the battalions of psychiatrists, psychologists, social workers, correctional staff, researchers and all sorts of dependent groups who do the dirty work of control and mopping up' (Cohen, 1985, p. 163). The roles played by specific groups of staff, say, in custodial institutions cannot be stereotyped, or analysed in a reductionist fashion, as simply the agents of repression. Barry Richards's discussion of the activities of applied psychologists in the Prison Psychological Service offers a more sophisticated understanding of such a cadre of expertise. He notes:

> Without historical understanding of its development and contradictions, we are not going to be able to inform political practice in struggles where applied psychology is involved – in education, health, production, prisons. The practice of applied psychologists is usually constituted by highly mediated contradictions at a number of different levels. Faced with the complexity of psychology as the reproduction of bourgeois ideology, we cannot make do with simplistic analyses of

psychologists as conspiring ideologues, or as direct agents of the repressive state, or as simple reflections, ideological effects.

(Richards, 1977, p. 9)

Applied psychology, within a fundamentally restraining penal apparatus, continues to offer opportunities for progressive practitioners to work creatively and in resistance to dominant ideologies. (see Chapter 9 for further discussion of resistance to punishment).

The Changing Spectacle of Punishment

The products of the punishment industry have changed markedly over the past 200 years. Linebaugh's study of the use of executions in eighteenth-century London refers in passing to two contrary global trends since the mid-1970s – towards the increased use of the death penalty and towards greater pressure for its abolition (Linebaugh, 1991, p. xv). However, since then, the public spectacle of the offender in the stocks, at the gallows, in the centre of the community, watched by a crowd, has become a rarity, in Western countries at least. The spectacle of formal punishments has played a prominent part in their staging. The description by Samuel Bamford of the public execution of two men in the early nineteenth century highlights its psychological impact on the spectator (Bamford, 1984, pp. 339–40). The staging of punishment, before the eighteenth-century public in many countries – with the notable exception of the Spanish Inquisition – became less and less a spectacle, and more a private act carried out within the prison walls (Arasse, 1991, pp. 109–10). The last public, formal execution in the USA was in Missouri in 1937, the last public guillotining in France in 1939. In Britain, it was probably the fear of riots as much as anything which led to the abolition of the procession through the London streets from Newgate prison to Tyburn from 1783, and to executions behind prison walls from the late 1890s.

But, if physically distanced, the drama and the exemplary force of the punitive act are transformed by various media into virtual realities. Law and order issues make news (Chibnall, 1977). A further, and more insidious, feature of punishment arises from the growth of an industry, using various media – films, books and television, for example – which may be claimed to express the gratuitous fascination of the spectator, the voyeur, of punishment. The stories of relatives of victims of crimes may be purchased by newspapers; writers may prepare books retailing the stories of murderers, and other serious offenders; books about serial killers may straddle the boundary between serious studies and voyeurism. The definition of research and entertainment thereby may be blurred. The popularity of studies of murderers, from the time of Jack the Ripper to the modern serial killers, attests to the interest of the public not having waned with the abolition of the public spectacle of corporal and capital punishments. The historian Philip Jenkins has documented the preoccupation with the serial killer (Jenkins, 1994). At the same time, changing public and professional attitudes towards some features of punishment have led to the growing importance of mechanisms such as distancing, proceduralism, hygienisation and the division of labour in the criminal justice system, for example, ensuring that multiple responsibilies exist for carrying out an execution, to say nothing of the roles of staff such as the custodians who relax with the prisoner on the last evening before the execution, or the priest in blessing the person just before the act of execution itself (Chapter 7). Such processes contribute to attempts to multiply, spread, or divert responsibility for the act of killing.

The Functions of Punishment

Formal punishments, such as those of criminal justice systems, function as a means of imposing social control, usually in circumstances where other sanctions have failed, or where likely failure is feared. Informally, punishments may serve to redress, but also may buttress, imbalances of power, which more often than not are intrinsically abusive. Though often subjected to rituals and procedures designed so that punishment can assume the mantle of neutrality, justice and apoliticality, the act of punishment is inherently political. Its application is shaped by political processes. Evaluation of the appropriateness of specific forms of punishment cannot be detached from its moral and political dimensions.

The use of punishment is a principal dynamic by which power is demonstrated. Punishment, like warfare, is more often than not a socially approved means of allowing one person to inflict physical or mental pain or discomfort on another. Punishment may be employed in a range of settings on the continuum from formal to informal punishment. The boundaries between punishment and social control are also blurred. Ewing acknowledges the distinction between the use of social control to coerce a person and punishment after the exercise of the law (Ewing, 1929, p. 47). The use of punishments in institutions, organisations, families, households and between individuals has expressed not only the feelings and thoughts of people, but, in the manner of punishing, the spirit of the age, the mentalities of key parties and the exercise of undue, or oppressive power by people over people.

Just as the crime figures represent one kind of vote winner, or vote loser, so the issue of how the state does, and should, respond to serious crime in particular, has contributed to the manipulation of electoral support over the years. Linebaugh suggests that execution in the USA plays a part in policing the underclass (Linebaugh, 1995b). Louisiana, a southern former slave state with a high incidence of black people, has the highest murder rate in the USA and at 505 prisoners per 100 000 people, the highest incarceration rate in the world (Linebaugh, 1995a, p. 29). High crime rates, murder rates, incarceration rates and high death rates go together, but whether they should do is a political decision rather than a social necessity or a moral imperative.

However, trends in any particular aspect of punishment are somewhat contradictory. For example, Gatrell's detailed exposé of the hanging histories of ordinary people demonstrates the horrific scale of executions in the period between 1830 and the abolition of public executions in 1868, during which more people were hanged than in the previous two hundred years or so (Gatrell, 1994a).

IS PUNISHMENT JUSTIFIED? PENAL THEORIES AND PRACTICES

The literature on the theory and practice of punishment has mushroomed since the early 1970s, as is evidenced by the range and depth of published work (instanced in Duff and Garland, 1994 and Garland, 1995). Debates about the justification or otherwise of punishment have tended to be located in the territory of criminal justice rather than in society as a whole. The past century of earnest endeavour by criminologists has produced remarkably few direct pay-offs in terms of demonstrations of the proven effectiveness over any others, of any particular penal sanction. Rather, criminologists, particularly in the dominant administrative rather than the somewhat marginal radical traditions, have all too often situated themselves alongside existing dominant practices, rather than outside them, from which vantage point it would be possible to sustain critiques of policy and practice (Jupp, 1989).

Western forms of criminal justice influence other countries, as is demonstrated not only through the imperialist replication of British penal policy and practice in India, Canada, Australia and other countries from the late eighteenth century. More subtle, though, is the influence of Western ideas and practices on other countries, such as China (Xui, 1995) and the export of ideas from the Third World to the West, notably in such areas as thought reform (see Chapter 3).

It must be acknowledged that criminologies in the plural rather than a single consensual discipline of criminology inform the study of penal policy and practice (Sack, 1995, p. 49). At the most mundane level, understandings of crime and responses to crime by politicians, professionals and academics are diverse in countries exhibiting a diversity of political regimes and cultures (Sack, 1995, p. 54). Some countries, notably in central Europe, have experienced dramatic changes since the late 1980s. It is unsurprising, therefore, that explanations of the varying incidence of crime in different countries remain rudimentary. According to Arthur and Marenin (1995), a country-by-country case-study approach may be the only way of addressing the diversity of features in different countries.

A great range of stances on the infliction of punishment has been adopted over past centuries. On the whole, commentators have tended to justify punishment. Some are cautious, however, and specify carefully the circumstances in which it is acceptable, or attack the use of particular punishments. A minority of commentators adopt the view that most or all punishments in particular circumstances are unjustified. Bernard Shaw opposes imprisonment, for example (see Chapter 6), and Ted Honderich argues that punishment cannot be justified in an unequal society where its pattern of use reflects those inequalities (Honderich, 1976, p. 183). Controversy about the uses and abuses of punishment often involves arguments conducted at different levels. Thus, one commentator may rely on moral arguments and another may use economic justifications, one way or the other. Structural inequalities may reinforce power differentials between different groups and interests in society, for example, along lines of class, gender, race and age. Thus, to give an example of gender inequalities, whilst Roman law did not permit the husband to kill his adulterous wife, if he did murder her, the crime was liable to be treated leniently (Treggiari, 1993, p. 284).

Traditionally, that is until the eighteenth century or thereabouts, the criminal law was regarded as the means to punish moral defects of character or action, or both. Walker (1991) distinguishes two philosophies of punishment: retributivism and utilitarianism. These complement a threefold distinction between classical, positivist and radical perspectives. Classical perspectives involve a focus on the offence. The emphasis is on retributivism, 'just deserts', compensation and reparation. Positivist perspectives divide into three main streams: teleological/ rehabilitationist, utilitarian – the modern equivalents of deterrence, protection and incapacitation, reformation, rehabilitation and correction – and teleological retributivist – or a mixture of these. Radical perspectives, which tend to argue for the reform or abolition of punishment, fall into four main streams: Marxist, abolitionist, realist and postmodern.

Whereas classical perspectives on crime focus on the offence, positivism concentrates on the offender. The dominance of positivism over criminology since the late nineteenth century coincided with, and found expression in, faith in the rehabilitative ideal which was progressively undermined by evaluative research in the second half of the twentieth century (see Chapter 8). A helpful distinction has been made in criminology between biological and more general positivists. Biological positivism, charted by Garland (1985a), maintains a tight causal relationship between the measurably distinctive and pathological features of criminals which distinguish them physiologically and biologically from non-criminals (Roshier, 1989, pp. 21–2). The dominance of positivism should not be exaggerated, since, as Roshier acknowledges, Bottoms (1983) rightly draws attention to the fact that the fine, in quantitative terms, has been the most significant initiative in penal practice during the twentieth century (Roshier, 1989, p. 35). The post-classical perspective on crime holds that everyone is capable of acting in a criminal way and that the criminal justice system may have a generally deterrent effect on most people (Roshier, 1989, pp. 116–17).

Arguments for the Use of Punishment

Moral arguments
Early penal theorists have attempted to set boundaries round the use of punishment. Beccaria (1764) proposed that the criminal law should not be applied in circumstances where retribution was the sole justification, on the grounds that prevention should be the aim of legislation. Bentham (1789) asserted that punishment should not be used in circumstances where the offence brought about no harm, where a different response would achieve almost the same purpose with less suffering, and where the harm caused by the penalty was greater than the original crime. Mill (1859 [1982]) based on Bentham's first principle his argument that compulsion or control should not be used when the individual was not affecting other people adversely.

Economic arguments
It may be argued that the criminal law should only be used in circumstances where the result, in absolute or in relative terms, justifies the cost. In respect of the former, a lengthy investigation aimed to secure the prosecution of young people of 15 in a particular community for having sexual intercourse might be considered an expensive waste of resources. Again,

the public reaction could be negative if resources were devoted to pursuit of a particular type of criminal offence, such as patrols to monitor the dropping of litter, at the expense, say, of responding to calls concerning crimes of violence.

Absolutist and relativist arguments: dealing with difference

From one perspective, there are fixed and inviolable values which underlie discussion of one or more aspects of punishment in any setting anywhere in the world. Within this, there is a widespread consensus that punishment may be justified as a means of prevention, deterrence or reform/moral education (see, for example, Ewing, 1929; Grupp, 1971). From another viewpoint, there are no absolute standards by which to judge many activities which fall within the criminal law. The kinds of behaviour which provoke disapproval in one era, country or culture, may be considered acceptable in another.

The relativity of limits to acceptable behaviour imposes cautions on the use of punishments through the criminal law and suggests that a more pragmatic approach be adopted to certain offences which do not transgress basic societal values, whereas a moral stand is taken on those which do. Whilst even this simple distinction will raise areas which are essentially contested, it may be possible to agree that, for example, violence against the person, or abusive action, is unacceptable in any circumstances.

The Platonic argument is that punishment provides an escape from the greater wickedness of doing evil (Plato, 1961, pp. 162–3). Hobbes asserts that 'a punishment, is an Evill inflicted by publique Authority, on him that hath done, or omitted that which is Judged by the same Authority to be a Transgression of the Law; to the end that the will of men may thereby the better be disposed to obedience' (Hobbes, 1909).

Pragmatic arguments in support of punishment invariably invoke anecdotal references to the small minority of more serious violent offenders – often with reference to particularly gruesome, or unique, crimes – who, it is felt, deserve heavy penal sanctions. More theoretically, punishment may be justified by criminologists and penologists on a variety of grounds. Ezorsky suggests that these are teleological, retributivist and a combination of these, which is teleological retributivist. Walker (1991 p. 7) has authoritatively considered the justifications for punishment.

Retributivism is inherited from ancient legal systems. It argues that it is a moral right and duty to punish wrongdoing; this is an end in itself and essential in a civilised society. The punisher should ensure, first, the correct identification of the person to be punished and, second, that the punishment is proportionate to the seriousness of the crime. Immanuel Kant argues that punishment is justified on moral grounds of retribution. According to this view, the severity of the punishment should depend on the wrongness of the offence, regardless of the consequences for the offender. However, such punishment is dependent on the person punished being cognisant of the implications, both of the offence and of the punishment.

The teleological justification is that the isolation and reform of offenders makes the world a better place by improving them, and other deterred potential offenders (Ezorsky, 1972, p. xii). Cloaked under this and other rationales for punishment may be the satisfactions gained by the perpetrators.

Utilitarianism was expounded by Jeremy Bentham in the late eighteenth century, who argued that punishment is a morally justified evil, where it brings about the greater good of the reduction of wrongdoing. Some utilitarians justify punishments with a reformative element, on the grounds that the future happiness of punished people who no longer offend, and otherwise potential victims, will be greater in the light of reformative actions than without them (Heath, 1963, p. 7). By the mid-1970s, at a time when the rehabilitative ideal was about to be dislodged, it was still at its peak. Andenaes, in an influential collection of essays, pointed out the problematic nature of the blanket adoption of treatment, in the sense of therapy, given the deterrent function of criminal law (Andenaes, 1974, pp. 156–7).

Capital punishment exercises a powerful hold on the consciousness of the general public, possibly because of its unique position as ultimate sanction. The functions of capital punishment, in classical criminal justice practice, include meting out justice to wrongdoers and, where possible, bringing each to a penitential state before the penalty is carried out. The utilitarian argument is that the punishment should fit the crime as far as possible.

> Utilitarian arguments for the restoration of capital punishment have been shifting from deterrence to the more tangible problems. How can society be secured against the repeated onslaughts of known and ruthless criminals in times when their numbers and their crimes are multiplying? Can they and must they be held in confinement virtually for the rest of their lives? If so, what will be the impact on the prisons? And how are we to combat the threat of intervention by terrorists to secure the release of their unlucky comrades?
>
> (Radzinowicz and King, 1977, p. 165)

Of course, deterrent punishment may be used without reference to the formal processes of criminal justice. Voltaire's Candide is disabused of

his hope of confirming his optimism about human nature when he journeys to England in the eighteenth century. On arriving in Portsmouth, he
witnesses the public execution of an admiral, apparently because this man
has not enough dead men to his credit, the justification for which is that:
'in this country we find it pays to shoot an admiral from time to time to
encourage the others' (Voltaire, 1988, p. 111). However, reductionism is
the more discriminating and customary use of deterrent punishment, to
discourage further offending by the offender or by others. Whereas retributivism relies simply on the proof that the offender deserves the punishment, utilitarianism requires the proof that the punishment is effective in
reducing wrongdoing. Retributivism produces the modern equivalents of
'just deserts', compensation and reparation. Utilitarian punishment produces the modern equivalents of deterrence, protection and incapacitation,
reformation, rehabilitation and correction.

At one extreme, mechanisms such as torture may be employed to base
the rule of the people by the state on deterrence. Such repressive means as
torture are not the prerogative of authoritarian dictatorships. McGuffin
parallels the use of torture by the British government in Northern Ireland
in the 1970s with similar practices by the French in Algeria, the Russians
in Hungary and what was then Czechoslovakia, the Americans in
Vietnam, Santo Domingo and parts of South America, as well as in Spain,
Greece, Brazil and South Africa (McGuffin, 1973, p. 21).

We can reconcile retributivist and utilitarian positions in the following
convergence: retributivists argue that the punishment of a particular
person is only justified if that person is regarded as guilty and aware
enough of the consequences of the offence to take responsibility for it.
Utilitarians justify punishment in terms of its deterrent character. This is
akin to teleological retributivism, which involves balancing complex arguments about whether the pain inflicted by punishing the offender should be
allowed to increase the total amount of suffering in the world in cases
where an horrific crime has been committed; this is in contrast with Kant's
principle of justice, that a person should not be punished as a means, by
administering punishment so as to benefit other people (Ezorsky, 1972,
pp. xix–xxii).

Attitudes to punishment are conditioned, among other factors, by cultural contexts. For example, incarceration rates vary between different
countries, notably in Europe, as do attitudes to capital punishment, abolished in the first decade of the century in Denmark, but not in Britain till
the mid–1950s. The retention of corporal and capital punishment, in
certain cases, are on demand fuelled by public opinion. This varies according to time and place.

Docking helpfully reviews perspectives on punishment in schools (Docking, 1980, ch. 9). Docking makes the distinction between punishment and discipline in an educational setting. He views discipline as simply conformity to rules, whereas punishment is the inflicting of pain – necessarily involving an act of retribution – on someone who has broken the rules. Docking views school-based punishment as 'at best a necessary nuisance. It is necessary as a deterrent, but its positive educational value is dubious (Docking, 1980, p. 279). Wilson (1971) sees punishment as positive – linked with discipline – in that it is part of a pupil's education in the existence of a moral order, rather than simply social control. Control involves penalties, whether or not the pupil acknowledges moral culpability. 'A rule-breaker is liable for a penalty whether or not he can see good reason for the rule, but a wrong-doer is liable for punishment *because* he can see good reason for the rules (and has nevertheless broken them)' (Docking, 1980, p. 117). Docking comments: 'Wilson sees punishment as primarily a moral matter with an educative function rather than simply a moral matter with a managerial function' (Docking, 1980, p. 208). He concludes that 'punishment is intrinsically bound up with justice and not simply with social expediency' (Docking, 1980, p. 208).

Abuses of Punishment

The phrase 'abuses of punishment' can be applied to any or all of the three arguments against it: that it is excessive, inappropriate or unjustified. However, it is necessary to clarify whether by abuses of punishment is meant *any* use of punishment. Whereas from classical, retributivist, Utilitarian and radical standpoints, punishment is part of the equation between acts deemed wrong by the state in due processes of law, from one radical standpoint at least – the abolitionist – punishment itself is considered wrongful. But whether it is judged as much a wrong as the crime itself is a complex question, dependent on the view taken of the relative wrongfulness of the crime and the punishment.

A particular difficulty arises over the lack of articulation of some abuses of punishment. Not surprisingly perhaps, the disciplines of research and practice in penality follow the contours of the male-dominated domains of knowledge to which they relate. In the hierarchy of importance, therefore, historically, public acts of violence attract more attention – whether from the mass media, police or researchers – than, say, violence in the home. Acts of criminal violence in the home, for example, remain largely hidden, and therefore unresearched, in many societies throughout the world. In many Western countries, whilst violence committed by men against women and children has been exposed increasingly since the 1950s, relatively little is known about acts of violence between women. In a study of violence between women, for example, it was noted that

> lesbians who are sexually abused by other lesbians often have difficulty in naming the assault as rape. We have no vocabulary for the crime. This was the area of our research that the women who told us their stories found it hardest to speak of. Often they would deny that they had experienced any sexual trauma with their former lovers, only to write later detailing scenes of extensive sexual brutality.
>
> (Taylor and Chandler, 1995, p. 18).

Literary, that is fictional and autobiographical, sources of insight into punishment are important, since the authorities are not always reliable sources of data on its nature and impact. Women may be inhibited from exposing these because they fear that investigations of such abusive acts by women against women may be carried out by men and used to contribute to masculine, and oppressive, interpretations of women as aggressors and as victims. Taylor and Chandler (1995) argue that criticisms of abusive acts by women against women have been used to undermine the feminist analysis of the structural power of men, rather than being viewed as occasions where abuse requires equivalent intervention to any other forms of abuse. As sinister are attempts to locate support for punishment in an interpretation of punishment and victimology which attributes the victim with attitudes justifying the punishment (Taylor and Chandler, 1995, pp. 28–9). Nurse Ratchett, in Ken Kesey's novel *One Flew Over the Cuckoo's Nest*, goads MacMurphy into violence to justify her own recourse to violent reprisals; she uses punishment as a means of evening the score with him. In an informal situation, in the research by Taylor and Chandler, Nadine describes how the reason she continued to stay with Claire, her abuser, had much to do with the mutual reinforcement between social pressures on her, her own ambivalent response partly because of the powerlessness and isolation she experienced, and pressure from the perpetrator, Claire herself (Taylor and Chandler, 1995, pp. 35–6).

The demarcation of the territory of penality as a discipline, and its discourse, appear less contested the further one moves away from a criticality based on sensitivity to divisions of power within society, in terms of gender, ethnicity and age. For centuries, the physical punishment of subjugated peoples, whether communally or in their roles as slaves or servants, was a taken-for-granted feature of many societies (Garlan, 1988), as was the routine punishment (see Chapter 7) of wives by husbands and children by parents.

In research for this book, the author wrote to the governments of more than 100 countries to ask for general data, including statistics, concerning the incidence of a range of punishments, including corporal and capital punishment. The paucity of detailed information about penal regimes in many different countries in the responses received is indicative of the lack of openness of governments rather than shortcomings in the quality of facilities. Often, the lack of direct information makes other sources – documentary and fiction – or a combination of the two – more important than they would otherwise have been. Henri Charrière's novel *Papillon* describes the formidable system of penal colonies – with Devil's Island as its infamous centrepiece – sustained by France in French Guiana in the first half of the twentieth century (Charrière, 1981). Jimmy Boyle documented solitary confinement in the special unit at Bairlinnie prison, Glasgow, in the 1970s, in his autobiographical books based on his diaries (Boyle, 1977; 1985). Clavell fictionalises life in Changi and Outram Road, the prisoner of war camps on Singapore Island during the Second World War (Clavell, 1975). Zhang Xianliang (1994) based the book *Grass Soup* on personal diaries written in a labour camp in China in 1960. He describes how his life, and the diary, were saved by his decision only to write ledger-like details in it, without indicating any incriminating thoughts, since he correctly anticipated that eventually it must be found by the authorities and searched for signs of anti-progressive thinking (Xianliang, 1994, p. 6). Solzhenitsyn's work (1963; 1984) on the system of Stalinist labour camps in Siberia combined his personal experience of serving a sentence in a labour camp between 1945 and 1953 with material gathered from other prisoners and from literature.

The moral dimension of justifications for features of particular criminal codes – such as long, exemplary custodial sentences for persistent offenders, corporal or capital punishment – tends to cloak their arbitrariness under the legalistic discourse of justice. Lady Constance Lytton diarised the three years to the end of 1911; during this period she became a convinced suffragette activist and spent several periods in prison. Most notable is her account of being force-fed at Walton prison, Liverpool (Lytton, 1976, pp. 268–70). Ivan Denisovich Shukhov, in the classic fictionalised representation of a Stalinist Siberian labour camp by Solzhenitsyn, resents being caught on his bunk at reveille by the sneaky guard, primarily because he is always one of the first prisoners up and the punishment is unfair (Solzhenitsyn, 1963, p. 11). Ray Rigby's brilliant novel set in a British prison for defaulters during the Second World War illustrates both the convergence of the abuse of power in both military and criminal jústice and the collusive avoidance of its reality by the officers in charge of the prison (Rigby, 1965). In these situations, institutional life imposes penalties on individuals in arbitrary ways, reinforced, or at any rate colluded in, by the apathy of the authorities towards justice. Goffman's inductive analysis links a vast variety of institutional forms with the single mental hospital in Washington, DC in which he carries out his anthropological research, and concludes that some features of total institutions – notably block treatment of inmates and the gulf in power between staff and inmates – contribute to the subversion of their formal goals (Goffman, 1967). It is not difficult, therefore, to find evidence confirming the view that institutional power and punishment corrupt.

In wartime, the traditional abhorrence attached to certain kinds of violent crime, such as attacking and killing an identified 'enemy', tends to be overridden.

> The state authorizes criminal conduct either because of its own designs on other states or its fear of the aggressive intentions of other states ... .
> Authorizing crimes in time of war has posed a problem for religions and ethical systems which proscribe conduct such as killing, wounding, kidnapping, destroying or carrying off other people's property.
>
> (Mixon, 1989, p. 5)

Whether or not similar kinds of justification are used for the 'just war' as for the 'just punishment', there are some similarities. In both cases, force may be used by one group of people to impose standards of behaviour on another. Also, officials – whether soldiers or executioners – may take life on behalf of the state. But in many countries, the elaborate codes governing judicial processes may be set aside in wartime; amnesties may be declared, for example, and certain classes of prisoner drafted into armed service. One by-product of Levi's documentation of the wartime experiences of Jews at the hands of the Nazis, is the insight that when the Russians counter-attacked towards the end of the 1939–45 war, the *Lager* (prison camp) of the fortress town of Glogau simply exchanged its former slave labourers of the Nazi period for all the wandering, suspect people encountered by the Red Army in the area (Levi, 1985, p. 232).

International agreements such as the Geneva Convention concerning the conduct of wars replaced earlier contracts and informal cultural norms governing them. From medieval times, it was customary for gentlemen and commoners to exact no mercy from each other if they fell into each other's hands during wartime (Contamine, 1990, p. 257). There is an arbitrary quality about the extremes of warfare, which contradicts the seeming independent objectivity of standards aspired to in the Hague Conference of 1907 which 44 states signed, the Geneva Conventions of 1949 which 62 states signed and the Additional Protocols of the Geneva Convention of 1977, to which 102 states gave their signatures (Best, 1983, p. 287). In his modern history of armed conflict, however, Geoffrey Best distances himself from what he sees as the arbitrariness of justifications for warfare; he views these as arguments which are capable of elasticity to suit the ends of the perpetrator (Best, 1983, p. 5).

The pressures against reform are very great. As in child abuse, the power of the perpetrator tends to be absolute. Solzhenitsyn introduces his massive indictment of the system – his image is that of the sewage disposal system – of dumping whole nations, through extermination, in a vast archipelago of prisons in the invisible country of *Gulag*, by saying he would like to acknowledge the many people who have contributed to his book, but 'the time has not yet come when I dare name them' (Solzhenitsyn, 1984, p. xi).

Most prison systems in Western countries are run by men, for men; even women prisoners and their prisons take on some of the macho characteristics of male prisoners and men's prisons: the forbidding buildings, the high incidence of violence. Only a tiny proportion of prisoners in countries such as the USA, South Africa and the UK are women, which makes their marginality in these systems even more pronounced; in contrast, although a significant proportion of prisoners in the UK and USA are black, these systems remain 'white' in their management.

Arguments against Punishment

The dominant conceptualisations of punishment tend to reinforce not only its continued uses, but also do nothing to disallow its abuses. Three main viewpoints may be taken: that punishment never involves abuse; that punishment may be abusive in certain cases and that punishment tends to be abusive, no matter what its rationale. The first seems implausible; the second and third are adopted in different parts of this book.

Often, campaigns against punishment have been conducted on the grounds that it is excessive, inappropriate, unjustified, or various combinations of these.

'Punishment is excessive'
One argument against punishment *per se* is that in essence it is qualitatively no different from cruel and unusual forms of punishment. The difference is

one of degree, rather than of kind. It is more straightforward to argue against excessive punishment than against punishment itself. Excessive punishment is widely regarded as punishment which is cruel and unusual, one form of which is torture.

The judge in the Gilbert and Sullivan opera *Trial by Jury* sings 'make the punishment fit the crime', the question being how to assess the border-line between what is excessive and what is not. At extremes, it may be relatively easy to determine. Thus, in March 1995, a young man in the USA was sentenced to 25 years' imprisonment for stealing a slice of pizza from some children on a beach. This was in the wake of a new federal law requiring offenders to be sentenced to long terms after their third 'serious' offence.

Examination of controversies about the use of corporal punishment, in the home, in school and in other settings is intrinsically relevant and also, given blurred boundaries between what constitutes punishment, control, discipline and abuse, inseparable from these wider considerations.

'Punishment is inappropriate'

In such cases, the argument tends not to centre on the abuse of punishment *per se*, but on the inappropriateness of particular forms in specific settings. Abundant evidence of the inappropriateness of punishment in such regimes as *Pindown* in children's homes (see Chapter 3) and in homes for older and disabled people, the punitive measures taken against immig-rants, including their extended detention in local prisons, all are features which need drawing together and their significance critically examined. But there are other areas, such as the use of physical punishments in behavioural therapy and monetary punishments as a deterrent, which have been under-examined, from the point of view of their ethical justification, as opposed to their efficacy.

One form of argument concerning the inappropriateness of punishment involves the complaint that after a certain number of years, delays in exe-cuting offenders may become unacceptable. The fact that many people wait on death row in the USA for more than a decade has provoked growing concern about this issue. Such concerns were reflected in the con-sideration by a seven-member judicial committee of the Privy Council, including Lord Justice Woolf who carried out the inquiry into the riot at HM Prison Strangeways (Woolf and Tumin, 1991), which considered delays in executions in Jamaica. This judicial committee took the view that delays of more than five years from sentence probably made the exe-cution an 'inhuman and degrading punishment' (letter to *The Times*, 6 April 1995) (see Chapter 7 for more details).

'Punishment is unjustified'

This argument is based on the fundamental belief that punishment is inherently degrading of humanity. One version of this is evident in the fears of the French revolutionaries that the guillotine, as much by the mass decapitations as by the type of spectacle it provided (Arasse, 1991, p. 65), would turn the people into 'a populace of cannibals' (Arasse, 1991, p. 64). It is arguably unacceptable for the state to order a person to execute another, whilst an individual who attacks the individual whom he alleges wronged him is tried and found guilty of murder. Here the arguments of what constitutes a just cause become important. For example, it can be argued that the process of execution is inherently and unavoidably unacceptable. In other words, even if it is theoretically justifiable that a person should be executed, an acceptable way of achieving this has not been identified. Further, making an execution ritual out of the process may be argued to be hypocritical.

A further argument against capital punishment may be put forward on the grounds that it is arbitrary, and therefore unjust. This was one of the principal forces driving the virtual abolition of capital punishment for half a dozen years in the USA from the late 1960s (see Chapter 7).

The next chapter deals with the ways the histories of punishment have been approached.

2 Histories of Punishment

The past is a foreign country: they do things differently there.
(L. P. Hartley, Prologue, *The Go-Between*)

INTRODUCTION

This chapter considers histories of punishment. It reviews different narratives and briefly visits the major eras of punishment, from pre-medieval to modern. It charts changing perspectives, rather than presenting a single, consensual history of punishment. It could be claimed that mere convenience makes the penal setting the main focus of this chapter. However, it has to be admitted that whilst the purpose of this book includes looking at punishments beyond criminal justice systems, the centre of gravity of debates about their histories remains in the penal system. This is not to say, however, that corporal punishment and other aspects of punishment do not deserve more detailed attention than they receive here.

THE PAST AND PRESENT OF PUNISHMENT: SOME DOMINANT THEMES

The nature of punishment in particular historical periods and geographical locations is shaped by economic, political and cultural factors. The tendency towards particular forms of punishment, such as corporal punishment, is likely to be associated with other features of an ethnic or cultural location, such as the status of children, women, different ethnic groups, people with impairments, religious beliefs, political ideologies, child-rearing practices and norms of adult, especially male, behaviour, as Miedzian's critique of the values of USA society demonstrates (Miedzian, 1992). Societies which are more imperialist, militarist, sexist and racist tend to differ markedly in terms of attitudes towards children and their punishment, from those which value non-macho qualities, cooperation, older and non-productive people such as those with impairments, and, of course, children. Perspectives on the rearing of children differ in terms of the extent to which the infliction of mental and physical deprivation, pain and punishment are considered to be essential to the nurturing of children.

36

Psychological theories buttress physical and mental violence, in the guise of the negative reinforcement of behaviour therapy, for example.

Comparison of different historical periods is not as straightforward as it seems at first sight. In Britain, in the late eighteenth century, for example, the increasing severity of punishments and notably the presence of capital punishment as the penalty for many, including minor, offences, led many juries to convict, apparently, in fewer cases than they otherwise would have done, in order to avoid the ultimate penalty being applied. Whether or not this is strictly accurate, it points to the need to draw a more complex map of the relationship between society and the criminal justice system. We cannot lump together the judiciary and the jury in the context of the politicians and senior officials who enact laws as their framework for action and appoint them. The participants in the criminal justice process reflect different, and at times conflicting, interests.

Further, it is not at all clear how some kind of index of the punitiveness of a society is to be assessed, and the extent to which an absolute scale can be drawn up which enables different eras to be compared independent of other social, economic, political and legal factors. Should the increased criminalisation of behaviour which took place in the eighteenth century in Britain be regarded as exceptional because it occurred during the period of the French Revolution? Or is this a benchmark of a historical moment of change? The interpretation of this needs to take account not only of the increased use of the guillotine in France, but also of the increasing recourse by the judiciary in Britain to punitive means of social control, fuelled in part, no doubt, by fears that, if unchecked, the infection of revolution might spread across the English channel?

Questions as to whom to punish, how to punish them, where, when, and why, have been central rather than peripheral to processes of social change in many parts of the world. Often, the means of punishment expresses the punitive, as well as the aspirant, mentality of the age, the circumstances of the particular incident, the punishers and the punished.

It would be misleading to present a one-dimensional account of the character of punishment in different eras. Nevertheless, some dominant themes are discernible. Cohen's view of the history of deviancy control systems purportedly stands outside the ideologies and narratives achieving dominance during each of the three phases he describes. During the first, pre-eighteenth century, period, moralistic, then classical, just deserts theories of punishment predominated and penal measures were sited in the community, witnessed by the public, rather than regulated by professionals in private. In the second, nineteenth- and early twentieth-century phase, positivist and medico-treatment ideals influenced an increasingly institutionally-based system. During the third phase, a partially successful critical onslaught on positivism by back to justice and neo-classical theories of punishment was exemplified by the dispersal of measures for controlling deviants, in a variety of community-based alternatives to custody (Cohen, 1985, pp. 16–17). Cohen (1985, pp. 13–14) identifies four cumulative changes featuring in the revisionist history of deviancy control systems, during the second major period of transformation whose parameters were established by the mid-nineteenth century: increasing state involvement through centralised, bureaucratic arrangements for the control and punishment of delinquents; increasing differentiation and classification of deviants; increased incarceration of deviants into different kinds of institution – whether for mentally ill, criminal, or criminally insane people; an increasing focus on tackling the mind and personality of the offender rather than punishment through the public infliction of pain on the body. Despite Cohen's certainty that the third phase of transformation is occurring during the second half of the twentieth century, he is appropriately cautious about its details and, presumably, eventual outcomes (Cohen, 1985, p. 14). Cohen's analysis provides a starting-point for an examination of dominant themes of punishment in different periods.

Before the Nineteenth Century

This period was dominated by the idea of punishment as an end in itself. This involved an absolutist belief in justice, sentences being specified in relation to particular offences.

Informal punishments, being traditional, by their nature have lain beyond the scope of written histories. Increasingly, as the law was written down, criminal and civil laws at least could be mapped in retrospect. Roman law was extensively documented. Roman law displayed a variety of forms in different parts of the Roman Empire and in the Germanic states and Byzantine Empire which succeeded it. The economies of many of these older societies were dependent on slave labour which was maintained in subjection by brutal punishments. Over the centuries after the arrival of Christianity, although not caused by this, the criminal law became stricter and its sanctions more brutal. Penalties varied with the social class of the offender. In Roman society, built on slavery and massive inequalities of wealth and power, poorer people from the lower classes who were found guilty of crimes could be sentenced to penal servitude in mines, quarries or Roman bakeries (Jones, 1990, p. 298). Torture gardually came to be applied not only to free men but also to *curiales* and senators. The death penalty was applied cruelly to a wide variety of offences (Vogt, 1993, p. 203).

In the Viking period, cash fines and outlawry were the main punishments for minor offences, for free people, but slaves could also be whipped and mutilated. Major offences such as theft, whether by free people or slaves, attracted death, by beheading or hanging. Witches could also be stoned, drowning or sunk into a bog (Foote and Wilson, 1979, p. 381).

From the eighth century, the Teutonic *Lex Baiuvarionum* has provided a written legal code for the regulation and punishment of people in society. Witchcraft was originally strictly controlled by Anglo-Saxon laws governing crimes against people and their property. Purgatory, whether or not intentionally, functioned as a means of subjugation, through punishment of religious deviance and nonconformity. The spread of Roman Catholicism led to increased prosecution of witches, for crimes against God, such as heresy. The Inquisition fostered the hunt to root out heresy.

The concepts of divine pardon and judicial intervention converged in the medieval notion of sanctuary. Often, sanctuary could be provided to a limited extent by a person reaching a cathedral. In the twentieth century, churches have provided sanctuary for people who otherwise may have been deported.

The history of punishment in Western 'developed' countries was dominated by the Church between the fifth and the nineteenth centuries, which, for the first 1000 years, in effect, meant Roman Catholicism. If images of religious discipline and instruction were fashioned from the surrounding landscape (Schama, 1995, pp. 436–7), the central idioms and metaphors of punishment were those of sin, atonement, punishment and the long road to purgatory and either heaven or hell. Peter Bruegel the elder in the sixteenth century depicted such images in his painting, drawing on the visionary work of Hieronymus Bosch (see cover illustration).

Treatment and reformation were more optimistic variants on the journey to redemption, offering milder alternatives to the harsher fatalism of Calvinism. The justifications for many of the more violent and gruesome forms of punishment were made more plausible by their embedding in the dominant religious imagery of sin, retribution and penance. The almost universal belief in the existence of heaven and hell emphasised the certainties of sprititually-induced punishment for spiritual crimes, overlapping with, and making more potent, the exercise of the law in circumstances where an earthly crime was committed. Into this calculus of just deserts, the invention of purgatory in the Middle Ages interjected a still more potent disciplinary measure, created and sustained, it could be argued, by the imperative of social control. Naturally, it involved then, as now, a weighty theological justification for beliefs reliant on the threat of long-term punishment in hell as an ultimate sanction, with heaven as the ideal to be realised by aspirants.

The penal code was influenced very largely until the nineteenth century by the dominant religious beliefs of the day. For centuries, it made little difference to the religious *cognoscenti* whether or not a person survived, died in prison or was executed; what mattered was whether the individual admitted guilt and offered penance for the wrong committed. It was only from the late eighteenth century, with the birth of the prison as a utilitarian, and increasingly large-scale, state-sponsored response to criminality, that another, essentially secular, focus developed on what happened there.

Inquisition: the process of punishment

In the Middle Ages, the Papal Inquisition was set up by Innocent III in a Papal Bull in AD 1199. This took the power of the Bishops for investigating heresy into the Vatican. Subsequently, the Vatican administered the process of the Inquisition. In 1204 the first investigation began with the campaign against the Albigenses in southern France and northern Italy. For the next five centuries, the Inquisition spread throughout Europe. By the fourteenth century, the activities of the Inquisition were extended to cover not only heretics but also witches and sorcerers. In 1252 Innocent IV approved the use of torture in a Papal Bull, as a last resort in extracting confessions. After confession, the offender was usually executed by the minions of the state. Following torture, the offender was usually required to repeat the confession without being tortured. In 1479 the Spanish Inquisition was set up. It was suspended in 1808 and recommenced its activities in 1814, finally finishing in 1834. The Spanish Inquisition was separately administered from the Papal Inquisition which was run from Rome. The Spanish Inquisition was set up by Ferdinand and Isabella as a Spanish remedy for sorcery.

The process of Inquisition involved the gathering of evidence, entailing sessions with Inquisitors over a considerable period of time, often extending to years. The accused person was able to discuss the case with a counsel nominated by the court. The role of the counsel was to persuade the prisoner to confess. Usually, the accused person was not informed who had made allegations of heresy. At the point when the accused person admitted the charges the Inquisitor would meet with the bishop and legal or theological experts to determine the verdict. If the verdict was reached immediately the prisoner was sentenced. In any cases of doubt as to the truth of the evidence, this court would use torture as a means of pursuing the truth (Lane, 1993, p. 291). The most common forms of torture involved the use of the pulley, the rack and fire. Additionally, flagellation was used, often for offences such as talking, singing, whistling and insolence to the jailers while awaiting trial (Van Yelyr, 1941, p. 32).

An important feature of many of these punitive sanctions was that they were exemplary, both in the sense that punishments took place in a public place, and also in the sense that the consequence of the punishment was visible, often horrifically so. Thus, the Englishman Isaac Martin was accused and found guilty in 1714 of being a Jew and was sentenced to banishment after being given 200 strokes with the whip. Martin reported later how 'stripped to the waist, with his hands tied, and a rope around his neck, he was mounted upon the back of an ass and led through the streets of Granada, his progress being punctuated by the administration of the 200 lashes, while the onlookers pelted him with such missiles as were available' (Van Yelyr, 1941, p. 32).

Some idea of the scale of activities of the Spanish Inquisition can be gained by the numbers burned in Andalusia, which amounted to 3000 in 1841, with a further 17 000 being tortured (Lane, 1993, p. 446).

Secular punishment
In 1426, the law proscribed vagrancy, punishable with three days in the stocks for the first offence. Within a few years, this punishment was relaxed. In the sixteenth century, in the reign of Henry VIII, the law decreed that beggars and vagrants could be whipped and returned to their parish of origin. Second-time offenders would have their ears cropped and for a third offence the person could be hanged (Byrne, 1992, p. 70). The application and removal of irons was a matter of commercial profit for the gaolers in the Newgate in the fifteenth century (Byrne, 1992, p. 27). Houses of correction were adopted in 1574 to try to curb the swelling tide of pauperism (Byrne, 1992, p. 70).

Slavery and punishment went hand in hand in the plantation economies of the New World, where an estimated 8 to 11 million slaves were imported between the seventeenth and nineteenth centuries. Sir Hans Sloane's stay in the West Indies from 1686 as personal physician to the Governor of Jamaica was followed by his two volumes of memoirs (Sloane, 1707 and 1725, quoted in Everett, 1991, p. 82) in which he noted the punishments of slaves he had witnessed:

For certain 'flagrant' crimes slaves were 'nailed to the ground with crooked sticks strapped to each limb. They were then slowly burned alive, first the hands and the feet, and then ... gradually up to the head.'

'Lesser' crimes were dealt with by castration, or chopping off part of the foot with an axe ... . Slaves were occasionally flogged to death, and often whipped until their bodies were raw, the more sadistic planters ordering salt, pepper or hot ashes to be rubbed into the wounds of their victims. Sometimes melted wax was applied or burning wood passed over the affected parts.

(Everett, 1991, pp. 82–3)

The Nineteenth and the First Part of the Twentieth Century

From the late eighteenth century the severity and scope of punishments administered through the law increased. In the nineteenth century they were largely confined to a new array of penal institutions, whereas in the twentieth century they diversified and extended to a range of community settings not previously envisaged as sites for punishment.

The tendency towards increasing the severity of punishments in Britain during the eighteenth century led, by 1800, to more than 220 offences being punishable by death. Some of these applied to children. Yet in the second half of the nineteenth century, and especially from the 1880s, there were other moves to remove children from the full rigours of adult life.

The eighteenth-century Hobbesian theory of social contract viewed force as necessary to impose order – the equation between powerful and powerless people – in society. In contrast, the Benthamite utilitarian viewed decisions about punishment and social control as the outcome of calculations balancing the justness of particular quantities of pain, against the possibilities of enhanced benefits to the individual and society on one hand, or increased criminality on the other.

Until the mid-nineteenth century, when the situation reversed dramatically, punishment, including prison and prisoners, was readily accessible to the gaze of the outsider (Gatrell, 1994b). Apart from a few sequestered prisoners in special categories – royalty or imprisoned clerics under Canon Law – the public could visit and converse freely with them, for example, at the house of correction, Holloway (Mayhew and Binney, 1862, p. 570).

Before the advent of penal servitude, many minor offences, as well as serious ones, attracted the death penalty. The relatively high rate of acquittals may be explained by the fact that in such circumstances juries were less keen to find offenders guilty.

Women were pardoned of capital crimes more readily than men, particularly if they were pregnant. The exception was crimes within marriage. A woman who killed her husband was hanged and burned, since she had committed a 'petty treason'; she, as the servant, had broken her master's trust. Between 1900 and 1949, of the 1080 men and 130 women convicted of murder, approximately 40 per cent of the men and 90 per cent of the women were reprieved (Ignatieff, 1983, p. 25).

As prison became established as a site for ongoing sentences to be inflicted, a range of new activities developed for prisoners. At times the rationale for these was reformative, at others it had the character of keeping idle hands from mischief, at others again, hard labour was unashamedly punitive.

Oakum picking involved untwisting and shredding hemp which had been tarred and used in ships to caulk seams on the sides and decks of ships to make them watertight. Oakum picking was often the only work in which prisoners could be employed. Adults and children alike tended to engage in it. The coarseness of the material caused the hands of the prisoners to be lacerated and blistered. In Cold Bath Prison, for example, 500 oakum pickers could be employed in one shed (Lane, 1993, p. 338).

To the Late Twentieth Century

The positivist revolution brought neo-classical criminology into alignment with the treatment paradigm which was to dominate penology from the mid-nineteenth century until the 1970s. Positivism did not just leave its mark on the proliferation of techniques and typologies for testing and classifying criminals, but also gave impetus to the efforts of the Home Office Research Unit in the 1960s and 1970s to measure, test and observe criminals and buttress proliferating policies of control and incarceration, rather than subjecting imprisonment *per se* to critical scrutiny. As Cohen notes (1977, p. 217), 'in more senses than the obvious one, the prison is the ultimate depository of changes that happen elsewhere', shifting since the mid-nineteenth century from being 'places of the last resort when all else had failed' to become 'the preferred solution, the pride of the nation'.

The collapse of the rehabilitationist ideal – fuelled by research findings concerning the equal irrelevance of pretty well every penal and treatment sanction, in terms of its ability to bring about predictable changes for the better in criminal behaviour – occurred more or less simultaneously in the 1970s with the brief flowering of Marxist criminology (Taylor, Walton and Young, 1973).

The 1980s witnessed the exhaustion of the rationale for imprisonment and a widespread search for a rationale to replace the lost hope of treatment or rehabilitation; the 1990s saw a renewed emphasis on building prisons and filling them with offenders, in the wake of the Strangeways prison riot of 1990, which ironically produced the clearest statement

(Woolf and Tumin, 1991) since the Gladstone Report nearly a century earlier (Departmental Committee, 1895) of a reformist agenda for prisons. There was an increasing tendency for punishment to be dispersed throughout the community, through a range of increasingly rigorous so-called alternatives to prison – suspended sentences, community service and various forms of supervision by the probation service.

Whilst corporal and capital punishment disappeared from the statute book in many countries, their retention often signified a willingness to employ such sanctions as exemplary warnings to potential offenders. Or, as in the USA, there was a tendency to retain the execution as a deterrent, but surround it with procedures which attempted to depersonalise and make hygienic the process of killing by the state.

NARRATIVES OF PUNISHMENT

Histories of punishment express more than one story of impositions of pain on offenders by the state. Some contributory features affect offenders 'from above', some from outside the actions of the state and some 'from below' through the culture of other offenders. Narratives need to take account of Berkman's history of the prisoners' rights movement in the USA. This contrasts the 'institutional history ... which is framed not only in terms of administrative and policy changes but also in the 'patterns of beliefs and activities of the clients – a historical phenomenon usually absent from institutional histories' (Berkman, 1979, p. 33). A meta-narrative is required which overarches particular perspectives.

Rothman's analysis of the origins of the asylum in the Jacksonion period is the starting-point for critical reflection on the revolutionary changes in the USA which ensured that institutions for poor, insane and criminal people, which were places of last resort in the eighteenth century, within 50 years became the first resort (Rothman, 1971). Ignatieff, after his historical study of the Quaker 'reforms' of British prisons at the end of the eighteenth century and beginning of the nineteenth century (Ignatieff, 1978), charts the challenging of liberal histories of imprisonment by different revisionist versions, challenged in their turn by counter-revisionist critics (Ignatieff, 1981).

McKelvey's summary of the history of prisons and rioting has echoes in Cohen's analysis:

Stocks, whipping posts, and grim gallows cluttered the background during the eighteenth-century prologue; the scenes of the first act, running through several decades of the nineteenth century, were staged in front of the massive walls of rival prisons; now in the second act the walls have been pushed aside, and we watch the officers and reformers debating before the open face of towering cell blocks in which the figures of convicts can be seen crouching silently behind the bars; in the next era the convicts will file out onto the front stage and take a major part in the drama; finally, in an epilogue an individual convict will remain standing in centre stage while keepers, teachers, doctors, psychologists, divines, and judges will make up a speechless background.

(McKelvey, 1968, p. 145)

Histories of punishments do not so much chart a single process of continuous evolution, or even revolution, so much as changed responses to changes in the social and cultural context and in the fabric of criminal justice. The lack of comparability in historical records, and in standpoints from which they are compiled in particular periods, means we can expect that there will be no necessary agreement among commentators about what has happened, or about the significance attributed to it.

Whilst at one level it is easy to portray the history of punishment by the state, in countries such as Britain, France and the USA and other European countries, as the fairly steady progression from a more barbaric to a less barbaric state, a more careful reading of the events suggests that this developmental narrative represents only one historical interpretation. It is a matter of debate, whether or not later forms of execution are less barbaric. For example, the argument that the substitution in the USA over the past century for the older forms of execution such as the gallows and the gun, of the uniquely USA-style execution by lethal injection, electrocution and gassing represents progress towards greater humaneness is a matter of opinion rather than objective fact. Traditionally, if statistics are brought to bear it is easy to argue that in some states, notably Texas, the execution rate actually imposes harsher punishments on the populace at the end of the twentieth century than 100 years ago. At the juvenile end of the spectrum, whilst the incidence of executions of offenders who committed a crime whilst juveniles has increased in the second half of the twentieth century, what may have been the first recorded execution of a juvenile took place in 1642.

Just as understandings of punishment need to be located outside the restricted perspective of its penological functions and purposes, so descriptions and interpretations of policies and practices of punishment – in the past and the present – are not products of the actions of offenders alone. Forms of punishment arise from a variety of social factors. They are neither totally dissociated from the issues of crime and responses to crime, nor exclusively derived from them. Garland notes that

> for one thing, it is not 'crime' or even criminological knowledge about crime which most affects policy decisions, but rather the ways in which 'the crime problem' is officially perceived and the political positions to which these perceptions give rise. For another, the specific forms of policing, trial, and punishment, the severity of sanctions and the frequency of their use, institutional regimes, and frameworks of condemnation are all fixed by social convention and tradition rather than by the contours of criminality.
>
> (Garland, 1995, p. 20)

Discussion of the abuses of punishment needs to be located in the context of the interaction between the concept of punishment and its environment. This carries the risk that the focus will be blurred at the boundaries between punishment, social control and social order, since examination of punishment informs understanding about how personal and social order are conceptualised and achieved. For example, the trend in countries such as Britain and the USA towards a mixed economy of penal provision, with an increasing proportion of facilities, notably prisons, provided by organisations in the private sector, necessitates careful consideration. In other words, the focus of this book on the abuses of punishment involves acknowledging, but referring briefly to this contextual chapter, to the detailed debates associated with sociological understandings of punishment, social control and social order, which have been the subject of extensive study, notably by Durkheim (1933; 1973), Rusche and Kirchheimer (1968), Foucault (1982), Garland (1985b; 1995), Ignatieff (1978) and Melossi and Pavarini (1981).

For punishment 'is necessarily grounded in wider patterns of knowing, feeling, and acting, and it depends upon these social roots and supports for its continuing legitimacy and operation. It is also grounded in history, for, like all social institutions, modern punishment is a historical outcome which is only imperfectly adapted to its current situation' (Garland, 1995, p. 21). However, it is necessary to acknowledge that there is no unitary, consensual account of the history of punishment and Garland's use of the term 'developmental' is contingent on this caution, when he states that punishment 'is a product of tradition as much as present policy: hence the need for a developmental as well as a functional perspective in the understanding of penal institutions' (Garland, 1995, p. 21).

The management of punishment, its originators, key technicians, the technology they wield, participants in its staged dramas, the degree of public or private implementation, as well as the significance given to it in the subseqent descriptions of it, all need teasing out. A mapping exercise is undoubtedly needed. The perspective on punishment adopted affects the way a particular history is narrated. Debates and controversies about uses of punishment take place in the context of a range of theoretical perspectives on the use and different narratives in the past and present.

Durkheim asserted the view that the notion of punishment is a central feature of society. He viewed the functioning of society as dependent on the existence of shared meanings and values, which sustain social solidarity. Thus, for Durkheim, punishment emerges as a necessary social activity, part of the moral framework operating consistently with social conditions, 'a moral phenomenon operating within the circuits of the moral life, as well as carrying out more mundane social and penal functions' (Garland, 1995, p. 24). Durkheim perceived punishment as the expression of the moral order of society (Durkheim, 1933; 1973). Garland's detailed discussion of Durkheim's interpretation of the nature and significance of punishment in society (Garland, 1995, pp. 23–81) amounts to a defence of its contemporary relevance: 'Durkheim's questions about the moral basis of penal law, about the involvement of onlookers in the penal process, about the symbolic meanings of penal rituals, and about the relationship of penal institutions to public sentiment, are all questions which are worthy of our close attention, even when the answers which Durkheim suggests are not themselves convincing' (Garland, 1995, p. 27).

Reformist narratives

Until the 1970s, with the notable exception of Rusche and Kirchheimer, the history of punishment tended to be written from within the reformist tradition (see, for instance, Rose, 1961). What are sometimes termed liberal criminological histories 'emphasised the conscience as the motor of institutional change' (Ignatieff, 1981, p. 154). They assumed that punishments based on reform improved on those based on retribution. They focused on changes in the act of punishment, rather than linking them with its wider social context (Ignatieff, 1981, p. 154). As Rothman put it, 'to describe the asylum as a reform takes for granted precisely what ought to be the focus of investigation' (Rothman, 1971, p. xv). The meticulous monitoring and measurement of the precise numbers of strokes of the birch or the lash administered, characterised the Victorian approach to corporal punishment, whilst the mistake-ridden art of hanging someone became a mathematically-vindicated science based on the equation between the placing of the noose, the weight of the body and the length of the drop being just sufficient to asphyxiate the victim by dislocating the neck without decapitation; these calculations were consistent with a Utilitarian view and surrounded what critics viewed as an inherently barbaric act with a halo of scientific authenticity and, its advocates alleged, justification.

Garland's seminal article in 1985 marked the beginning of a serious attempt to develop 'a "critical" account – as opposed, perhaps, to an "impartial" one' (1985, p. 110). By this he meant accounting for 'the theoretical formation of the criminological programme', examining 'the *theoretical framework* of criminology, asking how this structure of problems, propositions and concepts came to be assembled, and how it related to the events and institutions of the social world'. Thus, he stands outside the features of the 'new', positivist criminology which in the late nineteenth century and early twentieth century 'promised an exact and scientific method for the study of crime, a technical means of resolving a serious social problem and a genuinely humane hope of preventing the harm of crime and improving the character of offenders'.

Whilst urging critical scrutiny of the history and impact of the discipline of criminology and scepticism of its over-identification with positivism, Garland refers to the work of Taylor, Walton and Young (1973), when he is properly critical of 'wholesale dismissals of the "reactionary purpose" and legacy of "positivism" with all the simplifications and overstatements which these entail' (Garland, 1985, p. 110).

The science and discourse of criminology challenged the territories of jurists and judges, rather than establishing itself alongside the interests of those directly affected by crime – notably victims and offenders. Criminologists rendered problematic hitherto taken-for-granted concepts such as freedom, responsibility, rationality and rights, but this struggle was to establish their own discipline, and the following comment by Garland should be viewed in this light: 'the technical armoury provided by the criminological movement thus amounted to a number of elaborate identification techniques, a range of eliminative means such as deportation, labour colonies, preventive detention, etc., which owed little to criminological theory, and a faith that medicine and psychiatry could be relied upon to provide effective rehabilitative techniques'. Yet, despite the preoccupation with statistics, measurement and testing, from the point of view of products of all this technological activity, 'the criminological programme offered an effective social defence – through eliminative means and police techniques – but little in the way of prevention or rehabilitation.

However much it described itself as a curative programme, what was actually on offer was a technology of segregative control' (Garland, 1985, p. 134). In the process, it shifted ideas away from classical criminological theory, and power away from judges and the judiciary, towards positivist theories and the widening arenas of medicine, psychiatry, psychology and sociology and the professions which drew on them (Garland, 1985, pp. 134–5).

Revisionist narratives

Sylvester considers two fundamentally different perspectives on penology which have informed penal policy and practice: first, the thesis of Rusche and Kirkheimer that the growth of the criminal justice system was shaped by economic forces, notably the growing productivity of labour, which, in turn, destroyed the economic rationale for penal servitude, houses of correction and the industrial prison; second, the motivation towards reformative and correctional philosophies, informed in part by religious ideals, which grew in prominence in the nineteenth and early twentieth centuries, but which ultimately failed to justify their case (Sylvester, 1977, pp. 5–8). Since then, as Sylvester acknowledges, neo-orthodoxy – resting on the assumption that human beings are essentially rational – based on various forms of justice (Morris, 1974; Wilson, 1975; Giller and Morris, 1981), have had their deterrent effectiveness undercut by the failure of the criminal justice system to keep up with the demand for crime processing (Sylvester, 1977, p. 9).

The book by Rusche and Kirchheimer (1968) originally published in 1939 and the essay by Rusche (1980) originally published in 1933, represent an important tradition of Marxist conceptualisations of the relationship between the role of penal institutions and changing economic conditions in society (Adams, 1994, p. 25). They are notable representatives of Marxist arguments which, from the early 1970s to the 1980s, occupied the foreground of Western criminological thought. Rusche and Kirchheimer correlate changing penal methods from the Middle Ages to the middle of the twentieth century, with changing social forms which lie beyond specifically penal purposes. This contrasts with Durkheim's view that punishment is 'universal and largely immutable' (Garland, 1995, p. 90), in that 'punishments are to be viewed as historically specific phenomena which only appear in particular, concrete forms' (Garland, 1995, p. 90). They view prisons as the epitome of the function of the penal system as a means of social control, notably of poor people. In this sense, prisons have functioned like the workhouses of early Victorian England. 'When society's surplus labour needed dumping, they provided living conditions just below those of the lowest working-class people' (Adams, 1994, p. 25). Rusche (1978) puts forward a simplistic hypothesis in his research into the relationship between economic conditions and crime and punishment. He argues that societies where the supply of labour is scarce will adopt punishment to make people work, whereas when there is a reserve pool of unemployed people, harsh corporal and capital punishments will be used (Rusche, 1978, pp. 4–7). Melossi and Pavarini have carried the Marxist analysis, in the working-out of the relationship between economic conditions, modes of production and penal forms, to its 'most resolutely orthodox' position (Cohen, 1985, p. 23). This analysis

> binds the nature of the prison in a tight cause–effect equation between the changing nature of capitalism, modes of production, fiscal crises and the demand and supply of labour. Melossi and Pavarini reduce the complexities of the narrative to economically determined equations. It is a functionalist account in which the motives of participating people are 'more or less irrelevant or only of derivative status'.
>
> (Cohen, 1985, p. 23)

In similar vein, Andrew Scull's analysis (1977) of the decarceration of criminal and mentally ill people has been criticised (Matthews, 1979, pp. 100–17) for presenting the complex narrative of changing mental health and criminal justice policy in Britain and the USA in a way which is reductionist and determinist (Adams, 1994, p. 31).

Economic reductionism is an important, but not the sole critique to be made of Marxist analyses of the role of punishment in society. It is necessary also to avoid the implication that the horrors of punishments occurring from the late Middle Ages were simply 'socially permitted sadism' (Garland, 1995, p. 107). However, the motives informing many changes throughout history, notably those of the Quaker reformers in the late eighteenth and early nineteenth centuries in Britain, may have contributed to the harshness of the separate and silent systems (Ignatieff, 1978), but 'even the most shocking penal atrocities were generally undertaken within a positive framework of political intent and social symbolism' (Garland, 1995, p. 107).

A further question needs to be raised about the assumption that modes of production and the standard of living of working-class people directly correlate with forms of punishment. Penal policies and practices, rates of imprisonment, and specifically the uses of physical, corporal and capital forms of punishment, vary greatly from one country to another, independently of the location of that country in relation to capitalism or socialism. Garland refers to data from China and the former Soviet Union (Kadish, 1983, pp. 182–214) when he comments that 'the penal methods and institutions adopted by countries adopting socialist or quasi-socialist economic forms do not seem to differ greatly from those used in capitalist states, though their penal ideologies, custodial regimes and target populations do show some important differences' (Garland, 1995, p. 108).

Further, the simplistic equation which presupposes that the penal system carries out the will of the strong state is not adequate to encompass the complex interaction between politicians, civil servants and the providers of penal services in the public and the independent – voluntary and private – sectors. In Britain, evidence of the need for careful exegesis of this complexity has its origins not in commentary on the contemporary popularity of privatisation with the Conservative government, but in historical analysis of the relations between the state and penal agenices 200 years earlier. Young, for example, observes: 'Penal relations were not always the expression of state relations, their administration and implementation sometimes being founded in "private" bodies who were in contest with the state precisely over the penal issue' (Young, 1983, pp. 90–1). Young notes Ignatieff's account of penal reform and the penal system provides evidence which, whilst capable of simplistic interpretation, importantly charts the complexity of these relations. Ignatieff simultaneously advances the theory that prison expresses the interests of the dominant, powerful classes and the state, arguing that the bourgeoisie were coopted as contributors to this process, and yet 'he contends also that some members of this very class, the magistracy, were able to resist government direction and find exemption from central controls'. Again, 'not only is evidence presented to suggest that there was not a homogeneous class response, but also that penal administration worked successfully outwith the state (for example, early local prisons)' (Young, 1983, p. 91). Young concludes that 'this is not simply a question of insensitivity to empirical detail and complexity. Ignatieff offers evidence pointing to the possibility of quite different relationships of power between the penal system and the state: the evidence will not bear the imposition of the strong state thesis entailed in recent sociological accounts' (Young, 1983, p. 91). Finally, it is important to state that, in contrast with the contribution of Durkheim or Foucault to conceptualisation about punishment in society, the contribution of revisionism has been to locate histories of imprisonment in the explanatory context of narratives of class conflict (Scull, 1977; Melossi and Pavarini, 1981), social control by the state (Foucault, 1982), or a combination of these (Ignatieff, 1978).

The analysis of the use of imprisonment, and over and above that, execution, provides the central location for the consideration of critical narratives. Camus's ambivalence towards capital punishment is a moral stand, but is probably based on bad history and, according to Linebaugh, may also be ahistorical (Linebaugh, 1995b, p. 22). Linebaugh's analysis of the death penalty in Louisiana develops a Marxist argument, based on the wholesale killing of black people in the 1860s and 1870s, in the campaign to confirm white supremacy (Linebaugh, 1995b, p. 27). Linebaugh writes of the devaluation of labour by the death penalty in the 'United States of Lyncherdom' (Linebaugh, 1995b, p. 28).

However, the contributions of Marxist commentators are weakened by the fact that they provide no insights derived from Marxist theoretical perspectives focusing uniquely on this area of society.

Marxism offers no concepts or analyses which are peculiar to this set of institutions, and it has no particular theory of punishment as such ... . Marxism provides us with an account of penality's relationship with its class-structured political and economic environment and the implications this has for penal forms and penal practices. In most societies, the impact of class divisions upon penality is pervasive and profound but in so far as penality has other determinants, or relationships or significance, the analyst needs to look beyond the Marxist framework.

(Garland, 1995, p. 129)

It is straightforward to envisage the punitive apparatus of the penal system within Foucault's framing of the tactics of individualising disciplines, and, broader than prison and prisoners – 'a whole set of techniques and institutions for measuring, supervising and correcting the abnormal' (Foucault, 1982, p. 199). Garland argues for the need to locate Foucault's influential analysis of criminology as a discipline legitimising and extending penal power, in its broader societal context (Garland, 1992).

The distinctive contribution of Foucault to an understanding of punishment in society lies less in its inheritance in Weber's and Nietzsche's ideas (Garland, 1995, p. 131), than in its concentration on the different levels at which disciplinary techniques operate, and the linkages between these. There are irregularities, and gaps, in the analysis, not least because it depends on making connections between ideas and events (Adams, 1994, p. 34; see also Sparks, Bottoms and Hay, 1996, p. 65). Inevitably perhaps, it is difficult to sustain the connections between broad-brush discussion of disciplinary mechanisms operating in society in the eighteenth, nineteenth and twentieth centuries in Western Europe, and the detailed exegesis of the supervisory, disciplinary activities of the vast range and number of staff comprising the workforce of armies, workshops, schools and, at the core of the apparatus expressing disciplinary power, prisons. Foucault regards disciplines as 'techniques for making useful individuals' (Foucault, 1979, p. 211). In this sense, the term 'discipline' does not refer to an institution or a specific set of equipment. It is 'a type of power, a modality for its exercise, comprising a whole set of instruments, techniques, procedures, levels of application, targets; it is a "physics" or an "anatomy" of power, a technology' (Foucault, 1982, p. 215). The workforce engaged in exercising power in such circumstances form a network which operates between the monarch and the most menial level at which power operates in society (Foucault, 1982, p. 215).

Counter-revisionist narratives
Ignatieff (1981) uses the term counter-revisionism for narratives attempting to incorporate the experiences and the culture of prisoners. The provisional nature of all these needs taking into account. The result is that 'we now get the histories (in the plural) of the losers as well as the winners, of the regional (and colonial) as well as the centrist, of the unsung many as well as the much "sung few"' (Hutcheon, 1990, p. 66). According to one interpretation, therefore, these are the fragmented voices of postmodernity. They gain in vociferousness through the somewhat sporadic, if at times tumultuous, phenomena of riots and protests by prisoners – the respective territories of these are not clearly demarcated – from the early years of the twentieth century (Adams, 1994). One point of access to these multiple voices is in the memoirs of people who are punished, and through fictional representations which may illuminate features of punishment in particular historical and social circumstances.

In the latter half of the twentieth century, the prisoner's autobiography gained increasing prominence, not only as an alternative to official sources of information about the relatively sequestered prison institution, but also – as in the case of Leech's account (Leech, 1993), given a foreword by His Honour James Pickles, or Jimmy Boyle (Boyle, 1977; 1985), who became a prominent campaigner for prison reform on discharge from Barlinnie prison in Glasgow – has acquired the aura of respectability reflecting the unique contribution to be made by the voice of the prisoner.

Novels have been a traditional medium through which to convey the perceived realities of crime and punishment. In Compton's futuristic novel *Justice City* (Compton, 1994), the eponymous prison housing 5000 inmates is run by no more than 300 prison officers, using minimal staff–prisoner interaction through such means as Audi-frequency

Treatment and Long-term Incarceration. Cooke provides a fictionalised history of the Strangeways prison riot, viewed from the vantage-point of a prison chaplain (Cooke, 1995). Crime, criminality, criminal justice systems and penal processes form an important stimulus for creative work, exemplified, for example, in the commentary on the Russian and Soviet experience provided by the novels of Tolstoy (*Resurrection*), Dostoyevsky (*Crime and Punishment*) and Solzhenitsyn (*A Day in the Life of Ivan Denisovitch*; *The Gulag Archipelago*). Material for the latter two novelists comes partly from those authors' experiences of imprisonment in Siberia, albeit a century apart. Dostoyevsky, returning from a four-year sentence of hard labour in Siberia for the crime of sedition – reading aloud a critical letter at a gathering of the so-called Petrashevsky group – writes empathetically with the circumstances of Raskolnikov, who has murdered an old woman for selfish, and objectively inexcusable, reasons. Dostoyevsky emphasises the importance of the feelings – such as guilt and remorse – of the the criminal after committing the crime rather than the possible deterrent impact on his behaviour by the sanctions of the court (Dostoyevsky, 1965). Many of the more penetrating insights in the novels of Georges Simenon – notably in *Act of Passion* (1965), originally published as *Lettre à mon Juge* in 1947, *In Case of Emergency* (1965), originally published as *En Cas de Malheur* in 1956 and *The Widower* (1965), originally published as *Le Veuf* in 1959 – arose from their emphasis on the personality and circumstances of the criminal up to the point of committing the crime, rather than on the process of its subsequent detection.

Howe (1994) conducts the debate between herself and postmodern perspectives, but not with any great commitment, since her lack of faith in the intellectual coherence and relevance of postmodernism to, for example, the harm done to imprisoned women, soon overpowers other aspects of the argument. This is a useful caution, which underlines the macho version of masculinity which permeates the field of punishment, as indeed it does criminal justice and criminology in general (Newburn and Stanko, 1994). As has been noted in respect of the history of protest by prisoners (Adams, 1994, p. 235), it is all too easy, as Fitzgerald has done, to follow the men engaged in the more dramatic and violent collective acts (Fitzgerald, 1977) and to neglect the less visible but no less horrifying stories around women's resistance to imprisonment. This is apparent, for example, in the account of the imprisonment of women in Ireland in the Troubles of the early twentieth century and the account by Lady Lytton of her force-feeding when on hunger strike (Adams, 1994, pp. 142–4).

We can see in acts of punishment, and protests against forms of punishment vivid illustrations of Sumner's comment that the modern criminal justice system is 'still an arena of contestation between unequal forces' (Sumner, 1990, p. 45). It is important to acknowledge, as Chapter 9 illustrates, that the gains are not all on the side of the authorities. Behind postmodern representations of fragmentation, there are enduring features of punitive oppression.

POSTSCRIPT: HISTORIES ARE PROVISIONAL

It is appropriate, though, to end this chapter with a disclaimer that histories of punishment can be anything more than provisional. In any event, the horror stories of past punishments should not be taken as implying that the nearer one comes to the present day the more progress is made towards enlightenment. Pollock observes that the fact that children were whipped at times, and corporal chastisement was allowed, should not be interpreted as signifying that parents in the nineteenth century were more cruel than their twentieth-century counterparts. They did not necessarily care less for their children, or nurture them less effectively. The harsh discipline in some English public schools in the nineteenth century did not necessarily imply a universal tradition of harsh punishment in schools, the extracts from the regulations for the schools in Dunbar and Penn Charter pointing to relative mild disciplinary regimes (Hoyles, 1979). In the postmodern world, the distinction between the punishing state and punished offender breaks down in the fragmented realities of internecine struggle which supersede the grand divisions between controllers and controlled. In the process, the state may stand as both accuser and accused. Sometimes the accusation is justified, as the persistence of terrorism as a feature of both ancient and modern societies confirms the continuance of this as a form of punishment invariably sanctioned by states (Lane, 1993, p. 28). States are capable of worse still. In the twentieth century, the Holocaust of the Second World War incidentally produced some of the most barbarous incidents of punishment in history. As much as anything, such atrocities gave impetus to the movement towards the Universal Declaration of Human Rights in 1948, by the UN, a statement much drawn upon by advocates for those subject to punishment. The publication in 1996 of a meticulously detailed book by Swedish Save the Children (Brett and McCallan, 1996) on the atrocious treatment of children recruited to military service in more than a score of countries, including their forcible involvement in executions, indicates that there is some way still to go in this area.

3 Psychological Punishment

Punishment can never be dealt out with justice, for no man can be just. Justice implies complete understanding. Judges are no more moral than garbage collectors, nor are they less free of prejudice.

(A. S. Neill, 1960)

INTRODUCTION

This chapter examines different types of non-physical punishment, such as imposed emotional stresses, refers to the judicial procedings of courts, trials, conviction and sentencing, mass sentences, suspended sentences, fines and death and life sentences; it examines community-based punishment, community policing, schooling, outdoor pursuits and residential child care; finally, it considers the use of behavioural approaches, with particular reference to timeout, as forms of psychological punishment, and thought reform or brainwashing. The lack of formal procedures in many situations for the monitoring of forms of psychological punishment contributes to the tendency for denial, distortion and deflection of the attention, not least of professionals, from their realities. The quotation at the start of this chapter is a useful reminder of this, since not only does it highlight incidentally the gendering which emphasises the centrality of men in all sectors of criminal justice; it also draws attention to the vulnerability of judicial processes; in this chapter, the argument is taken still further, in the suggestion that these processes may be experienced as inherently punitive, even before their outcomes, punitive or otherwise, are considered.

PSYCHOLOGICAL PUNISHMENT: A CONTINUUM OF OPPRESSIVENESS

Psychological punishment permeates society; it is a feature of the socialisation of children and young people, and males in particular; it finds expression in activities for personal and professional development, as well as in systems of youth justice and criminal justice, the courts and in the treatment of mental health problems. Punishment emerges as a key determining feature of relations between workers in the human services and people with whom they work. Most of the aspects of punishment considered in later chapters – physical, custodial, corporal and capital – have a psychological dimension. Even areas of the human services whose manifest purpose is therapeutic, may be experienced by clients or patients as punitive.

It would be gross misrepresentation to refer to all work in the human services as punitive. Nevertheless, this chapter selects those areas of the human services where aspects of psychological punishment are more apparent. This is appropriate, since this book implies that abuses may arise other than in areas where formal punishment is the rule.

The continuum of punishments ranges from the infliction of mild to severe psychological pain and discomfort. This is not a one-dimensional continuum, for punishment is not a monolithic concept which applies identically in every setting. For example, in the highlighting of the trial as punishment, it is the process which may be experienced as punitive; the impact of the sentence may be punitive, but as the outcome of the process and a number of decisions. Further, the location of a particular punishment on the continuum is problematic, since judgements and experiences vary. The experiences of both punishers and recipients are likely to differ. What is mild punishment to one person may be experienced by another as very severe.

In Britain, the use of non-physical means of imposing punishment, whether on children, young people or adults, has a long history. Their uses are by no means confined to the penal system, or to enforced custody. Neither are they restricted to the working classes. For example, in accommodation for older people defined as a hotel by providers, punishment may be outlawed. In different settings, this may lead to a range of practices.

Psychological punishments, as aspects of discipline or control, have been deployed traditionally in social care, social work, psychiatry, policing, youth work, teaching and many other professions. Many of the so-called skills in administering psychological punishments are not handed down through training courses, or procedures approved by the agency and issued by line managers, but passed on from generation to generation, from one practitioner to another.

The ideological link between repression and love in child care expressed in the work of Mary Carpenter (Carpenter, (1851) in the mid-nineteenth century and the apotheosis of community-based social work – the Children and Young Persons Act 1969 – is well-established (Adams, Allard, Baldwin and Thomas, 1981, p. 11). John Heron identifies several functions of interpersonal work which have a control–authority-based function, alongside those which are facilitative and more directly therapeutic (Heron, 1990). It follows that psychological punishment is likely to be encountered in many formal settings – that is, where professionals deliver services: child care, youth custody, counselling, criminal justice, mental health, residential, day care and community care. In addition, psychological punishment has a prominent role in the discipline of the household and the workplace.

Though the criminal justice process is the obvious focus of attention, selected first below, clearly it is not the only one possible. The criminal justice system exhibits similar features of division, inequality and oppression to those operating in wider society. The law, in contrast with the myth that its operation stands above criticism (Braye and Preston-Shoot, 1992), is problematic in its measures and applications, reflecting as it does the processes of government – policymaking and lawmaking – in a society subject to debates and conflicts over injustices and their rectification.

The processing of police investigation may be experienced as punitive by those on its receiving end. Interrogation by the police has been subject to severe criticisms, associated with the strengthening of safeguards for its subjects, in the Police and Criminal Evidence Act 1984. Subsequently, in such notable cases as the Guildford Four or the Birmingham Six, the overturning of the original convictions on appeal has been due largely to the police malpractices and failure to follow recognised procedures when interviewing suspects (see below). Similarly, the entire process of trial and sentence can be considered as inherently punitive, rather than simply its outcome. We consider these aspects next.

Courts

Dickens subjects the injustices of the processes of law to grim scrutiny in the novel *Bleak House* (Dickens, 1956, pp. 2–4). The court setting, its culture, rituals and language, is as much likely in the late twentieth century as it was in mid-Victorian London to be foreign, oppressive and as punitive to the uninitiated. Pat Carlen's research into magistrates' courts has relevance also in crown courts (Carlen, 1976). The court system is no more intended to be a punishment *per se* than are prisons *for* rather than *as* punishment. But 20 years on, due process only thinly overlies crime control in court processes and procedures which are likely to be experienced as unintelligible and punitive (Sanders and Young, 1994, pp. 304, 346–8). The trial of the Knave of Hearts in *Alice's Adventures in Wonderland* occupies the last two of the 12 chapters in that book. In a parody of the injustice of the court system, the Queen shouts 'Off with her head!' at Alice's assertion that it is wrong to sentence before the verdict (Dodgson [Lewis Carroll], 1933, p. 86). Leaving aside the general question of the appropriateness of the criminal justice process, at one extreme, there are circumstances in which children may be called to give evidence in cases where they allege abuse, or women in cases where they allege rape. At the other extreme, parallels have been drawn between the use of internment by the British government in Northern Ireland, under the Northern Ireland Special Powers Acts of 1922, 1933 and 1943 and the Offences Against the State Act 1939 (amended in 1972 to increase the powers of the gardai and the courts) (McGuffin, 1973, p. 25), the use of internment in Sri Lanka (then Ceylon) and the use of indefinite detention without charge, trial or sentence in the Philippines and Zambia (McGuffin, 1973, p. 21).

The so-called Diplock Courts were established by the Northern Ireland (Emergency Provisions) Act 1973 (subsequently amended several times and replaced by a more rigorous Emergency Provisions Act in 1991, extending police powers to stop, search, arrest, detain and question people), following the recommendations of a commission chaired by Lord Diplock, which reported in 1972. Between 1974 and 1979, Diplock Courts achieved a 94 per cent success rate (Foley, 1995, p. 107). Diplock Courts were formally introduced as a measure to counteract intimidation of jury members, but because most convictions were achieved on the sole basis of statements signed whilst in police custody, allegations grew concerning the intimidation and torture of defendants by the police whilst being interrogated, in efforts to get them to sign confessions. In 1978, in response to a deeply critical report by Amnesty International (Amnesty, 1978), the British government initiated an inquiry chaired by Lord Bennett which concluded that the injuries of some detainees could not have been self-inflicted (*Report of the Committee of Inquiry into Police Interrogation Procedures in Northern Ireland, 1979*). The United Nations subsequently criticised the regimes in the holding centres of Northern Ireland (*Summary Record of 92nd Meeting of UN Committee on Torture, 1991*, quoted in Foley, 1995, p. 107) and the Council of Europe (Council of Europe, 1994, quoted in Foley, 1995, p. 107) criticised the British government for 'permitting psychological and physical ill-treatment of detainees, including assaults and death threats, during police questioning' (Foley, 1995, p. 107).

Diplock courts were subject to criticism throughout their duration, from their setting-up in the wake of the events known as Bloody Sunday, to their abolition. Irish activists and their sympathisers tended to view such measures as punitive over-reactions, whilst their campaigns for political and social reform were ignored. The Bloody Sunday Justice Campaign was ignored by the mass media for years. In contrast, the life sentence of Private Lee Clegg for the murder of 18-year-old Karen Reilly, joy-riding in

Belfast, was followed by a campaign to free him, which, with support from senior army officers and much of the tabloid and right-wing press, reached a crescendo in the winter of 1994–95 (*Guardian*, 26 January 1995).

Trial

The argument of this section is that trial procedures in themselves constitute a major feature of psychological punishment. Borges (1970, pp. 234–6), the outstanding Argentinian novelist and visionary, examines the paradox that 'every writer creates his own precursors', by finding in the work of Zeno of Elea, Kierkegaard and Robert Browning some literary antecedents of the maze-like, never-ending convolutions of bureaucratic processes which Kafka applies to the law (Kafka, 1966). Joseph K., the central character in Kafka's novel, which by its unfinished state, mirrors the seeming interminable experience of some trials, is arrested one day for an unknown offence and eventually dies at the hands of two mysterious companions without his trial ever having reached the highest court (Kafka, 1966, p. 251). Nabokov, between the experiences of bolshevist and Nazi regimes, wrote the novel about Cincinnatus C., condemned to death, in effect, for the crime of being a person (Nabokov, 1959).

Critical appraisal of trial procedures has been the domain since the 1970s of campaigning organisations in the fields of criminal justice – notably the Howard League for Penal Reform and the Prison Reform Trust – and human rights – such as Amnesty International and Liberty, formerly the National Council for Civil Liberties. Amnesty International has located debate about the inadequacies of trial processes in the broader context of the protection of human rights through the law, pointing out that the founder of Amnesty International, Peter Benenson, was a practising English barrister who drew on his practice throughout his working life (Staunton and Fenn, 1990, p. 65). Particular concerns have included the vulnerability of the independence of the judiciary in some political regimes (Staunton and Fenn, 1990, p. 66). The independence of judges is a crucial constituent of the justice of the trial process (Staunton and Fenn, 1990, p. 72) and this area is addressed by the Centre of the Independence of Judges and Lawyers (CIJL), based in Geneva. Concerns have been expressed for many years over undue, or indefinite, delays in bringing a person to trial, the loss of evidence for the defence through delays in collecting it, the existence of laws which are discriminatory or which violate human rights, inadequate representation of an accused person in court and inadequate provision of legal aid (Staunton and Fenn, 1990, pp. 67–70). Inadequate trial procedures have been a particular focus of criticism, with the right to silence being subject to erosion in the early 1990s, the right to silence having been accepted as long ago as 1827 as equivalent to a not guilty plea. Amnesty International stated that since the foundation of the Islamic Republic of Iran in 1979, there was not one known instance where a political prisoner facing the death penalty was defended by a lawyer. 'In some cases, a presumption of the guilt of the accused meant that the trial lasted a matter of minutes and consisted only of the reading out of the charges and the passing of sentence' (Staunton and Fenn, 1990, p. 71). The extent to which trials are open and subject to public and media scrutiny may be an important indicator of their fairness (Staunton and Fenn, 1990, p. 73). Liberty has also campaigned for radical reforms of processes of criminal justice, notably the strengthening of the right to silence, outlawing convictions solely based on confessions, providing all arrested people with immediate access to independent legal advice from qualified solicitors, imposing a maximum of 24 hours on the period of detention without charge, requiring police and prosecution to disclose all evidence to the defence, giving the accused person equivalent access as the prosecution to forensic evidence, not requiring black defendants to face all-white juries, giving defendants the unqualified right to challenge prosecution witnesses and requiring judges not to comment on evidence during trials (Foley, 1995, pp. 27–8). Cretney and Davis (1995) have found major dislocations in criminal justice processes, preventing perpetrators of violence, especially males, of violence being brought to justice. Liberty has campaigned against homophobia, evidenced through the negative attitudes of some police towards lesbian, gay and bisexual prisoners and, subsequently, through hostility from other prisoners and staff (Foley, 1995, pp. 56–7).

Conviction and Sentence

In some circumstances, the acts of convicting and sentencing should be viewed *per se* as having a significantly punitive psychological dimension, arising from the manner in which they are imposed. Amnesty International criticises the practice of carrying out sentences without the right of appeal, against conviction or against sentence. 'At least 37 countries have special or military courts empowered to pass death sentences without safeguards or without the right to appeal. Executions have been carried out within hours or even minutes of sentencing, leaving no time for those concerned to appeal or ask for clemency' (Staunton and Fenn, 1990, p. 71).

The organisation Liberty has compiled a list of more than 200 cases in which the conviction of a person for a crime is claimed to be in doubt

(Foley, 1995, p. 25). By way of illustration, in the early 1990s in Britain there were a number of notable cases of convictions being quashed, following allegations – upheld by the courts – of police malpractice during the processes of gathering evidence. These included the quashing in October 1989 of the convictions of three Irishmen and an Englishwoman – the Guildford Four – imprisoned for bombings in Guildford and Woolwich in 1974; the overturning of the convictions of three men – the Tottenham Three – imprisoned for killing a police officer during a riot in North London; the quashing in March 1991 of the convictions of the six Irishmen – the Birmingham Six – imprisoned for bombing two public houses in Birmingham in 1974; the quashing in February 1992 of the sentence for murder of Stefan Kizako, who had spent 16 years in prison; the overturning in December 1992 of the convictions of three men – the Cardiff Three – imprisoned for the murder of a prostitute in Cardiff in 1990 (Foley, 1995, pp. 25–6).

Four examples of sentences with a psychologically punitive dimension are discussed here: mass sentences, suspended sentences, fines, and death and life sentences.

Mass sentences
The psychological impact on people at the time – and on subsequent generations – of symbolic punishments such as mass sanctions, can only be guessed at. This aspect of the history of punishment is replete with examples. For instance, in France, collective punishment was exacted on the people of Thiviers in France in 1638 after an outbreak of rioting, in the form of the razing of the walls and gates of the community to the ground. In Abjat, in 1641, the vice-seneschal of Périgord supervised the dismantling of the town bells, the destruction of the market and the setting-up of a memorial pyramid as a warning in its place (Bercé, 1990, pp. 190–1). The sanction employed by the Nazis at Oradour-sur-Glâne involved the massacre of many of the inhabitants of the village. Some measure of the impact of this incident may be gathered from the fact that, in remembrance and as a museum, to this day the village has been left exactly as it was on the day of the massacre.

Suspended sentences
Suspended sentences were introduced in 1968, under the Criminal Justice Act 1967. Under certain conditions, less serious offences could be suspended – that is, sentences of imprisonment enforced only if a further offence was committed within a given period. The early years of the use of suspended sentences showed a shift from the use of immedi-

ate imprisonment and also a decrease in the proportionate use of other non-custodial sentences such as fines and probation (Oatham and Simon, 1972, p. 233). On the other hand, early evaluation suggested that the proportion of offenders whose suspended sentence was activated was less than the number who would originally have received immediate imprisonment (Oatham and Simon, 1972, p. 235). The longer-term problem of suspended sentences, however, was that a delayed log-jam effect was created; as former sentences of suspended sentence were activated following the commission of a further offence, the numbers of people sent to prison increased, as a delayed further punishment. Without doubt, in some cases suspended sentences embody the psychological punishment of the Damocletian sword, hanging over the person (Coutts, 1994).

Fines
A continuum exists from the informal use of fines, for example, in schools, to their formal deployment in the criminal justice system. A complex web of factors affects how people experience, and respond to, being fined (Bose, 1995) and generalisation is difficult. So, although fines could be regarded as out of place in this chapter, it has to be acknowledged that their psychological impact on the person fined may be as great as their financial consequences. Chu (Chu and Jiang, 1993) shows that the combination of imprisonment with a less than maximium fine may be a more effective deterrent from future offending than maximum fines. As long ago as 1969, short-term imprisonment in the Federal Republic of Germany was almost entirely replaced by fines. This led to an immediate decrease in the proportion of prison sentences, from 23 per cent to 7 per cent, between 1968 and 1971. Incarceration rates declined by about a third between 1969 and 1971 (Albrecht, 1984). However, in the longer term, the use of imprisonment for recidivists increased, keeping the Federal Republic of West Germany near the top of the league of incarceration rates of countries in Western Europe (Adams, 1996b, p. 177). At the informal end of the continuum, the headteacher of James Oglethorpe primary school, Upminster, Essex, imposed 120 fines on 37 pupils whilst on a five-day school holiday on the Isle of Wight. One boy was fined 30p for failing to find his clipboard, pen and notepad in a room inspection; a girl was fined for asking 'where are we going?' as the ferry reached the harbour. The headteacher justified the fines as 'a light-hearted way of encouraging children to take responsibility for their belongings and actions' (David Wooding, 'Head fines kids 10p for each mistake', *Sun*, 10 July 1995).

Death sentences and life sentences

The funnelling effect of sentencing in relation to capital crimes is discussed in Chapter 7, but it should be noted that it takes place in relation to black and female offenders, especially with regard to the award of custodial sentences.

Cases which arouse more public antagonism towards the offender in the USA are more likely to lead to serious penalties such as the death sentence. There is a public mood favouring retributive justice rather than rehabilitating the offender. Juveniles charged with murder tend to be tried as adults, making them subject to the death penalty. Officials, such as prosecutors, often have to stand for political office. It is common for appeals to be made, at first to the local court, then to the Supreme Court or to international justice. Such appeals can take years, often more than a decade passing while various levels and kinds of appeals take place.

Many offenders on death row in prisons in the USA are poor, male, and include a disproportionate number of black people. Most of them will be unable to pay for a lawyer, and have probably, therefore, been defended by an advocate appointed by the court who may not oppose the death penalty and who, being on a low fee, may have no incentive to put effort into their defence. Those sentenced, and their relatives and friends, may experience great psychological distress at this stage in their processing by the criminal justice system (see Chapter 7). Prolonged waiting on death row contradicts the cruel and unusual punishment clause of the Universal Declaration of Human Rights.

The case of Nicholas Ingram, aged 32 and convicted on his twentieth birthday of shooting and killing a man, after tying the man and his wife to a tree during a robbery in Cobb County, Georgia, took headlines in the British mass media for the month prior to his execution on 8 April 1995. The case reawakened debates about the US system of criminal justice, which leads to around 3000 prisoners sentenced to death waiting on death row for more than a decade whilst their cases move through tortuous appeal processes, which over the past two decades have led to more than 50 men and women being declared innocent and released. In January 1994, of the 2802 people on death row in the USA, only 44 were women, but a disproportionately high 1102 were Afro-American (Linebaugh, 1995a, p. 29).

The Home Secretary in the UK for many years exercised a wide area of discretion, not accountable to Parliament, in the judgement about whether a person convicted of a capital offence was executed. In contrast, the European Commission of Human Rights in Strasbourg ruled in 1994 that the exercise of discretion by the Home Secretary over when a murderer under 18 detained at Her Majesty's pleasure is released violates the European Convention on Human Rights, because such a decision should be taken by a judicial body and not a politician. Lord Donaldson, Master of the Rolls 1982–92, is cautious over the erosion of the the Judiciary's independence from Parliament, pursuant on the Home Secretary's plan in 1995 to increase the influence of the Home Secretary over sentence lengths. Donaldson sees this as a covert attempt to exercise Parliamentary authority to ensure judges pass life sentences in certain cases. Donaldson argues that this undermines the basic principle of the rule of law, namely that the Judiciary enforces the will of Parliament, through the criminal and common law. Transferring some powers of the Judiciary to the Executive would threaten the freedom of the citizen. 'It is one thing to be governed by the rule of law. It is quite another to be governed by a despotic, albeit no doubt benevolent, Government. And any Government which seeks to make itself immune to an independent review of whether its actions are lawful or unlawful is potentially despotic' (Donaldson, 1995).

The cases of women such as Myra Hindley, tried in 1963 at Chester Assizes for murders committed with Ian Brady, are redolent of similar attitudes as those which hanged Ruth Ellis, the last woman to be hanged in the UK for murder. In December 1994, Hindley was informed that the Home Secretary had decided she would never be released from prison. The grounds for such a decision do not have to be revealed and can only arouse speculation: has the prisoner failed to respond to the rehabilitative element of her imprisonment? Will prolonging imprisonment make it more likely that she will be reformed? Is there a need to inflict a longer, even indeterminate sentence, in order to vent society's feelings against her? Is there a risk that otherwise she will commit further offences? Would it prove impossible to make appropriate arrangements for her on release?

Following the conviction of two boys for the murder of James Bulger in 1993, trial judge Mr Justice Morland, who had sentenced the two boys, had recommended that they serve a minimum of eight years on grounds of punishment and deterrence, later increased by Lord Chief Justice Taylor to ten years. Following a petition from the Bulger family and the receipt of more than 21 000 cut-out coupons from readers of the *Sun* newspaper, Michael Howard, then Home Secretary, directed that the boys should serve at least 15 years. This was criticised by Edward Venables, QC for one of the boys, as misconceived, in that it was unlikely to impact on the average of one killing by children under 14 every 5 years, it was in excess of judicial recommendations and it failed to take account of mitigating circumstances and the need for rehabilitation of the boys (*Guardian*, 18 April 1996).

Two particular weaknesses exist in the British system for imposing and reviewing life sentences. First, the involvement of the executive rather than judicial procedures such as a tribunal, in reviewing life sentences and deciding on the release and recall of life sentence prisoners. Second, it has been suggested in a series of Parliamentary reports since the 1970s that the mandatory life sentence for all murders, irrespective of whether committed in the heat of a domestic argument or in cold blood in pursuit of another crime, should be replaced by a discretionary life sentence.

The remainder of this chapter considers a range of interventions in the human services with a punitive psychological dimension, including community-based punishments, community policing, schooling, residential child care and behavioural therapies such as timeout, and other behaviourally-based activities. The inclusion of community-based activities such as community policing may seem to rest uneasily alongside behaviour therapy. But their inclusion in this chapter is intended to highlight their punitive psychological impact on some people, in some circumstances.

Community-based Punishment

The collapse of the rehabilitative ideal in the 1970s, due largely to research demonstrating the ineffectiveness of treatment, hastened a convergence between radical critiques of the treatment paradigm and right-wing advocates of law and order. Certain features of the work of the probation services were moving towards tougher and more punitive sanctions for offenders even before the Conservatives came into power in May 1979 (Harris, 1977; King, 1979). The Probation Control Unit in Kent, the outcome of planning which began before May 1979, opened in 1980. Probationers attended for six days a week over six months, including evenings; they had to conform to curfew arrangements when they went home to sleep. They had also to report to the unit more or less straight after leaving work.

It would be a distortion to assert that in the mid-1990s the probation service has become, in effect, the means by which intended government policy from the late 1980s has become translated into the practice of punishment in the community. For a start, to many probation officers, such policies are anathema. Nevertheless, the shift of the probation service towards the practice of community-based punishment is sustained and significant, whether or not it will be reversed in future. There has been a concerted push in this direction, led by Ministers and Home

Office officials, and acceded to by some probation managers. The Government's proposals for greater use of non-custodial options were set out in the Green Paper *Punishment, Custody and the Community* (Home Office, 1988). At the same time, it proposed tightening the procedures for breaches of community service orders. A new supervision and restriction order would involve compensation, reparation, community service, judicial supervision, attendance at a day centre or restriction of liberty using 'tagging' or electonic monitoring. These restrictions on the offender's freedom of action were described by the Home Office as a punishment (Home Office, 1988). After some political manoeuvring, during which some senior managers in the probation service actually came up with even more punitive proposals (Beaumont, 1995, p. 59), the White Paper *Crime, Justice and Protecting the Public* (Home Office, 1990) combined measures concerning the release of some prisoners with the essential features of the Government's punishment in the community proposals still preserved. National standards on community penalties were proposed which affected both probation officers and offenders, since, as far as probation orders were concerned, they increased the number of times offenders on probation had to see their probation officers. As far as community service was concerned, it was proposed that work carried out by offenders should fall into one of four categories: safeguarding the community against further crime; repairing damage due to crime; physically improving the environment; and caring for disabled and/or older people. Sanctions for offenders not complying also would be made tougher.

In early 1996, the Government considered increasing house arrest by the use of electronic tagging, as a means of containing an unexpected rise in the prison population (*Guardian*, 1 February 1996).

In 1994, the Home Secretary Michael Howard announced his intention to inject demanding physical labour into measures taken for dealing with offenders in the community, such as community service and probation orders. This included ensuring that community sentences leave young offenders 'wet, tired and hungry' so that they are too exhausted to engage in criminal activities (*Guardian*, 13 October 1994), and increasing the punitive element in imprisonment (*Guardian*, 19 September 1994). Parents of young offenders who failed to carry out community sentences could themselves face the prospect of punishment (*Guardian*, 23 September 1994). The impact of such changes on the role of the probation officer continues to reinforce the long-standing tendency away from treatment and towards them becoming agents of social control (Harris, 1982; Griffiths, 1982).

Community Policing

Policing in the community, and the running of custodial institutions, increasingly are carried out by private contractors alongside employees of the state. The police are likely to be 'patrolling with a purpose' alongside holders of franchises to maintain public order in society. 'Operation Swamp' involved police challenging people – inevitably this meant Blacks – they encountered on the streets of Brixton in the lead-up to the Brixton Riot of 1981 (Scarman, 1981). This was experienced by many black people as stigmatising and punitive. Michael Keith's impressive study of the interaction between black communities and the police more than justifies the case for explanations of such complex phenomena to be based on empirical – in his case ethnographic – data, in order to generate historically and socially situated analysis. He argues that there are dangers in academic, as well as public generalisations, not based on geographically specific data (Keith, 1993). Similar points may be made about the applications of punishment.

The army moved into Northern Ireland in the wake of Bloody Sunday in August 1969. The peak of the involvement of the British army in Northern Ireland was Operation Motorman, when some 30 000 soldiers were deployed. By 1995, there were about 17 600 soldiers, 1000 RAF and 250 naval personnel there. The fact that the government regarded the threat to national security posed by the Irish Republican Army (IRA) and other republican and loyalist groups as its first priority, can be gauged from the estimated 2000 MI5 officers – almost half of its current resources – and up to 100 metropolitan police officers in the anti-terrorist branch, devoted to security in Ireland (*Guardian*, 1 September 1994). Between the introduction of British army forces to Northern Ireland on 14 August 1969 and 31 August 1994 when the IRA announced a ceasefire, there were more than 3150 deaths, more than 36 600 injuries and more than 10 000 explosions. Armed checkpoints supervised by City of London police in the City of London (*Guardian*, 1 September 1994) were still in evidence in 1996.

Schooling and Outdoor Pursuits

The twin virtues of imposing hardship and deprivation on people being groomed for leadership, or – in the case of delinquents – being equipped for good citizenship, by means of outdoor pursuits and intermediate treatment (Adams, Allard, Baldmin and Thomas, 1981), were enshrined in British culture long before the first Outward Bound School was established at Aberdovey in 1941 (Roberts and White, 1972, p. 337) and have persisted despite a lack of empirical evidence of their character-developing potential (Roberts and White, 1972, p. 350). Despite this fact, such public schools as Gordonstoun – which established the Aberdovey school – continued to advertise the virtues of the development of self-reliance through a combination of physical and intellectual challenges. This was exemplified in the Training Plan at Gordonstoun, which some 30 years ago took the form of 'a chart, which the boy fills in every evening recording whether or not he has done certain duties and kept certain rules. These duties and rules are of a very simple and definite nature, such as: "two cold showers", or "not eating between meals", or "special exercises". Introspection is not to be encouraged: no probing of one's conscience is necessary to answer the simple question on the Training Plan' (Gordonstoun School, n.d., p. 8).

The changing conception of childhood over the past two centuries has linked with changes in disciplinary structures of family life. Donzelot has developed the concept of tutelage of children (Donzelot, 1979) to support the argument that the history of childhood since the early nineteenth century has witnessed enforced dependency and decreasing autonomy and responsibility (Burchell, 1981, p. 94). Children's resistance to aspects of their status as immature persons tends to be pathologised, that is, defined – as when they protest about their schooling – in terms of the problems they represent, rather than as indications of problems rooted in society and in the system of schooling (Adams, 1991). The curbing of behaviour of school pupils considered too difficult for teachers to discipline has become a growing issue since the prospect in the 1970s of the banning of corporal punishment, and then its realisation in the mid-1980s.

School rules may extend beyond the school premises and school hours, for instance, where a pupil is punished at school for violations such as smoking in the street whilst wearing a school uniform. Many institutions have strict rules and regimes, in the making of which young people have little or no say. A further layer of injustice is geographical, in that local authorities have very varied rules and procedures about discipline and punishment in their areas. Some schools have rules which are geared towards control rather than education and learning.

Since the 1960s, the number of units for curbing so-called disruptive pupils grew quickly. According to the HMI's Report on Behavioural Units in England (1978), the first unit was established in 1966 and by 1977 there were 239, 199 of which were set up between 1973 and 1977. The majority – 172 – catered for secondary school pupils, providing an estimated 4000 places. Two-thirds of these were for secondary school pupils who had been suspended from their schools and who were unlikely to return to school before reaching school-leaving age. Facilities for dealing with so-called disruptive pupils increased rapidly, as schools' tolerance of deviance decreased, and the literature from commentators and researchers mushroomed accordingly (Booth and Coulby, 1987).

The measures taken by government to curb disruptive pupils included pupil referral units, heavily criticised by school inspectors for failing to provide adequate education for pupils excluded from schools who attended them. In 1993, when the Government banned indefinite exclusion, the number of expelled pupils rose rapidly, to 15 000 per year. Gillian Shephard, Secretary of State for Education and Employment, ruled that the parents of a child expelled from two schools would no longer be able to exercise a choice of school and would be directed by the local authority. Gillian Shephard announced that parents would have to sign up to the discipline policies of a school before they could send their child there (*Guardian*, 13 April 1996, p. 12). The contracts referred to in Chapter 10 are an illustration of this approach.

The psychological and social impact of these punitive sanctions – especially repeated, or long-term exclusions from school, which is an increasing likelihood in the mid-1990s – on pupils, their families and friends, will vary according to circumstances, but is likely to be significant. Difficult, and even disruptive, pupils may be portrayed as anarchistic, but this is a simplification. In an unequal, class-ridden education system and society where young people are presented with increased educational demands in a lengthened process of pupillage (Adams, 1991) and no guarantee of a job at the end of it, they tend to inhabit cultures which are indifferent, or hostile, to the dominant values of schooling (Willis, 1977). Amazingly, despite this, pupils suspended in Grunsell's survey, to the extent that they espoused anti-school values, demonstrated an implicit commitment to their own ethical beliefs, even offering their own versions of rewards and punishments (Grunsell, 1980, p. 64).

Proposals to extend the powers of headteachers to exclude pupils from schools were discussed at the Conservative Party Conference of October 1996. In that same week, the *Doncaster Free Press* gave over its page one headline to the news: 'Hundreds of Pupils Banned by Schools', referring to the use of a policy of mass exclusion of pupils, by two Doncaster schools (*Doncaster Free Press*, 3 October 1996, p. 1). In mid-October 1996, controversy erupted over the Ridings school in Bradford, where teachers demanded the suspension of up to 60 pupils for a range of claimed disciplinary problems. This sharpened the ongoing debate about various strategies not involving corporal punishment for curbing indiscipline in schools. The Government's Education Bill published at the beginning of November 1996 proposed strengthened sanctions in schools, including extended powers to expel for drug-taking, to exclude from certain lessons, for writing lines and detentions.

Residential Child Care

Punishment and discipline in institutions such as schools and residential homes for children and young people are often administered in situations where they have very little say over the way they are treated. Where this involves an adult and child, the standpoint of the adult usually prevails, at the time, and subsequently when each accounts for it, at a hearing or investigation. Regimes in such institutions may be strict, and in any case invariably are imposed on children and young people rather than negotiated with them.

Abuses by residential child-care staff constituting psychological punishment have been catalogued in a series of major inquiries and investigations since 1945 (Adams, 1997, ch. 6). The most infamous in the 1990s is the inquiry into the so-called Pindown regime in children's homes in Staffordshire (Levey and Kahan, 1990). This involved restrictions on what children could do and how they could dress, most notably through the practice of keeping so-called offenders in their nightclothes for long periods of time. The Children's Homes Regulations – that a child should not be required to wear distinctive or inappropriate clothes – were broken by staff implicated in the Pindown inquiry (Levy and Kahan, 1990, p. 127). At that time, these regulations did not protect children in England and Wales, but those in the rest of the UK were protected even less, since they did not even apply in Scotland or Northern Ireland (Gulbenkian, 1993, p. 79).

Evidence by Millham and others to a DHSS Working Party on discipline and control in residential child care noted that inappropriate discipline may increase psychological damage already suffered by children (Millham *et al.*, 1981). It was also noted that boys on occasions were kept in pyjamas for several days to discourage them from absconding. Inspections concluded that children and young people should be controlled by other methods and also that threats of, or actual, transfers to other residential settings were unacceptable sanctions, as were sanctions imposed on groups of children for the offences of one or two, or sanctions used to 'persuade' small numbers to own up to offences. Children should not be picked out in front of the group, or forced to behave differently, or wear different clothes (DHSS 1981).

Informal subcultures among children and young people may be exploited by staff and used as a means of psychological oppression of others. The former proprietor of Castle Hill School, Ralph Morris, following an inquiry

(Brannan, Jones and Murch, 1993), was sentenced to 12 years' imprisonment in 1991 for offences of abuse against young people in his school, where he headed a power structure, harnessing a dominant subculture among the boys to his own authoritarian management style.

> He operated a hierarchical system whereby some older and more senior boys were afforded special privileges ... . These favoured pupils presented as a fearful and vindictive corps and were used to control those who dared to go beyond the clearly defined limits. There are many examples of boys being assaulted by members of this elite task force at Ralph Morris's instigation. This group was referred to, by Mr Justice Fennell at the trial, as Ralph Morris's 'Republican Guard'.
>
> (Gulbenkian, 1993, p. 71)

Many children and young people in care perceive child care as synonymous with punishment as the method of achieving control, by restricting their freedom and depriving them of their basic needs and rights. The imperative of maintaining control is the justification for staff imposing authority, by such means as drugs – the 'liquid cosh' – transferring to other establishments, which may be less accessible for visits, suspending, that is ejecting them, from homes and leaving them to cope for themselves, sometimes for lengthy periods of time.

At the Life in Care Conference 1981, children spoke about their experiences of punishment. Several stated that withholding visits and visiting parents should not be used as a punishment, drugs should not be used to control or punish children, children who wet the bed should not be made to sleep in the wet bed all night and those who smoked should not get their mouths washed out with carbolic soap or detergent. One delegate reported that she had been in a lock-up for four years for the 'offence' of running away.

One girl said,

> I have never broken the law, but I was living with girls from prison who were disturbed and often violent. The place was surrounded by high walls and was patrolled by dogs. The superintendent in charge was a really sadistic man and he tried to convince me that I was mad. He used to make us get up in the night and scrub floors, and he used to beat us up. Once, he twisted a girl's arm behind her back and threw her into the bath. There was no point in hitting back because he used to be a psychiatric nurse and knew all the holds.
>
> (Life in Care Conference 1981)

Behaviour Modification

Behavioural theories have informed social work practice for many years (Sheldon, 1982, 1995; Hudson and Macdonald, 1986). The use of deprivation to extinguish behaviour and bring about attitude change in inducing new behaviour, is common to therapeutic regimes based on behaviour modification. Those based on learning theory tend to wait for desired behaviour to appear and then to reinforce it. Somewhat ironically, the traditions of behavioural work – involving changing a person's behaviour – and cognitive work – involving working from the basis of a person's own experience – have converged in the social work literature (Sheldon, 1995).

This does not lessen the fact, however, that the use of behavioural modification in social work, to bring about changes in clients' behaviour, may involve tensions between the accountability of the behavioural social worker, the experience of the client, the effectiveness of the intervention and its ethical justification. A social worker may achieve ethical behavioural practice by working with a client to identify shared goals and then working out an agreed programme of behaviour modification to enable the person to achieve these goals. However, some behavioural practice may conflict with this empowering approach. Some commentators attempt to distinguish punishments in behaviour therapies from the non-therapeutic use of behaviour-shaping work with people, based on behavioural psychology and to which they may not have given informed consent (Griffith, 1983, pp. 318–20). But this distinction is difficult to maintain in practice since an autistic child, for instance, may not be able to give informed consent, as is instanced in the use of behaviourally-based therapy by Lovaas in work with autistic children (Lovaas, 1987), psychotic children (Lovaas and Newsom, 1976) and children with learning disabilities (Lovaas and Simmons, 1969). The technique may be experienced by the child as punitive and its goal may be that of imposing or changing behaviour by putting the child under duress. This runs counter to the anti-oppressive principles of practice (Dalrymple and Burke, 1995), involving the process of empowering the person, at the levels of feelings, thoughts and actions. From a range of behavioural techniques, timeout is selected here for particular examination. The use of electric shocks is discussed in Chapter 4.

Timeout
Timeout (TO) is an iconic concept in the field of psychological punishment. Specifically, TO is a term used in behavioural work, often referring to techniques used to punish children. Thus, 'TO can be defined as a

period of time in a less reinforcing environment made contingent on a behavior' (Brantner and Doherty, 1983, p. 87). More generally, TO occipies a continuum from discipline as an informal and minor means of punishment to formal and major aspects of punishment. We can locate on this continuum the three main types of TO distinguished by Brantner and Doherty: isolation, exclusion and nonexclusion (Brantner and Doherty, 1983, p. 88). Although isolation TO in its pure form involves no more than separating the person from the source of reinforcement, typically in another room, there is a danger of lack of a clear boundary between segregating the person in this way and solitary confinement: exclusion involves removing the person from the area of reinforcement. For example, a child may be placed in the 'naughty corner' of the classroom, or have 'to face a corner or sit behind a screen' (Brantner and Doherty, 1988, p. 88). It may involve putting a physical barrier such a latched door between the person and the activity (Brantner and Doherty, 1983, p. 122). Nonexclusion involves removing the person from the situation and making him or her observe it, rather than being able to continue participating.

The three major weaknesses of TO can be examined in turn: its proneness to abuse, ethical and legal objections and its social acceptability. With regard to the first, the boundary between TO as a legitimate means of exclusion and as an abusive act is imperfectly delineated. 'This type of TO has historically been confused with the term *seclusion*, an unethical and illegal procedure used as an excuse for solitary confinement' (Brantner and Doherty, 1983, p. 88). TO may be regarded as contingently or absolutely unethical. The former rests on a view that inherently it is acceptable, but, for example, its overuse can be abusive. Brantner and Doherty quote the case of *Wyatt* v. *Stickney* (1972) as concluding that 'legitimate timeout procedures may be used under close and direct professional supervision as a technique in behavior shaping programs' (1983, p. 121). Further, in the case of *Morales* v. *Turman* (1974) it was noted that a TO procedure lasting less than one hour did not necessitate a due process procedure.

Concerns about the second, ethical and legal, objections led to a set of standards for the use of TO being developed in California, for the use of aversive or restrictive behavioural techniques. Three levels of aversiveness and restrictiveness were distinguished: level 1, mildly restrictive or aversive, level 2, moderately restrictive or aversive and level 3, highly restrictive or aversive. Exclusion TO and contingent observation involving nonexclusion are regarded as mild in this context (Brantner and Doherty, 1983, p. 122). What the California standards describe as 'locked TO' is regarded as highly restrictive or aversive. Concerns revolve around the need to limit the time over which this is applied and to monitor continuously the person locked out in this way. Additional safeguards include review by a senior staff member if the time exceeds one hour and recording the circumstances of the incident as well as the time the person left and entered the room. The California standards attempt also to address the issue of the rights of the person, by attaching to each of the three levels of restrictive and aversive techniques a corresponding level of review committee. 'The first level consists of a case management team and requires general consent. At the second level, an agency review is implemented, and the third level consists of state review personnel as well as lay persons' (Brantner and Doherty, 1983, p. 122).

The third area of concern, the social acceptibility of TO, transcends debates about its effectiveness. Thus, the California standards illustrate a shift towards questioning the inherent legitimacy of such techniques. For example, TO methods may be considered unacceptable because they violate the rights of persons (Brantner and Doherty, 1983, p. 123).

Thought Reform and Brainwashing

Nokes comments (1967) that if the authorities were serious about the methods of treatment they employ to change offenders' behaviour, they would adopt more effective techniques such as thought reform, ethical, moral or political considerations being equal. Thought reform in the Korea of the post-war era grew more sophisticated than the brainwashing of the Chinese during the 1930s and 1940s (Lifton, 1961). Such approaches depend on the development of disengagement from previous norms, through the dislocation of depriving a person of information about the former world she or he inhabited. Then, group pressure, punctuated in some cases by further disorientation to ensure that the person ceases to rely on previous judgements, is accompanied by building up the contemporary reference group and its value base.

The impact on people in Lifton's study varied. Those least affected were able to shrug the experience off following repatriation, because of their orientation to their everyday lives being fairly instrumental. Ironically, those such as priests with the most deeply-held, well-thought-through beliefs before undergoing the process, had the greatest difficulty readjusting afterwards (Lifton, 1961).

Dr James V. McConnell proposed in 1970 combining the use of brainwashing techniques of sensory deprivation with 'drugs, hypnosis and astute manipulation of reward and punishment to gain almost absolute control over an individual's behaviour' (McConnell, 1970 quoted in

Mitford, 1977, p. 129). Whether another technique – the use of intrusive surgery to burn out electrically those areas of the brain believed to be responsible for aggressive punishment (Mitford, 1977, p. 139) – constitutes punishment is a matter of semantics rather than substance. Dr Martin Groder, prison psychiatrist at Marion federal prison, USA, used thought-reform methods to impose on agitators, 'suspected militants, writ writers, and other trouble makers' using 'intense group pressure ... so that [their] emotional responses and thought-flow will be brought under group and staff control as totally as possible' (Mitford, 1977, p. 127).

This chapter has dealt with some areas which consistute the least tangible, and therefore, most often marginalised or ignored, aspects of punishment. Paradoxically, it has also demonstrated the core relevance of other psychological aspects of punishment. The next chapter examines the imposition on people of those physical constraints which may be considered punitive.

4 Punishment by Physical Constraints

> Violence and insensitivity have been reinforced throughout most of human history, especially in men. Isn't it time that we began to counter-act cruelty, xenophobia, war, and genocide with lessons in empathy and critical thinking?
>
> (Miedzian, 1992, p. 166)

INTRODUCTION

The tendency of professionals in the human services to rationalise the use of physical constraints in the interests of therapy or good order and disci-pline makes it almost impossible to segregate such punishments from aspects of treatment or control. It is difficult also, given the segregation of knowledges – notably the compartmentalisation of discussions about crim-inal justice from, say, punishment in the home – to contextualise consider-ation of punitive physical constraints in a critique of the dominant macho culture of masculinity which pervades the field. The quotation at the start of this chapter puts down a marker, which is elaborated in the illustrations which follow.

This chapter deals with restraints or constraints including traditional constraints, curbs on meeting basic needs, body searching, bodily restraints such as leg-irons and chains, and methods such as gas to inca-pacitate people; it also discusses the punitive use of drugs, and the use of electric shocks in behavioural programmes; finally, it considers some ethical issues which arise in the application of these forms of punishment.

There is an overlap between the wide range of circumstances in which restraints are used and their specific use as means of punishment. The use of physical constraints as punishments imposes indirect physical hurt on people, that is, other than by hitting them. Physical constraints are likely to have a psychological as well as physical impact on people. The boundaries between psychological punishment, physical punishment and corporal punishment are debatable, but however imperfectly delineated, they differ significantly. There is a degree of overlap also between this chapter and Chapter 3, in that many punishments have both physical and psychological aspects which impact on people.

VARIETIES OF PUNISHMENT BY PHYSICAL CONSTRAINTS

Physical means have been used to punish people for many years. Their use is most commonly associated with custodial settings in the penal system. They are characteristic rather than exceptional features of penal systems, past and present, throughout the world. A continuum exists from the more mild varieties such as requiring prisoners to wear similar clothes, or 'prison uniform' – to the more severe – such as using chains or irons to restrict people's movements. However, the lack of literature on the less dramatic forms – often indirect rather than involving inflicting direct blows on a person – obscures this issue rather than indicating there is no problem. Physical restraints are used in many other circumstances as an informal means of punishment, as in the locking of children in a room by their parents, or through the tying of small children into baby seats in a nursery. In some circumstances such as where psychologists and psychiatrists converge with social workers and others to undertake behavioural work, professional ideologies actually support and justify punitive activity.

Physical constraints imposed by staff in a total institution such as a prison may lead to a range of intensities of denial of human rights to freedom and choice. The denial of a person's humanity occurs on a lesser scale, but may be experienced as no less real, in other institutions with a custodial dimension. The pupil in the novel *Kes* is portrayed by the novelist as reasonable in his rebellion. His humanity and sensitivity in befriending and training a kestrel are counterpointed by the uncouthness and oppressive victimisation of some teachers in the school (Hines, 1976).

It would be impossible to give comprehensive coverage to the full range of punishments which fall within the scope of this chapter. The following are dealt with here: traditional constraints, curbs on meeting basic needs, body searching, bodily restraints, incapacitation, use of drugs, use of electric shocks and torture.

Traditional Constraints

The range of traditional constraints includes such methods as the stocks and various head cages and bridles, all of which involve restricting movement of the head and neck and are likely to cause great pain and distress. The stocks were an ancient form of punishment involving pinioning the legs and arms of the offender in heavy wooden cuffs, which were often located in the middle of villages and which remained in use until the latter half of the nineteen century. The Bethlehem Royal hospital, or Bedlam, in London charged a fee of 1*d* up to 1770 for visitors to view the 'lunatics'.

A report to the House of Commons in 1815 found that 'one inmate was chained to her bed for eight years, the matron feeling the prisoner would murder her if released'. William Norris 'for twelve years ... was chained with a strong iron ring round his neck. His arms were pinioned by an iron bar and he could only move twelve feet away from the wall. In this position he lived as normal a life as possible before dying shortly after his release' (Jones, 1993, p. 57).

Hard Labour and Less Eligibility

Prisoners sentenced to hard labour could be working in a quarry, say, at Dartmoor prison, breaking stones. Or, they could be in a comparable situation to the inmates at the Andover workhouse in the 1950s, gnawing the rotten bones they were sent to crush on a near-starvation diet (Rose, 1986, p. 122). A range of measures imposing great physical and emotional hardship on paupers, criminals and mentally ill people were common in custodial institutions in the nineteenth century. The treadmill was used in prisons in the early nineteenth century (Mayhew and Binney, 1862). But its consequences when inflicted on pregnant women or sick inmates, could be fatal (Ignatieff, 1978, p. 177). The use of the treadmill had been abandoned by the early years of the twentieth century.

In the second half of the nineteenth century, prison managers in the USA made money from hiring prisoners out to contractors, the Connecticut Penitentiary, for instance, making a profit of more than $90 000 between 1833 and 1850 (Hibbert, 1966, p. 196). However, such practices led not only to protests by labour unions but also to notorious abuses, such as the chain gangs (Hibbert, 1966, p. 197) and virtual slave labour of the Southern states.

Chain gangs
Physical restraints in the USA have been associated traditionally with some forms of labour, notably in chain gangs. The history of chain gangs is most prominently associated with slavery and life and work on them was portrayed vividly in the film *Cool Hand Luke*. However, sentences of hard labour have had currency in parts of the USA, and in other countries such as Britain, where slavery was not a feature.

In the last two decades of the twentieth century, reform groups in Britain and the USA have made increased efforts to outlaw the use in the penal system of physical restraints as a form of punishment.

But chain gangs of manacled convicts are on the increase. This contributes to appeasing the public view that prisoners should be punished.

Several states in the USA had reintroduced chain gangs by the mid-1990s, for the first time since the 1930s (*Observer*, 4 February 1996). Chain gangs for men were introduced in Phoenix, Arizona in 1995 and for women in 1996. 'The women weed and pick up rubbish in the city streets. They work eight hours a day, seven days a week for 30 days to win release from "lock down", where four inmates share an 8ft by 10ft cell' (Reed, 1996, p. 10).

The tabloid press used the circumstances of a British citizen, Marcell Harpin, imprisoned for stealing cheques and obtaining £2000 in 1995, as the occasion to report the decision in Alabama to recommence chain gangs at Limestone Correctional Facility. Apparently, prisoners 'are chained to a hitching rail usually used for horses. Most don't stay conscious in the 100 degree heat for longer than a few hours ... . Deputy warden Tom Davis said: "We're kinda proud of Harpin. It sends a message that we don't care who you are, we won't take any nonsense"' (*Sunday Sport*, 17 September 1995).

Curbs on Meeting Basic Needs

The deprivations of custodial institutions in themselves operate as punitive constraints. The main deprivations concern custody itself (dealt with in Chapter 5), food, choice over participation in the regime – notably in the degree of association with other people – and freedom of choice over personal appearance – notably in such aspects as dress, hairstyle and make-up – this last a particular issue in girls' schools, and the subject of many sanctions by staff and protests by pupils (Adams, 1991, pp. 125–6).

No issue is more central to, or symbolic in, institutional life, than food. Deprivation of food may be used informally in the household as a means of punishing people, as well as formally in institutions. Dietary deprivation is an aspect of psychological punishment which resonates with the links between people's power – or lack of power – to express their individuality and the preoccupation with eating, and starvation, in society. Until they were banned in 1971 in Britain, penal institutions for adults, such as detention centres, employed dietary deprivation as a punishment for offences against the code of discipline. For example, the Borstal Rules published in 1964 specified that a restricted diet of 1*lb* of bread each day and sufficient water could be given alternately with normal diet, for three-day periods, without any time limit (Borstal Rules, 1964, Rule 53, page 15). At the same time, dietary deprivation, notably the use of Complan as a substitute for a full diet, was used in residential child care. The ironic inversion of dominant values ensures that the abusive, stigmatising punishment of the person who challenges societal norms by the unregulated indulgence of pleasurable eating is not questioned; the label of food abuser is imposed on that person. Eating is a threat, to control and privacy (Ellmann, 1993, p. 56). Dietary curbs are a weapon for the authorities, with the pay-off that the person deprived in this way becomes weaker as the punishment proceeds.

> The imposition of dietary restrictions aim to bring the person – of whatever physique – under control. The fat person and the thin person are both signifiers of bodies, and therefore people, out of control. The fat person is 'out of control': fat is the enemy within the body, like Communism in the body politic, which threatens to subvert the very notion of self-governance. But fat also stands for the return of the repressed, for something that *should not show* but has come to light. What exactly is the dreadful secret? Can it be so appalling that we *like to eat*? The crime is scarcely worthy of the punishment, except that fat has now become the symbol of a welter of anxieties ensnarled in the term 'abuse'.
>
> (Ellmann, 1993, p. 57)

Dietary deprivation – as in the British penal system until the 1970s – may be imposed directly on offenders as a means of punishment, or, as in some prisoner of war camps between 1939 and 1945 – for example, those run by the Japanese (Clavell, 1975) – left to percolate through an institution where the total amount of food supplied is simply not adequate to feed the prison population.

Ellmann comments:

> the very notion of the self, the unified integral individual, is founded on the model of incarceration. It was in the seventeenth and eighteenth centuries, the age that Foucault calls the Great Confinement, that workhouses, asylums, and penitentiaries were built in order to conceal the criminal, the destitute, and the insane from public view; and it was also in this era that the modern conception of the individual was born. To be a person is to be a prison, this historical coincidence suggests; and in the keep of subjectivity, the solaces of privacy are always counterbalanced by the terrors of eternal solitude.
>
> (Ellmann, 1993, p. 94)

In the total institution (Goffman, 1967), the hair of the inmate may be a focus of staff concerns about good order and discipline. If hair is too long or too short, it may be a threat, because of the presumed correlation between bad behaviour and long, flowing locks at one extreme or a skin-head cut at the other. Clothing and make-up often acquire significance in the school and become symbols of conformity or rebellion. Pupils who dress differently may be punished in school, or, in extreme cases, simply be excluded from school (see Chapter 3).

Poor living conditions
Gaol fever – which was probably typhus – replaced leprosy as the feared disease, in the prison hospital rather than the lazar house of the fifteenth and sixteenth centuries, as the reformer Samuel Tuke endeavoured to replace regimes based on punishment and coercion with hygiene and education (Pietroni, 1991, p. 152). Gaol fever was a disease widespread in British prisons, whose spread into society beyond the prison was much feared, until the late eighteenth century, when Quaker reformers set to work to improve the physical conditions of imprisonment. Andrew Rutherford, however, draws a comparison between this gaol fever and 'a new and virulent gaol fever (which) is endemic in many societies, including some which set high store on democratic values and aspirations'. This

> has every appearance of being beyond political control. Like its eighteenth-century predecessor, it may be curbed only when it is widely recognized that the uses made of imprisonment and the conditions within modern prison systems have consequences which transcend the experience endured by persons who become society's prisoners. The scope and administration of criminal law is a measure of the weight given by any society to humanitarian values including liberty. Prison systems are the deep-end of the process of criminal justice. As the prison system expands the ultimate values of democractic society are threatened.
> (Rutherford, 1986, p. 3)

The most visible symptom of the new gaol fever identified by Rutherford is the gross overcrowding of prisoners (Rutherford, 1986, p. 3) – conditions of two or three to a cell being far worse than, for example, in the silent and separate systems characterising the mid-Victorian period (Rutherford, 1986, p. 98). Prisoners experience gross violations of their humanity, to the extent that they are deprived of liberty and are compelled to live in appalling conditions. The critical report by the Chief Inspector of Prisons on conditions in Preston prison in the early 1990s is typical of dozens of similar reports (HM Inspector of Prisons, 1994).

Body Searching

The physical searching of people invades people's privacy, infringes their rights and has a punitive dimension (Adams, 1994, p. 148). Strip searches were introduced to Armargh prison in November 1982, after a gap, according to the prison chaplain, of almost forty years (London Armagh Group, 1984). David Mellor of the Home Office responded in March 1983 to parliamentary questions by Kevin MacNamara, with the information that in Armagh prison between 1 November 1982 and 11 March 1983 772 strip-searches were carried out, an average of 32 strip-searches per woman, compared with one per woman in prisons in England and Wales (London Armagh Group, 1984). In the autumn of 1996, there were witnessed discussions by Home Office officials about the possibility of introducing searches of the underwear of women visitors to prisoners, to try to intercept drugs – contradicting the widespread view that there are many routes in and out of prisons apart from formal visits, not least using contact with staff.

Bodily Restraints: Leg Irons and Chains

'Instruments of restraint' is the term used by the Prison Reform Trust in their publication (1984) covering a range of physical restraints, from those attached to the person, such as handcuffs and canvas restraining jackets, to restraints by means of accommodation, such as isolating rooms, or padded cells.

The export of equipment from the UK, such as leg-irons and gang-chains, was exposed by the *Daily Mirror* in 1983, but continued as late as 1991. Such practices violate international standards for the treatment of offenders and, despite the banning of export licences by Parliament (Amnesty, 1992, p. 11), constitute a form of penal imperialism with a dubious inheritance. A firm in Birmingham claimed in advertising material that they had been 'making leg-irons for over two hundred years and that the firm began its operations by making leg-irons for the slave trade' (Amnesty, 1992a, p. 9). The use of leg-irons, which are intended to severely inhibit prisoners' movements, is forbidden by Rule 33 of the United Nations' Standard Minimum Rules for the Treatment of Prisoners (Amnesty, 1992, p. 9).

The use of bodybelts and similar restraints is concentrated in local prisons, remand centres and closed training prisons, including dispersal prisons and closed youth custody centres (Prison Reform Trust 1984, p. 6). Their use is uneven between establishments, though statistics of their use may not always be readily available. However, Parliamentary Written Answers (7 March 1994, p. 6) revealed that five prisoners were restrained at Wandsworth prison during 1982, the special cells were used 70 times, body belts 7 times and ankle straps 3 times (Prison Reform Trust, 1984, p. 6). The Howard League for Penal Reform stated that body belts were used for prisoners 96 times during 1994 ('Bodybelt restraint "routine in jails"', *Guardian*, 16 November 1995). Press coverage of the use of body-belts was followed by disclosure of the use of physical restraints for pregnant women in prisons, in a letter from several authoritative researchers and practitioners, including Mary Barnard, chair of the National Childbirth Trust, Sheila Kitzinger, Caroline Flint, president of the Royal College of Midwives and Ann Oakley, to the *Guardian* (*Guardian* Letters, 17 November 1995): 'In April last the Home office issued an instruction that all women prisoners should be handcuffed to a prison officer when outside the prison. For many women this includes being shackled while attending for maternity appointments and during the birth of their babies ... . Latest statistics show that 56 women gave birth in outside hospitals whilst imprisoned during 1993/94.' Quoting the press release of a report by the Howard League for Penal Reform (Travis, 1995, p. 12), the authors state:

> One woman was shackled to two officers, one of whom was male, during her antenatal examination. The same woman subsequently was handcuffed and chained throughout a three-day stay in hospital, including when she used the lavatory. Her baby is due next month. Such treatment of pregnant women is barbaric. Pregnancy and birth are an intensely emotional and personal experience. Treatment during this time is likely to have a profound effect on women's self-esteem and mothering abilities. This practice ensures that it is an inhumane process, which degrades the child-bearing woman and all those involved in her care.

The Howard League report quotes Home Office statistics indicating that special restraints, including bodybelts, handcuffs and special cells were used 3200 times in 1994, an increase of 700 on 1993. The use of special cells or strip cells has increased fivefold in the past decade (Travis, 1995, p. 12).

Television and press coverage early in 1996 of a similar case, involving covert filming of a pregnant prisoner from Holloway being chained to a bed in Whittington hospital, north London, when she arrived to give birth, and chained and handcuffed every time she left the bed, showed a sharp division between government officials and critics. Anne Widdecombe,

Home Office Minister, defended these procedures on Channel 4 television: 'We have had one woman abscond when she was fairly well into her pregnancy. She went to an ante-natal appointment and jumped out of a first floor window ... . But we have an absolute rule that we don't handcuff women or restrain them while they are actually in childbirth' (*Guardian*, 6 January 1996, p. 5). The prisoner's reported treatment during the birth refers to the fact that

> as she lay in the labour ward, the guards sat on the other side of a screen and could be heard chatting ... . Beverley Beech, chair of the Association for Improvement in Maternity Services, who was with Annette during the birth, said last night it was a humiliating experience, which pregnant prisoners across Britain have to endure. 'For any woman to give birth successfully she needs to feel secure, confident in her attendants and unstressed. Annette [full name of prisoner not revealed, to preserve confidentiality] was very stressed by the presence of the guards.'
>
> (*Guardian*, 6 January 1996, p. 5)

Subsequently, Michael Howard gave in to political pressure arising from media coverage and organisations such as the National Childbirth Trust and the Association for Improvements in Maternity Services, and announced the relaxation of the policy of using chains and handcuffs on women prisoners visiting hospital (*Guardian*, 19 January 1996). Within two months, fresh controversy over shackling erupted, with press reports of the two accompanying prison officers refusing to remove shackles from a woman held at Holloway prison, at the funeral of her ten-day-old baby. An official complaint was sent to Holloway prison by the chaplain, the senior nursing sister previously caring for the baby, the hospital social worker and the bereavement services coordinator, stating they were 'disturbed by the affront to the dignity of a newly bereaved mother by the inflexible approach to the use of handcuffs at her child's funeral' (*Guardian*, 6 March 1996). In September 1996, the Prison Service modified the practice of chaining prisoners to their beds when they received treatment in NHS hospitals (*Guardian*, 27 September 1996). In contrast with the extensive mass-media coverage of such cases involving adults, the punitive restraint of children remains largely unreported. The Gulbenkian working group illustrates from a study of children in care the case of a 'fifteen year-old mentally handicapped and apparently very difficult girl being bound by her ankles and wrists to a hospital bed to stop her self-injury and disruptive activity' (Stewart and Tutt, 1987, quoted in Gulbenkian, 1993, p. 79).

Incapacitation

The most direct form of bodily restraint involves staff using *force majeur* to enforce compliance. In 1993, the Police Complaints Authority issued guidelines to all police forces after Oliver Pryce died following a neck hold, in a struggle with Middlesbrough police. Such holds are not allowed in penal establishments in the UK. However, a post-mortem on the death of a man in Blakenhurst private prison near Redditch, Hereford and Worcester, suggested that he may have been subjected to an illegal neck hold (*Guardian*, 3 February 1996).

The use of other incapacitating restraints by police officers may be experienced as at least as punitive as the use of similar constraints by staff in penal establishments. There have been increasing debates about use of incapacitating weapons in mid-1990s in Britain. Tear gas has been used in prisons in the USA for many years, for example, in suppressing the riot at Howard state prison, Rikers Island on 19 April 1930 (Adams, 1994, p. 64). The first use of CS gas in a public order situation in Britain appears to have been during the 1981 urban riots; the use of handled truncheons has become common since the late 1980s. CS sprays were approved by the Home Secretary Michael Howard in August 1996, for use by police forces in Britain, after trials in 16 of the 43 forces in England and Wales. The substance known as CS, after Corson and Stoughton who first synthesised it in 1928, is squirted from an aerosol canister; it 'causes streaming eyes and nose, eyelid spasm, salivation and a burning sensation in the throat and nose. There may also be some reddening and blistering of the skin, similar to severe sunburn' (Campbell, 1996, p. 3).

Use of Drugs, Substances and Allied Techniques

Drugs are a major contributor to the arsenal of methods of punishment and social control available to staff in residential and day-care settings, whether social care, penal custody or protection are the main purposes. Drugs may be used simply to knock prisoners out, or as part of a behavioural programme (Cohen, 1977, p. 223), similar to the use of smells, sounds and electric shocks as aversive techniques in the form of the use of ammonia capsules for children who bite their fingers (Bailey, 1983, p. 254), emetics for ruminating infants (Bailey, 1983, p. 255) and the use of isolation and darkness as negative reinforcers for an autistic child

(Bailey, 1983, p. 262). Bailey reports the use of cold baths, shots of shaving cream in the mouth, citric acid, ammonia or tabasco pepper administered in food, on children aged from three months upwards, and the use of high-decibel noise, in behavioural programmes to reduce such 'undesirable behaviours' as crying and 'idiosyncratic hand mannerisms' (Bailey, 1983, p. 257).

Following the death of Larry Winters in Barlinnie prison, Glasgow, as a result of a drug overdose, there were allegations that he had become an addict as a result of huge doses of drugs used over the years to control him in prison. PROP, the organisation for the preservation of the rights of prisoners, began an investigation into the use of drugs as a means of control. In the USA, drugs have been used to control prisoners for many years. The use of drugs in behaviour-modification programmes can only be described as harsh and punitive. For example, in the 1970s drugs such as anectine – a powerful drug which causes a loss of muscle control and even the cessation of breathing – were used to curb the anger of prisoners (Mitford, 1977, p. 131).

Primo Levi, in the afterword to *The Truce*, expresses great concern at the Soviet practice of, if not actually punishing dissent, attempting, in effect, to destroy dissenters with drugs (Levi, 1985 p. 392). The distinction between the use of drugs by professionals in the criminal justice system, for therapy, control or punishment, is to an extent a matter of semantics. Critics tend to allege that drugs are administered to control whilst advocates assert that treatment is necessary. Undeniably, for many years, the use of drugs has formed a significant feature of the life of offenders in many settings. If the usage of prescribed drugs is added to the estimates of extensive usage by prisoners of illicit and self-administered drugs, the total incidence of drug-taking can be seen to be even more widespread.

Over the years, the Home Office has been secretive, to say the least, about revealing hard data on drug usage, of whatever kind (Fitzgerald and Sim, 1979, pp. 8–9). However, some indication of the growing significance of officially administered drugs can be gathered from the fact that between 1971–72 and 1975–76, according to a Home Office response to a Parliamentary question, the cost of drugs, medications and dressings used by the prison medical staff more than doubled (Veitch, 1977, p. 11).

Administration of drugs is far higher in the UK for women than for men prisoners. The sexist comment on this may take the form of the argument that women are more prone to mental illness than men. It is more likely, though, that women are more subject than men to being defined as disturbed if they resist the way they are dealt with, and staff thereby may tend towards medicalising the response to them and prescribe drugs.

In the second half of the twentieth century, drugs have become an increasingly widespread method of addressing the problems of controlling prisoners, curbing the misuse of alcohol and other drugs and securing attitude and personality changes. Tranquillisers have been used, sometimes in association with psychotherapy, and the use of drugs as a means of therapy in themselves has been practised for many years. In evaluating a probation-based programme of group meetings for sex offenders, Roger Shaw, who led it, advocated the use of drugs alongside the programme, to reduce the libido of those attending (Shaw, 1978, pp. 9–13). However, evaluation of such programmes concludes that the use of tranquillisers on their own is clearly inferior to other types of treatment and even the use of drugs in association with other forms of therapy is likely only to produce short-term benefits (Lipton, Martinson and Wilks, 1975, p. 597).

Cohen draws attention to the use of hormone implants, chemical castration or psycho-surgery, the use of drugs such as Prolizin, 'which produces a zombie-like effect', to curb violent behaviour in prison, and in California, brain surgery, advocated 'in such institutions as the MPDU – the Maximum Psychiatric Diagnostic Unit – to reduce trouble-makers to a state referred to by the California Department of Corrections as "temporarily dormant"' (Cohen, 1977, p. 223). Both Bentham's Panopticon prison and the behaviourist psychologist apparently have the goal of achieving complete control over the prison as a social environment. Cohen illustrates with reference to the operant conditioning regime in Patuxent Institution, a 'total treatment facility' in Maryland for more than 400 prisoners, where 'the behaviour modification programme consists of promotion from filthy roach-infested punishment cells, through various level of "reinforcement", up to the final luxury of TV and family picnics' (Cohen, 1977, p. 224).

It may be difficult to distinguish the use of drugs as therapy from their use as a means of controlling behaviour – both involving significant deprivations and even elements of torture. Techniques of behaviour therapy or behaviour modification, based on behavioural psychology, may involve the use of drugs to discourage unwanted behaviour. Such negative reinforcement – a euphemism for punishment – may involve the administration of drugs which produce very unpleasant effects. Antabuse, often used as part of a behaviour modification programme to combat drink problems, induces sickness when the person takes an alchoholic drink. Whilst the use of such drugs may be justified as part of treatment programmes, it is easy to see how in an institution tranquillisers, anti-depressants, Antabuse and similar drugs 'seem to effect no long-term cures and are fundamentally control devices that make it easier to manage "disturbed" inmates in institutions' (Lipton, Martinson and Wilks, 1975, p. 599). It is easy to understand, therefore, the strength of opposition to the use of drugs, from those recognising their ineffectiveness in changing behaviour, and from those opposed to their use for control purposes rather than as a specific treatment under medical supervision.

Use of Electric Shocks in 'Treatments'

The use of other techniques than those discussed in Chapter 3, based on behavioural theory, includes shocks which inflict physical harm. This form of punishment should not be confused with the use of such techniques as electro-convulsive shock treatment (ECT), which also may be experienced as punishment. Electric shock is more overtly punitive, being used as a source of aversion in behaviourally-based interventions. Its advocates claim that 'electric shock can be an effective intervention for serious behavior problems that have proven refractory to other forms of treatment' (Carr and Lovaas, 1983, p. 221). 'The shock is delivered from a hand-held device, similar to the goad used for herding farm animals into wagons, sometimes referred to as a "shock-stick". This device contains from three to five 1.5-volt flashlight batteries and it is most typically designed to deliver a peak shock of 1400 volts at 0.4 mA (Harris and Ersner-Hershfield, 1978). The shock is administered through two protruding ter-minals located at one end of the stick and separated half an inch away from each other. The shock travels between these two points along the surface of the skin. The pain has been described as being 'similar to that experienced when one is hit with a leather strap or a willow switch' (Carr and Lovaas, 1983, p. 221).

Electric-shock punishment has been widely used, for example, in the USA as a behavioural technique in the treatment of children regarded as having behaviour problems, including autistic children and those with learning disabilities. It may be justified, as Carr and Lovaas attempt to do, by reference to its use in curbing self-injurious behaviour such as head-banging, but also is used in situations where children are aggressive or are displaying other chronic symptoms:

> One child with whom we are currently working has hit his ears repeat-edly so that they are swollen to the size of tennis balls. He has broken his nose and injured his kneecap by striking his face with his knee. Further, by repeatedly pummeling the side of his body with his elbows, he has produced kidney damage. Clearly, such behaviour is dangerous, so much so that individuals exhibiting this behavior are usually institu-tionalized and often placed in physical restraints to prevent extensive

self-inflicted injuries from occurring. Although shock has been used primarily to control this type of behavior, it is sometimes also used to control severe aggression or chronic, non-organically based vomiting.

(Carr and Lovaas, 1983, p. 222)

It is ironic, as well as perhaps repugnant, that electric shock treatment is used to impose hurt on people with the claimed utilitarian justification of reducing the possible harm they may do to themselves.

Electric-shock treatment typically involves the use of a shock stick on the limbs:

> To begin with, as soon as the client hits him- or herself, the shock stick is applied for 1 or 2 sec (*sic*) on the client's leg or arm. Simultaneously, the therapist shouts 'No!' Typically the client will now delay the next self-injurious response for a period of 5–30 sec. During this delay, the client should receive a great deal of reinforcement for non-self-injurious behavior. That is, a contingency is put into effect as soon as the client stops the self-injury. When the next self-injurious response is made, the procedure is repeated. This cause an even greater delay. After 5–10 shocks, the rate of self-injury should be virtually zero, at least in one situation. However, if the client should be put in a new situation, there may be no generalization. That is, the client may continue to engage in self-injury.
>
> (Carr and Lovaas, 1983, p. 228).

Medical or scientific experiments may not be carried out on people without their free consent, according to Article 7 of the International Covenant on Civil and Political Rights. Thus, the forcible imposition on prisoners and patients of such techniques of behaviour modification (see also Chapter 3) is outlawed (Amnesty International, 1984, p. 16).

Torture

Torture is the term applied to a form of punishment regarded as cruel and unusual. Torture was never legal in Britain and was illegal in Russia since its abolition in 1742 by Frederick the Great and in France since 1792. Traditional tortures include picketing – in itself a method of execution, if the offender was left impaled on the picket or spike and then hanged – plunging the hand or arm in boiling water, carrying a piece of hot iron or walking blindfold over burning coals as a test of innocence provided the wounds healed in three days, the use of thumbscrews, and the rack, used to stretch the arms and legs of the offender until the joints were torn from their sockets. Much more recently, torture was outlawed by the United Nations on 9 December 1975, in Article 1 of the (somewhat gendered) UN Declaration against Torture:

> For the purpose of this Declaration, torture means any act by which severe pain or suffering, whether physical or mental, is intentionally inflicted by or at the instigation of a public official on a person for such purposes as obtaining from him or a third person information or confession, punishing him for an act he has committed, or intimidating him or other persons. It does not include pain or suffering arising only from, inherent in or incidental to, lawful sanctions to the extent consistent with the Standard Minimum Rules for the Treatment of Prisoners.
>
> (Amnesty International, 1984, p. 13)

The Standard Minimum Rules for the Treatment of Prisoners were adopted by the First UN Congress on the Prevention of Crime and the Treatment of Offenders, in Geneva in 1955. They set out 'what is generally accepted as being good principle and practice in the treatment of prisoners and the management of institutions' (Amnesty International, 1984, p. 13). Despite the existence of such guidelines, the Amnesty International Report *Torture in the Eighties* (Amnesty International, 1984) gives details of torture in more than 90 countries, amounting to one-third of the world's governments.

Not only the physical but also the psychological dimension of torture needs to be considered. The main elements identified by Amnesty as constituting torture include 'the severity of physical or mental pain or suffering caused to the victim, the deliberateness of the act, the fact that the act has a purpose, and the direct or indirect involvement of state officials in the act' (Amnesty International, 1984, pp. 13–14). The inclusion of mental pain means that psychological torture is included in the definition. There may be difficulty in interpreting these statements, as the case of Northern Ireland considered by the Council of Europe from 1971 to 1978 indicates. In 1976, the European Commission of Human Rights reached the unanimous conclusion that the UK had used torture when applying interrogation techniques in 1971 involving hooding, wall-standing, subjection to continuous noise, deprivation of sleep and deprivation of food and drink (Amnesty, 1984, p. 14). But in 1978, the European Court of Human Rights overturned this judgement by a large majority of 13 to 4, even though it agreed by 16 to 1 that these practices constituted inhuman and degrading treatment.

Amnesty International argued that this latter judgement was flawed, since the law relating to torture should reflect the ability of contemporary methods, for example, to inflict severe psychological suffering, and since the unequivocal condemnation of these practices should not become caught up in a debate about the distinctions between one form of cruel and degrading treatment and another (Amnesty International, 1984, p. 15).

However, in 1979, the intention of the UN to interpret the phrase 'cruel, inhuman or degrading treatment or punishment' broadly was confirmed when a commentary was added to Article 5 of the Code of Conduct for Law Enforcement Officials, stating: 'The term "cruel, inhuman or degrading treatment or punishment " has not been defined by the General Assembly but should be interpreted so as to extend the widest possible protection against abuses, whether physical or mental' (Amnesty International, 1984, p. 14).

Inge Genefke, medical director of the Rehabilitation and Research Centre for Torture Victims in Denmark, offers the view of her organisation, that the carrying out of torture by any person can never be justified, including the claim that the person was only carrying out the orders of another person (Genefke, 1995, p. 98). The centre has rehabilitated survivors of torture from 46 countries of the world. This experience suggests that methods of torture are 'the same all over the world' (Genefke, 1995, p. 101). Genefke's organisation finds it necessary to refine the definition of torture adopted by the Twenty-Ninth World Medical Assembly in October 1975 ('the deliberate, systematic, or wanton infliction of physical or mental suffering by one or more persons acting alone or on the orders of any authority, to force another person to yield information, to make a confession or for any other reason') to include government-sanctioned tortures (Genefke, 1995, pp. 97–8).

Thus, physical torture may include

the application of electric shocks to the most sensitive areas of the body; the suspension of the victim by an arm or by a leg, which can last for hours; the immersion of the victim's head under water until the point of suffocation; the burning of the victim's skin with cigarettes or red-hot iron rods; beatings aimed at specific parts of the body, such as under the feet until the soles are badly damaged. Sexual abuse is common, particularly against women, though men are also sometimes harmed in their ability to function as men; dogs can be trained to rape both men and women. Sanitary conditions in detention are usually extremely poor, any request for visiting the toilet becoming a pretext for torture; the victim is kept alive with filthy food and drinking water; freedom of movement is limited, with prisoners often packed so closely as to force them to sleep in turns. (Genefke, 1995, p. 100)

The manufacture in the UK of electric-shock batons and rods, whose use is banned in in the UK under the Firearms Act (1988), and leg-irons, for export to other countries such as China, Saudi Arabia and Turkey which use torture techniques, was reported in 1995 (Anon., 1995b, p. 9).

An electric shock from a baton can cause severe pain and affects muscle control; victims often feel nauseous and may have convulsions or faint under the shock ... . Shocks with batons are often applied to sensitive parts of the body, such as the inside of the legs, soles of the feet, inside of the mouth and ears and the genitals. Sonam Dolkar, a 26-year-old woman in Tibet, was detained for months on suspicion of being a Tibetan independence sympathiser. She was repeatedly tortured with shocks from wires attached to her body. Electric batons were applied to her face and every part of her body including her vagina. Eventually she was vomiting and urinating blood daily and was moved to a police hospital from where she managed to escape to India.

(Anon., 1995b, p. 9)

In 1996, according to a documentary screened on Channel 4's *Dispatches* programme on 13 March 1996 (Pallister, 1996, p. 4), manufacturers in the UK were still giving quotations to supply electric-shock batons abroad. 'Last year the same television team revealed that Royal Ordinance, part of British Aerospace, was prepared to supply thousands of the 60,000 volt sticks to the Lebanon and boasted that RO had sold 8,000 to Saudi Arabia. RO's suppliers were German' (Pallister, 1996, p. 4).

Psychological torture includes methods such as 'sleep deprivation, blindfolding and isolation' (Genefke, 1995, p. 100). These may produce

a deep sensation of fear and helplessness and can also provoke hallucinations. Total isolation can be maintained for years, in which time the victim is uncertain of their fate, and their family is ignorant of their condition and whereabouts. Many victims are coerced to say or do things which violate their ideology or religious convictions, the purpose of which is to destroy fundamental parts of the victim's identity related to their self-respect and self-esteem. Political and ethical values are attacked by techniques such as the coercion to sing songs which praise the very things which the victim is against. Mock-executions lead the individual from a sense of reality into a nightmarish state of almost suspended animation. The breaking down of the victim's personality begins with their arrest. Names are replaced with numbers. Personal belongings are removed, including glasses, life-saving drugs, etc., and are replaced with ill-fitting uniforms.

(Genefke, 1995, p. 100)

This description is similar to those of people subjected to cruder attempts at brainwashing, rather than the more sophisticated thought reform (see Chapter 3).

The participation of medical professionals may legitimate coercive punishment, of which torture is an extreme illustration. The reasons why physicians take part in torture, for example, are complex, as Hernán Reyes observes:

Experience has shown that medical participation often comes about in an oblique way. Although there often may be some degree of coercion (fear of losing position, rank, other benefits or, in extreme cases, even their freedom or lives) many doctors convince themselves that their actions may actually be beneficial 'within the circumstances' to the victims. This is the slippery slope that doctors sometimes take, some perhaps even naively thinking that they are 'only trying to help'. Some doctors may sincerely believe that their presence can be beneficial and allieviate some of the suffering. Paradoxically, some of the victims may also be 'comforted' by the fact that a doctor is somehow involved. This should not, however, cloud the essential fact that doctors should never get involved in any form of repression for any motive whatsoever.

(Reyes, 1995, p. 46)

Ellmann highlights the insidious mimicry of the everyday by the apparatus and procedures of torture. 'Domestic objects are perverted into instruments of pain: tables and chairs are used as racks and bludgeons, contradicting their hospitable associations; electric lamps blaze day and night, destroying time and using light to dazzle rather than to see' (Ellmann, 1993, p. 100).

The disturbance of the person's intuitive grasp of the normality of interpersonal interaction is heightened by interrogative techniques which alternate quickly, sometimes employed by two interrogators displaying contrasting effect, between kindness and brutality, empathy and total disregard for personal dignity or mental and physical well-being. Thus, the language and culture of hate and affection may become intertwined and often confused. In a bizarre twisting, suggested by the word 'torture', there may be 'a disturbing kinship between the language of torture and the language of love' (Ellmann, 1993, p. 101). There is a nauseous but palpable resonance betwen this relationship and that between care and control, in social care. The difference between these descriptions and those of interrogation by the police are in degree rather than in kind.

Torture also provides a spectacle. Guards in the torture chamber are voyeurs, just as prison officers watch whilst others strip-search prisoners (Adams, 1994, p. 148).

> The torture room provides the mise-en-scène where power materializes in the spectacle of pain. The fact that it was called the 'cinema room' in South Vietnam signals the importance of the ocular and voyeuristic aspects of the ritual. ... Bobby Sands records as sexual assault a search in which the prisoners were forced over a table and 'the cheeks of their behinds torn apart by the screws' hands.' .... One could argue that the inmates of Long Kesh starve in *eyes*: for staring and starving both have the effect of reifying bodies into spectacles. These spectacles, moreover, mystify the true relationships of power, because it is the individuals who are humiliated rather than the social forces that they represent. But it is precisely this confusion of the symbol with the symbolised which underlies this rhetoric of laceration.
>
> (Ellmann, 1993, p. 102)

The extent to which the company of other prisoners is denied, discrimination between prisoners in terms of treatment, the age, sex and health of the prisoner, the duration of a particular treatment or punishment, its known or likely physical and mental impact on the prisoner, reduction of diet, denial of adequate medical care, forcible feeding, compulsory labour, are all ways of dealing with people which may be cruel, degrading or inhuman (Amnesty International, 1984, p. 16).

Experiences of torture include extreme psychological and physical abuse, involving 'isolation, abduction, secret detention, incommunicado detention beyond the reach of family, friends and legal assistance ... the sense that the interrogator controls everything ... degradation, insults, sexual threats or assaults, forcible eating of one's excrement, humiliation of one's family ... breaking down under extreme pressure and severe pain' (Amnesty International, 1984, pp. 18–20). Torture victims often require psychological, medical and social help and treatment after release (Amnesty International, 1984, p. 25). Some experience such post-traumatic shock that they can never revisit their experiences, and it takes decades before they can speak about them, as was the case with one man who was able eventually to write about his experiences and visit Japan to meet his former interrogator (Lomax, 1995).

ETHICAL CONSIDERATIONS IN THE USE OF BEHAVIOURAL TECHNIQUES

Ethical issues apply directly to humans being punished and indirectly to animal experiments designed to test such punishments before they are applied. In relation to both, Singer sets out the ethical principle of the equal consideration of the interests of all animals and people (Singer, 1991, ch. 1). The human dignity of the person punished may be undermined by punishment and also that of the humanity of the society in which punishment occurs, diminished by the manner of its application. Carr and Lovaas attempt to set three ethical boundaries to the use of aversive techniques: first, that their use is only justified 'if the *individual* is the primary beneficiary of treatment', that is, they 'should not be used solely for the convenience of the institution at which the individual resides' (Carr and Lovaas, 1983, p. 226). Second, they should not be used where the person's anticipated response presents 'threats to the client's biological survival' or endangers 'the client's social, emotional, and intellectual growth to a degree that ensures lifelong institutionalization', or where there are 'serious threats to others who are physically weaker than the client' (Carr and Lovaas, 1983, p. 226). Third, that where electric shock, for example, is used, 'it must entail a small amount of pain and discomfort relative to the amount of pain that would result if the behavior problem were left untreated' (Carr and Lovaas, 1983, p. 226).

All the above ethical considerations proposed by Carr and Lovaas are matters of judgement on which the use of punishment is contingent. As they admit in relation to this third point, 'the key question is how long treatment will take' (Carr and Lovaas, 1983, p. 226). Carr and Lovaas justify such punishment, for example, with reference to relativist and utilitarian arguments. They are reminiscent of the attempts by utilitarians such as Bentham to calculate what constitutes a just measure of pain to inflict, for the benefit of others. Relatively greater amounts of shock, apparently, are unacceptable, whilst smaller amounts are. For example, 'unless there is a marked decrease in the rate of self-injurious behavior in at least one situation in the presence of at least one therapist following 5–10 shocks, the procedure will probably fail and should be discontinued' (Lovaas and Newsom, 1976). 'In consulting work, we have seen cases in which a thousand or more shocks have been applied with minimal effect. This level of shock use violates the ethical dictum that the amount of pain due to treatment must be less than the amount of pain that the client would experience if the problem behavior were left untreated' (Carr and Lovaas, 1983, p. 228). Thus, in Benthamite terms, there is a need to estimate whether the benefits of the treatment exceed any harm it does:

> In the case of severe self-injury, a small amount of pain resulting from brief, effective shock treatment is justifiable if one considers the lifetime of pain in the form of physical restraint and drug-induced stupor that would occur if the behavior were left untreated. By the same token, shock treatment is warranted for high-frequencty aggression, such as that involving severe biting of others, when the only other alternatives are physical restraint, forcing the client to wear a face mask, extraction of the teeth, or psychosurgery. Finally, shock is indicated in the case of chronic, uncontrollable ingestion of dangerous objects that necessitates multiple abdominal surgeries.
>
> (Carr and Lovaas, 1983, pp. 226–7)

Similar ethical questions to those occurring in behavioural techniques are raised by the use of drugs, whether as a means of treatment or control, even when their effects are allegedly minor and short-lived.

> For some types of more chronic offenders – such as sexual offenders and alcoholics – there is a tendency to ignore ethical questions and to make use of more drastic methods such as castration and severe forms of negative conditioning. (One study, for example, used chemically induced apnoea – the inability to breathe – as the unconditioned stimulus and combined this with the subject's favorite alcoholic beverage.) Although negative conditioning alone may have little effect, it can always be argued that this is because the treatment was not sufficiently draconian. Hence, if the argument proceeds solely on the grounds of expediency, there is no limit to the kinds or intensities of experiences that may be proposed under the label of 'medical methods'.
>
> (Lipton, Martinson and Wilks, 1975, p. 599)

Perhaps the most incredible feature of the imposition of physical pain by professionals on clients is the willingness of the former to do it. Milgram's much-quoted experiments (Milgram, 1963, 1974) purporting to demonstrate the willingness of a cross-section of 'typical' males in the USA seemingly willing to inflict pain and potentially fatal harm – in the form of electric shocks – on others, were more widely publicised than their critiques (Mixon, 1989). Arguments, however, over the experimental correctness and predictive power of Milgram, or indeed, concerning the ethics of his experiments, are rendered somewhat sterile by the fact that physical punishments such as behavioural therapy and torture are already widespread and are not outlawed by the countries in which they are practised.

5 Punishment by Custody

Imprisonment as it exists today is a worse crime than any of those committed by its victims.

(Shaw, 1922)

INTRODUCTION

This chapter deals with three main kinds of custodial setting: prison, custodial establishments for children and young people, and, in a brief addendum, hospital custody for people with mental health problems. These are not a comprehensive view of the vast scope of custodial settings, but they enable the examination of typical uses of punishment as custody. In examining them, this chapter encounters a striking ambiguity which lies at the heart of the tension in all three types of custody, between their claimed therapeutic purposes and functions, and their actual punitive ones. The dichotomy is rarely as sharply defined as this, however, which makes the task of clarifying, describing and interpreting the significance of forms of punishment that much more difficult. The chapter touches also on the desired nature of custodial regimes, as opposed to their unintended consequences, in terms of increasing rather than reducing offending behaviour or in producing a significant rate of suicides; it also deals with the use of custody for such groups as asylum seekers and attempted immigrants; finally, it considers a number of non-penal settings in which children, older people, people with mental health problems and people with learning disabilities are dealt with. It should be noted that the discussion of corporal punishment in Chapter 6 contains much of relevance in relation to boarding schools, especially public schools.

PRISON

The prison is the stomach of the state, according to Coetzee, a state which stamps Michael K. with a number and gobbles him down. But punishment in prison is a waste of time, for he 'has passed through the bowels of the state undigested; he has emerged from its camps as intact as he emerged from its schools and orphanages' (Coetzee, 1990, p. 221).

Rothman's brilliant historical exposition of the birth of the asylum in the USA identifies the ideological sleight of hand by which the prison insitution was legitimated, despite its failure as an engine for reforming criminals. Not surprisingly, given this fundamental failure of the rationale for the massive prison systems of the USA, euphemisms cloak the extension of the prison system in the USA during the twentieth century, where there was a proliferation of correctional institutions which were not called prisons (Adams, 1994, p. xii). In fact, the portrayal of the prison regime in the British mass media as akin to that of the holiday camp contrasts with the reality that it is a fundamentally punitive and controlling institution, the central response to crime.

> Most of us see prison as *the* punishment for crime. Of all the alternative forms of sentence open to our courts, it figures most prominently in the public imagination. Other forms of disposition, like a fine or a term of probation, are seen as acts of leniency: as relaxations of the full punishment of imprisonment, allowed because of some mitigating circumstances in the particular case.
>
> (Jones, 1967, p. 106)

Expansion of the Prison System

The popularity of prisons as a means of punishing offenders remains as undiminished in Western countries as in the third world. If anything, the relative prosperity of the former has enabled the expansion of prison-building programmes to accelerate since the early 1980s, as is evidenced by the UK and the USA. In the USA, for example, more than 1.5 million people were locked up in prisons early in 1996, 90 000 more than a year previously.

Rutherford critically contrasts the 1930s, when the prison population fell in the UK, with its slow increase in the 1950s and 1960s and the quickened pace of increase in the 1980s (Rutherford, 1989, p. 27). He aligns this with Winston Churchill's scepticism, in his brief period as Home Secretary in Asquith's Liberal government, of the justification for imprisonment, expressed in his speech in the House of Commons in 1911, when he stated that even when conditions in prisons had been brought to a decent standard, 'the convict stands deprived of everything that a free man calls life ... . The mood and temper of the public in regard to the treatment of crime and criminals is one of the most unfailing tests of the civilization of any country' (H.C. Debates, 5th Series, vol. 19, cols. 1353–4, 20 July 1910, quoted in Rutherford, 1989, p. 27).

Overcrowding

Between May 1993, when Michael Howard became Home Secretary and the prison population was 43 500, and October 1996, the prison population rose by almost a quarter. In October, the number of prisoners exceeded 5000, 4500 more than the predicted peak. In 46 prisons, by February 1996 a state of emergency was declared, as they were required by the Home Office to take more prisoners than their operational capacity normally allowed.

> Some jails are being asked to find space for 10 per cent more prisoners than their official capacity. Hospital units and offices are expected to be converted into cells, more single cells will be occupied by two inmates and in some cases prisoners will be put in dormitories as governors try to house inmates in jails which are already officially full.
>
> (*Guardian*, 29 February 1996).

It was announced in October 1996 that a former nuclear airbase in Suffolk, England would probably become an overflow prison to relieve the pressure on existing prisons, staffed by Ministry of Defence police (*Guardian*, 19 October 1996).

Hyper-security and Restrictiveness

There is an enormous body of research evidence to support the view that prisons are primarily warehousing institutions, whose punitive classifying and controlling functions take precedence over any claim to rehabilitative activity (Morris and Morris, 1963; Irwin, 1980; MacKenzie, 1989; Human Rights Watch, 1993). The violence with which the authorities in the USA have suppressed the major riots by prisoners of Attica in 1971 (Adams, 1994, pp. 83–7) and Santa Fe in 1980 (Adams, 1994, pp. 94–8) attests to their primarily punitive character.

Prisons are exemplars not only of the application of penal principles, but also of the extent to which prison systems are designed and run by men. Prison cultures – whether staff or prisoner, in male, female or mixed institutions – tend to be dominated by aggression and machismo, associated with a version of masculinity, running counter to the values of humaneness, softness, openness, trust and anti-oppressiveness. Sexual abuse – between males and of women by male staff – is a particularly characteristic feature of such environments (Weschler, 1991, pp. 41–2). The more general shortcomings of penal institutions in general are epitomised in their treatment of women – often housing them too far from their families for frequent visiting, providing inadequate pre-natal care and post-natal facilities for mothers and babies, as well as inadequate recreational and educational opportunities. Thus, if prisons are inadequate for men, they certainly 'do not take into account several of the vital needs of women' (Weschler, 1991, p. 85). The failure of the penal system of Britain to take account of the situation of women in prison is epitomised in the lack of specific reference to women or girls in prison, in the inquiry into the prison system chaired by Mr Justice May, which reported in October 1979 (May, Committee of Inquiry into the United Kingdom Prison Services, 1979). Purpose-built six-foot-square cells for women in a new prison, Eastwood Park, near Bristol, were condemned in 1995 by the then Chief Inspector of Prisons Judge Stephen Tumin. They were below the minimum standard of 5.5 square metres set by the Prison Service itself. Jeremy Mallinson, director of Jersey Zoo, an international centre for research into primates, said 'No zoo would confine an ape in an area measuring 6 foot by 6 foot. This would certainly not be acceptable, and indeed would damage both the psychological and the physical wellbeing of the animal.' Slightly bigger, 10-by-6-foot cells in another wing of the prison were reserved for prisoners who behaved well, as an incentive to good behaviour (*Observer*, 25 February 1996).

The prison of the late twentieth century displays some of the anarchic features of the lack of order in the medieval-style institution, where the guards simply provided token supervision from outside the prison or the asylum. This is characterised by the no-go areas for staff and the proliferation of internecine conflict between various subcultures and gangs of prisoners. This may be one consequence of the fragmentation of groups, the diversity of interests between prisoners and intense, often violent, conflicts between different groups (Adams, 1994, p. 229). In the USA, for example, in Stateville maximum security prison, Illinois, it has been estimated that as many as 85 per cent of prisoners may be affiliated to the large number of mutually hostile gangs operating in the institution, which was designed as a panopticon, so that one guard, in theory, from a central point could see into every cell, and control every activity in the institution (Weschler, 1991, p. 39).

In prison systems akin to the UK and USA, the majority of prisoners are held in conditions of medium or maximum security. Security classifications of prisoners tend to ratchet up the judgement of how far they are at risk, to the extent that staff are anxious. Andrew Rutherford quotes the example of Texas, to illustrate his argument that expanding prison systems tend to over-use maximum security facilities and under-use those which are minimum security. Thus, 'in Texas the state system categorizes ninety-five per cent of its prisoners as maximum security, despite the fact that the head of the system has testified to the legislature that forty per cent of the male population do not need to be imprisoned' (Rutherford, 1986, p. 66).

Elliott and King documented in detail a case study of the impact on a new prison of the growing emphasis on security in the English prison system during the 1970s (Elliott and King, 1978). By the end of the 1970s, the rehabilitative rationale for imprisonment was replaced in many Western countries, notably the USA and Britain, by 'a focus on retribution, incapacitation and deterrence' (Weschler, 1991, p. 11) 'Big House' prisons, many built around the turn of the century, are human warehouses, using punitive methods to coerce inmates into compliance (Wright and Goodstein, 1989, p. 264) and suppress riots (Adams, 1994, pp. 58–71). What Cohen refers to as the Chinese box effect (Cohen, 1977) has been termed 'Marionisation' in the USA. More than thirty states since 1983 have followed the example of the federal prison at Marion, Illinois, where a super-maximum security institution – referred to as 'maxi-maxi' – was created.

The confinement in 'maxi-maxis' is administered by prison officials without independent supervision and leads to a situation in which inmates may in fact be sentenced twice: once by the court, to a certain period of imprisonment; and the second time, by the prison administration, to particularly harsh conditions. This second sentencing is open-ended – limited only by the overall length of an inmate's sentence – and is imposed without the benefit of counsel.

(Weschler, 1991, p. 3)

The debate about prison standards reaches a low at the point where there are calls – reminiscent of the principle of less eligibility of the Poor Law Amendment Act 1834 – for conditions to be made less palatable than the most modest community-based housing. In contrast, Casale and Plotnikoff (1989) argue for a programme of reform in standards of life in prisons which should focus on three core conditions – time, occupancy and space in the cell; sanitation; and personal hygiene – and locate 'a reasonable strategy to ensure the implementation of minimum standards' in 'a larger exercise in re-examining the assumptions behind traditional concepts – security, control, staff/prisoner relations and prison design' (Casale and Plotnikoff, 1989, p. 21).

The nature of the prison changed markedly during the twentieth century, shifting first towards a pattern in the USA of concentrating offenders considered high-risk in massive, fortress-style security prisons and second, in the later years of the twentieth century, dispersing this enhanced security throughout the system as a whole (Cohen 1977). Prison institutions retained their character as hierarchical, militaristic forcing-houses for macho power and demonstrations of violence by staff and inmates alike. This is a persistent feature of prisons as total institutions (Adams 1994, p. 228). Even the most progressive policy is likely only to reduce the basic dichotomy between managers and workers in the institution into an intricate power-play between progressives and traditionalists (Mathiesen, 1965; McCleery, 1961).

Diversification and Imperialism: Hulks, Prison Ships and Transportation

Overcrowding and poor conditions were features of other methods developed for incarcerating prisoners. For example, conditions were appalling in the hulks moored in estuaries round the coast of Britain during the early nineteenth century, from one of which the escaped convict comes whom Pip meets on the Essex marshes in the early pages of Dickens's novel *Great Expectations.* When Pip asks about the nature of these prison ships, Mrs Joe responds unequivocally: 'People are put in the Hulks because they murder, and because they rob, and forge, and do all sorts of bad; and they always begin by asking questions' (Dickens, 1953, p. 12). Conditions on the prison ships used to transport prisoners to other countries, notably Australia and the USA, were so bad that mutinies – generally repressed with punishments of great brutality with whippings and executions – were not uncommon (Adams, 1994, pp. 109–11). Thus, the mode of enforcement of penal sanctions itself produced secondary deviance, which attracted further punishment. The idea of prison ships is not entirely anachronistic, as is indicated by the plans of the Home Office to transfer to Portland in the spring of 1997 a modern 'hulk' formerly intended to be used as a prison ship in New York (Adams, 1994, p. 103), but found to be too expensive by the authorities there.

'Less Eligibility' in Prison Regimes

Whereas in the early nineteenth century in Britain and the USA, advocates of prisons argued for their reformative qualities, by the mid-nineteenth century the failure of prisons to eradicate crime had already led to widespread disillusionment. This was expressed in a shift towards developing prison regimes along similar lines of less eligibility to those applied in the nineteenth-century British workhouses. In essence, the workhouse regime in the wake of the Poor Law Amendment Act of 1834 was intended to be no more attractive than the least attractive option for the lowest-paid labourer. In similar vein, the Prisons Act 1865 marked a return to severity of punishment as a deterrence from crime, rather than attempting to reform. It endorsed the system of keeping prisoners in separate cells so that they could not communicate with each other and authorised hard labour on the treadwheel, shot-drill, crank and capstan and the use of irons and chains (Sindall, 1990, p. 140).

Twentieth-century prison systems bear testimony to the historical role of the penal institution as a utilitarian structure designed to discipline what nineteenth-century commentators regarded as the 'dangerous classes', and what a century later has been presumed to be, in part at least, a criminal 'underclass' (Irwin, 1985). Margaret Atwood, developing a case study of Grace Marks, interweaves history with contemporary fiction to show the total failure of criminal justice to address the complexity of the oppressions experienced by the individual. She illuminates the career of Grace, from being the accomplice to murder at sixteen, through custody in Kingston prison and to subsequent experiences in 'respectable' mid-nineteenth-century Canada (Atwood, 1996).

The Conservative government was influenced in the mid-1990s by two of the more negative features of the penal system in the USA, to introduce tougher and more controlling prison regimes in top security, for prisoners serving longer sentences, and bringing in longer and more deterrent sentences. The first of these brought some Home Office officials and Home Secretary Michael Howard into conflict with more progressive prison governors, with Derek Lewis, whom Howard may have sacked from his post as Director-General of the prison service, in the summer of 1995, and the Chief Inspector of Prisons Judge Stephen Tumin, whose contract the Home Secretary did not renew when it expired in the autumn of 1995. The second of these was exemplified in the announcement in 1995 by Michael Howard of plans to introduce minimum prison sentences for burglars and dealers in hard drugs, on the lines of the USA formula of 'two strikes and you're out', giving automatic life sentences for rapists and violent repeat offenders. This brought him into conflict with many professionals and academics, including Lord Donaldson, former Master of the Rolls and Lord Ackner, former law lord, who stated:

> It is a complete reversal of policy. In 1991 it was said judges were being too tough and sending more people to prison than any other European country except Turkey. Their discretion had to be removed by making

them sit in blinkers. The Home Secretary will never get it through the Cabinet because he is following the American experiment which has gone disasterously wrong. It will be incredibly expensive to build the prisons which will be necessary.

(Travis and Dyer, 1995, p. 5)

In support of this view, Paul Cavadino, chair of the Penal Affairs Consortium, commented: 'Judges already have the power to pass life sentences for such crimes when the gravity of the offence or the dangerousness of the offender justifies this. But sentences must reflect an assessment of the individual circumstances and of the offender's just deserts' (Travis and Dyer, 1995, p. 5).

Bernard Shaw's (1922) opposition to prison as a means of punishment, quoted at the beginning of this chapter, is as unrepresentative of public opinion in Britain in 1996, when this book is being written, as when it was first published 70 years ago.

Pre-trial Custody

Many criminal justice systems use custody as a principal means to detain people before trial. In some parts of India, for example, up to four-fifths of the prison population may be remanded for up to two years (Vakkalanka, 1996). Whilst there is a prima-facie case for minimising numbers of pre-trial prisoners, there is ample evidence also for addressing the injustice of housing them in sub-standard conditions, which are unacceptable for convicted offenders, let alone those subsequently found innocent. The shortcomings of pre-trial conditions habitually include physical deficiencies made worse by overcrowding and inadequate privacy, a lack of personal safety, deficiencies in the regimes in aspects such as activities, food, health and contact with the outside world (King and Morgan, 1976; Weschler, 1991, pp. 20–31).

In the USA, over half of more than 367 000 prisoners in the total of more than 3300 jails – administered by counties and located in local communities – are estimated to be occupied by people awaiting trial (Weschler, 1991, p. 17). Many jails are overcrowded, with over-occupancy rates highest in the larger institutions – that is, those housing more than 1000 prisoners. By no means the worst accommodation is the oldest. Thus, Weschler's survey visit revealed that

the Criminal Justice Center in Nashville, Tennessee was built in 1982 with a capacity for about 3000 inmates. At the time of our visit in

1990, it held more than 800 inmates and we were told that at some point recently it had held 1,100. For over six months, a staff member told us, the facility's gymn was used to house several hundred pre-trial detainees. They had two bathrooms and two showers at the gymn. At the time of the greatest overcrowding, additional space in the under-ground tunnel leading to the courthouse was used to house 200 inmates. There were no showers and no bathrooms in that area. When we visited, inmates were housed in cells. The cells we visited, however, had no windows and were very crowded (for example eight women in a cell of 174.20 square feet, or less than 22 square feet per prisoner)

(Weschler, 1991, p. 19).

These conditions amount to punitive custody for both innocent and guilty prisoners on remand.

Detention of Attempted Immigrants

The phenomena of social upheaval, war and civil strife produce global problems of diaspora, hundreds of thousands of people at any one time leaving their homes and their countries and seeking refuge elsewhere. At the same time, there is a constant tendency for people to seek to live in another country, for many reasons, not least because of the desire for improved opportunities and, perhaps, with the aim of joining friends and relatives already there. In 1958, the Supreme Court of the USA observed that the policy of not detaining 'alien' people entering the country without the necesssary papers reflected the 'humane qualities of an enlightened civilization' (Weschler, 1991, p. 91). In contrast with this ideal, refugees entering the country often attract a punitive response, in the form of detention in penal-style camps or actual prison accommodation.

Thus, the response by the authorities in Hong Kong to 'boat' people fleeing from Vietnam, or by the USA to Cuban, Haitian and central American aliens seeking entry has been to set up detention facilities to house them on arrival. The USA employs many city and county jails to this end, the early 1980s during the Reagan administration having reversed the policy of non-detention which had held sway since 1954. Conditions in such detention facilities all too often fall below the stand-ards of the worst custodial facilities in the country elsewhere, as is evi-denced by the Human Watch Report on conditions in the USA (Weschler, 1991, pp. 92–9).

Asylum Seekers

A lack of justice is evident in the punitive treatment to which asylum seekers in the UK – regardless of whether they have committed, or whilst in detention commit offences – are subjected, both on arrival, and in detention centres. Asylum seekers who have come to the UK without prior permission from the authorities tend to be confined in immigration detention centres on their arrival, whether by boat or by air. There was evidence in the early 1990s, that the policy of detaining asylum seekers, regardless of whether they have committed a criminal offence, was deterring people from seeking asylum in the UK, applications declining from 44 800 in 1991 to 24 600 in 1992 (Amnesty International, 1994, p. 61). In the mid-1990s, in Campsfield House detention centre,

> there is no internal disciplinary procedure ... and, as a result, the only real sanction against 'indiscipline' or 'disruptive' behaviour" by detainees is enforced transfer to Haslar HOHC, where the regime is more controlled, or to a criminal prison. However, in the absence of any formal disciplinary procedure, it is clear that the imposition of such 'punishment' by Immigration Service officials is not subject to any form of due process. This is a violation of international standards, which provide that detained persons 'shall have the right to be heard before disciplinary action is taken', and 'shall have the right to bring such action to higher authorities for review'. (UN Body of Principles [Principle 30]) It is also in marked contrast to the situation in criminal prisons themselves, where The Prison Rules, made under the authority of the 1952 Prison Act, set out 22 offences against prison discipline and the Manual on the Conduct of Adjudications governs a formal disciplinary procedure, including the right to representation, oral hearings, and a review mechanism.
>
> (Amnesty International, 1994, pp. 44–5)

Isolation and Segregation

Prisoners may be isolated as individuals, or segregated in small groups from the rest of the prison. This isolation may be temporary, perhaps as a consequence of offences against prison discipline, or permanent because of the classification of the prisoner, perhaps following being assessed as requiring segregation from other prisoners. The origins of the segregation of prisoners lies in the silent and separate systems which became popular in the nineteenth century in the prisons of Western countries and those of other countries which were modelled on them. Whereas segregation may be reserved for prisoners viewed as posing a threat to good order and discipline, solitary confinement may be used over and above this either as a means of protecting the prisoner from assaults by other, or as a means of control.

Franke, a notable scholar of corporal and capital punishment in the Netherlands, interprets the changing use of solitary confinement in the light of prevalent societal and cultural ideas (Franke, 1992). Thus, he reinforces Garland's (1985b) impression of England and Wright's (1983) view of France, that liberal, *laissez-faire* individualism was consistent with locating causes of poverty and criminality within such notions of individualism, freedom and self-help, problems such as unemployment, poverty and criminality being viewed as morally rather than as socially-based – that is, as 'traits of individual character, righteousness and responsibility' (Garland, 1985b, pp. 40–5; 50–1; quoted in Franke, 1992, p. 141).

A detailed exposition of the changing nature of segregation in prisons is not relevant here. Two aspects are highlighted as particularly abusive. First, in the early 1980s, women's prisons made disproportionate use of segregation in special cells. In 1982 a disproportionate number of women were restrained (Table 5.1), relative to the total prison population. Special cells were used 259 times compared with 892 times in all-male establishments (Prison Reform Trust, 1984).

Second, the use of special units within prisons must be viewed critically, in the light of the research by Cohen and Taylor (1972) on the impact on prisoners of long-term imprisonment. However, aspects of imprisonment need to be viewed in relative rather than absolute terms. It is

Table 5.1   Prisoners restrained on non-medical grounds in 1982

	Males	Females
In local prisons	297	
In remand centres	77	83[1]
Closed women's prisons	21	
Dispersal prisons	89	

[1] That is, women on remand in custody were 31 times as likely as men to be subject to restraint in similar prisons (Prison Reform Trust, 1984, p. 7).

difficult to compare different units at different periods in time. To some staff and prisoners, the prospect of remaining in some special units where a relatively positive and relaxed regime was established, would be preferable to remaining in solitary confinement. The closure of the special unit at Parkhurst prison's C wing revived for the most intractable prisoners in 1986 after a review by the Control Review Committee (CRC), led a psychiatrist who worked in that unit, on his resignation, to write an open letter of protest to the Home Secretary:

> The harshness of your current prison policy has finally ground my therapeutic endeavours at Parkhurst to a sickening half – I must now resign on principle. Against overwhelming evidence you maintain a bizarre attachment to 'austerity', which bears especially hard on mentally ill offenders, who include the most unpredictable and dangerous of all. Those too violent and dangerous for Broadmoor had been successfully accommodated in Parkhurst's C wing Special Unit until you decimated it two weeks ago by expelling all category A prisoners. Now they have nowhere to go, and must face a degrading move every three months from prison to prison in solitary confinement for decades – I can no longer support such an inhumane, dangerous and expensive prison policy. As a doctor, my five years' work on C wing has been exhilarating. We reduced the rate of violent assaults by 90 per cent and heavy medication by 94 per cent. This open letter is unlikely to deflect you and your ministerial team from your current folly. Nevertheless, as I leave the Prison Service under protest, I hope others will take encouragement from the fact that treating human beings with humanity rather than brutality makes them, and us, safer, more secure and above all more civilised.
>
> (*Guardian*, 27 January 1996)

CUSTODY FOR CHILDREN AND YOUNG PEOPLE

Since the 1850s, there was more or less continuous growth in the custodial systems for dealing with children and young people considered to be at risk of harm from others, to themselves or to others. Also, residential accommodation for educating largely middle- and upper-class children grew, through boarding schools, and establishments dealing with children considered to have educational special needs, problems of maladjustment, autism, health, mental health, learning difficulties and physical disabilities (Platt, 1969; National Institute for Social Work, 1988a, 1988b). The report of a working group convened by the Gulbenkian Foundation commented: 'The restriction of the liberty of children accommodated by health, social services and education authorities, or in residential care – nursing homes or mental nursing homes – is extremely inconsistent, both between different services and categories of institution, and between different jurisidictions within the UK' (Gulbenkian, 1993, p. 78). The report refers to tighter regulation of children's homes run by local authorities than health-authority establishments, or the government-administered special treatment centres (Gulbenkian, 1993, p. 78).

The fragmentation of service provision and the numbers and diversity of providers, as well as the difficulties of monitoring quality and maintaining standards, to which the Gulbenkian Report refers, have been exacerbated in the 1990s by the introduction of quasi-markets in the personal social services (Adams, 1996a, ch. 3). A full consideration of the full range of custodial institutions for young offenders would be beyond the scope of this section, since it includes reformatories, later redesignated as Home Office Approved Schools and then as community homes with education, borstals and detention centres, later redesignated as young offenders' institutions (YOIs), the two special youth treatment centres at Glenthorne and Brentwood, and, currently, the facilities for secure treatment orders and so-called 'boot camps'. The following discussion makes selective references to this list.

The history of custodial institutions for young offenders – reformatories, Home Office Approved Schools, borstals, and young offenders' institutions, has been marked by a succession of attempts to innovate and reform, which by and large did not transform them into progressive, humane establishments.

Long, Dull Pain: Borstal Training/Youth Custody

Borstal training, introduced in the Prevention of Crime Act 1908, began as a therapeutic endeavour, but by its transformation to youth custody 70 years later, had become a negative label (Behan, 1958; Hood, 1965; Sillitoe, 1959). In borstal, goals and activities which were part of the treatment philosophy were increasingly likely to be perceived by inmates as means of social control which, ultimately, were punitive. Staff tended to use the indeterminacy of the 9- to 36-month sentence – later 6 to 24 months – as a means of inducing compliance in the borstal boys (by the 1970s euphemistically referred to as 'trainees'). Value-judgements about so-called 'progress' towards reform from delinquent behaviour contributed to claims of successful treatment. Indeterminacy was likely to involve decisions about home leaves and discharges being dependent on reviews of responses to casework, group counselling, trade training or institutional rules and norms. (Hood, 1965). Measures such as group counselling were also wielded by staff as a means of individual and social control in these formally treatment-based, but in practice often punitive, regimes (Taylor, Lacey and Bracken, 1979).

Short, Sharp Shock: Detention Centre

The short, sharp shock of the detention centre (DC), created – though this phrase was not invented then – by the 1948 Criminal Justice Act and brought in from the early 1950s, was based on the notion of discouraging delinquency through punishment in custody, rather than simply by custody. That is, the regime of the DC was intended to be punitive and thereby deterrent. This notion underwent further reincarnations in the 1980s in the experiments with tougher regimes (Thornton, Curran, Grayson and Holloway, 1984) and again in the early 1990s with secure training.

Young Offenders' Institutions

The persistently macho culture of custodial institutions resonates with dominant values in the community. These have historically reinforced the provision of rigorous physical education for trainees and competitive sports, with progress measured in terms of similar criteria to those obtaining in the public school system. These values are rich in metaphors which sustain machismo and violence. The argot and culture of the custodial institution, reminiscent of the violence of life in the public school, provides a vehicle for this (Adams, 1991, pp. 30–1).

There is an argument for considering all custody as punitive, whether or not those imposing it claim that custody is as, and not for, punishment, or claim some overarching rehabilitative/therapeutic philosophy which benefits prisoners/inmates. Inspections and investigatory reports initiated by the authorities – for example, after a number of suicides at Glenochil young offenders' institution in Scotland (Scottish Home and Health Department, 1985) – provide a key source of independent corroboration of conditions in custodial institutions. Documentary exposés include such as that accompanying the campaign by Amnesty International concerning conditions in a labour camp for young offenders in Almaty, the capital of Kazakhstan, where young boys mutilated themselves to gain the sanctuary of the hospital and escape the brutality of the regime and institutional culture ('True Stories of the Cross', Channel 4, 30 July 1996). This provides a rather more dramatic means by which conditions in penal institutions in particular settings can be portrayed and subjected to public scrutiny.

Solitary Confinement for Children and Young People

The use of solitary confinement in locked cells – sometimes referred to as single separation – for young people in custody was achieved in 1972 in detention centres, by an amendment to the detention centre rules. As late as 1981, 66 of these rooms were still being used in the care system. Such cells were liable to be used, particularly by the less experienced staff, as a form of control, and on occasions young people could be locked in solitary confinement for long periods.

Cellular confinement may be used as a punishment. Even where it is not, it may still be experienced as punitive. C. A. Joyce, the then head of the Cotswold Community, told the author that he frequently used to put a refractory boy in solitary confinement for a day or two, with only a chair and a prayer book, and occasional visits from himself and the chaplain to relieve the isolation. He viewed this as part of the treatment approach, rather than punitive. However, such facilities – single rooms for confinement and secure facilities – inevitably take on a punitive character and, to the extent that they impose isolation and limit social interaction, are likely to be experienced this way by children and young people.

Tougher regimes apart, the other major category of custodial facility is secure accommodation. The Criminal Justice Act 1982 provided criteria, in a section inserted as Section 21A of the Child Care Act 1980, to limit which children 'in the care of a local authority' could be placed in accommodation provided for the purpose of restricting liberty; it allowed the Secretary of State to issue regulations providing arrangements for a judicial review by the juvenile court of placements in secure accommodation within the community home system.

Section 39 of the Child Care Act 1980 and the Community Homes Regulations 1972 restricted the liberty of children in community homes; they specified the need 'to obtain the permission of the local authority or voluntary organisation in whose care the child is'. But voluntary organisations were exempt and could restrict the liberty of children on their own account. Two 'Youth Treatment Centres' at Brentwood and Glenthorne were provided under Section 80 of the Child Care Act 1980 under the direct control of the Department of Health. There was a consensus in the Social Services Inspectorate and Department of Health by the 1980s that limiting access by children and young people to their parents and friends should not be used as a form of punishment or control.

Secure accommodation may be developed either within an existing establishment or in a separate establishment. Evaluations of secure accommodation confirm unambiguously that they act punitively to confirm delinquent careers rather than deflecting or halting them (Millham, Bullock and Hosie, 1978; Harris and Timms, 1993).

Secure Training Institutions and Boot Camps

Following the sentencing of two boys for the murder of James Bulger, the Government introduced measures to contain persistent young offenders in a small number of new secure training centres, with a deterrent regime. Government plans to introduce secure training orders with quasi-jails for juvenile offenders were incorporated in the Criminal Justice and Public Order Act 1994. They were aimed at young offenders who had committed at least three offences within a year. Research commissioned by the Northern Ireland Office (NIO) into the effectiveness of the Lisnevin secure training school in Ulster, reputedly the model for the British institutions for secure training orders, was not allowed by the NIO to be published when first completed. Thus, the Parliamentary debates on this aspect of the Criminal Justice and Public Order Bill, during 1994, were not informed by the largely negative findings of this research report, produced by the Belfast Adolescent Psychology and Research Unit. The research tracked 592 former inmates of Lisnevin and found that 86 per cent reoffended within three years of discharge and 95 per cent thereafter. The comparative statistics for young people who were not locked up were 71 per cent and 83 per cent. The negative impact of the institution on the predisposition of offenders to serious offences is demonstrated in the fact that only 6 per cent committed violent crimes before admission, whereas 20 per cent did so after discharge (*Observer*, 20 November 1994). Mary Honeyball, general secretary of the Association of Chief Officers of Probation, visited Lisnevin secure training school in 1994 and commented that it was 'bleak beyond belief. The children sleep in cells with bars, on mattresses on the floor' (*Observer*, 20 November 1994).

Boot camps developed in the USA and provided a model which impressed members of the Conservative Government in Britain in the 1990s. The first 32 young offenders aged 18 to 21 to attend a tri-service Military Corrective Training Centre at Colchester in the autumn of 1996 were due to experience an almost identical regime to the 'corrective training' given to service personnel. 'They will wear the same working clothes – though without military insignia. They will be supervised by a sergeant major and 10 sergeants, get up at 6.30am to face room and kit inspections, training runs and marching drill. Their hair will be cut short, and for the first six to eight weeks there will be no television' (*Guardian*, 15 April 1996, p. 4). The tensions between harshness and rehabilitation in this regime were similar to the detention centre regime of the 1950s. Alongside the 'hard but not harsh' regime, there were elements of 'teaching life skills' and 'building self-esteem' (*Guardian*, 18 April 1996, p. 11). Further descriptions of the regime were of graded stages of progressively less punitive regimes within the institution:

> The declared purpose of the centre is rehabilitation, though inmates are subjected to discipline that is daunting by civilian standards. The centre also runs courses in bricklaying, painting and engineering. The regime will be based on a 'stick and carrot' system. If the youngsters co-operate, they will switch after six to eight weeks to an easier routine in which they are not locked in at night and have brief access to black and white television. The final phase – when they are no longer escorted around the camp – is heralded by the arrival of colour television. Traditional big military dormitories are to be replaced by centrally-heated and double-glazed six-man flats with kitchen space and drying rooms in a £30 million scheme.
>
> (*Guardian*, 15 April 1996, p. 4).

The Prison Governors' Association put in jeopardy plans to open the boot camp at the Military Corrective Training Centre, Colchester, by threatening court action to insist that legally only a trained prison governor rather than an army officer could assume responsibility for such an establishment (*Daily Telegraph*, 19 October 1996).

Tougher regimes are contra-indicated by the increasing incidence of psychological as well as social problems, which may lead to suicide – currently running at about one per week, in circumstances where those incarcerated are deprived of such facilities as visits, access to leisure and educational facilities and the opportunity to interact informally with other people.

HOSPITAL CUSTODY FOR PEOPLE WITH MENTAL HEALTH PROBLEMS

The history of mental hospitals parallels prisons in that the use of moral reformation programmes succeeded the widespread use of restraining chains and strait-jackets (Scull, 1991, p. 110), as the posivitist revolution gathered pace from the mid-nineteenth century (Bean and Mounser, 1993, p. 4). Later still, the large mental hospitals built at a respectable distance from many towns in Britain during the latter half of the nineteenth century became, in effect, warehouses for storing mentally ill – and non-mentally ill – people for increasingly long periods.

The history of the psychiatric hospital shows an ironic contrast between the ideals of Bettelheim (1970), who was reacting in part to the Holocaust and the grimness of the concentration camp, and the subversion of the ideal, expressed relatively mildly in Goffman (1967), who reserves much criticism for the, albeit loosely defined, total institution, and more devastatingly in the film of the book *One Flew over the Cuckoo's Nest* (Kesey, 1977). Within the so-called treatment regime of the mental hospital, this film portrays group therapy as a nightmare form of social control by nurses.

The four special hospitals – at Ashworth, Broadmoor and Rampton in England, and Carstairs in Scotland (Adams, 1996a, pp. 144–5) for several decades have provided accommodation which is quasi-punitive in nature, staffed as they are by a combination of medical, nursing and prison officer grades. They have attracted many critical studies (Gostin, 1977), inquiries and investigations, the most noteworthy of which, the Rampton Inquiry (Boynton, 1980), upheld allegations that staff were using several illegal and unprofessional sanctions to control patients. These included the so-called Rampton cocktail – a concoction of different courses of food, mixed together – and throttling out – a coiled towel tightened round the neck till the patient passes out. The punitive practices of staff in hospitals are very difficult to eliminate by legislation or procedural regulation. In the late 1980s, a social work student from the author's university, who visited a mental hospital, found one patient on a locked ward sitting facing the wall. On asking why this was, she was told the patient had committed some minor misdemeanour on the ward and this was the regular way of sanctioning patients. Such treatment is a function of institutional culture, rather than an aberrant act by an individual. The only effective way to extinguish some practices, or malpractices, may be to close the institution down.

In the mental hospital, as in other total institutions, Goffman observes that order is maintained by a system of rewards and punishments, 'petty by outside standards but assuming Pavlovian dimensions in a situation of deprivation. Rules may not be made fully explicit. The inmate cannot appeal to them for protection, and he may break them unwittingly, and be punished for it' (Jones and Fowles, 1984, p. 15). By the nature of their mental health problems, many people do not go entirely voluntarily into a locked ward or secure unit in a hospital setting. Roger Clough argues that the lack of the purely voluntary element in admissions contributes to these institutions becoming second-class. He comments that this can generate problems 'more difficult to eradicate than the original reason for admission' (Clough, 1981, p. 7). One consequence is the persistent tendency of staff to develop institutional practices, perhaps involving social pressures towards conformity (Clough, 1981, p. 8), which may be experienced by residents as punitive.

6 Corporal Punishment

You can whip vice into a boy, but you can't whip it out.
> (Walter Parsons, Chairman of Leeds Juvenile Court 1933–37, *Yorkshire Evening News*, 4 August 1937, quoted in Scott, 1938, p. 187)

INTRODUCTION

This chapter deals with the nature, history and incidence of corporal punishment, its widespread use, such as in work, education, penal and household settings, its deployment in behaviour modification and other treatments. It deals also with issues raised by the use of corporal punishment, including controversies, particularly over its use on young children at home and in playgroups and nurseries. Corporal punishment is defined quite narrowly in this chapter, as comprising direct punitive blows inflicted by one person on another, including those which lead to amputation.

CONTRADICTIONS OF CORPORAL PUNISHMENT: BANNED YET WIDESPREAD

Corporal punishments such as flogging and punitive amputations are prohibited by a ruling of the Human Rights Committee; this is the United Nations committee which monitors the Covenant by States Parties, made in July 1982, that corporal punishment falls into the prohibited category of cruel, inhuman or degrading treatment, punishment or torture (Amnesty International, 1984, p. 16). Amputations typically involved chopping off hands or legs for the offences of theft or trespass in medieval England, cutting off one or both ears for non-church attendance in the reigns of William the Conqueror and Henry VII, and cutting off a hand for seditious libel in the reign of Queen Elizabeth I. Despite more modern prohibitions, corporal punishment remains deeply ingrained in the cultures of countries in many parts of the world. One indication of the embedded nature of corporal punishment in societies, is the widespread tradition of stories illustrating the taken-for-granted place of corporal punishment, in folk tales and fairy-tales. The UN Committee on the Rights of the Child has also

118

recommended the banning of all physical punishment of children, at home or in institutions. More than 180 countries had ratified the UN Convention on the Rights of the Child by January 1996, committing them to taking all appropriate measures to protect children from all forms of physical or mental violence, injury or abuse (EPOCH Worldwide and Rädda Barnen, 1996, pp. 4–5).

In the face of these efforts, however, corporal punishment of children, in particular, persists. It is still legal in British households and is a part of growing up for children in many other countries (Korbin, 1987). Corporal punishment of children is particularly well entrenched in the culture of Britain and the USA (McFarland, 1995). In the autumn of 1996, amid concerns about school discipline, the controversy concerning whether or not to allow corporal punishment is unabated. The *Sunday Telegraph* went so far as to link together Dr George Carey, Archbishop of Canterbury, Lord Tebbit, former chairman of the Conservative Party and David Blunkett, education spokesman for the Labour Party, as all supporting the moderate use of corporal punishment (*Sunday Telegraph*, 27 October 1996, p. 11).

For many years, adults have referred to the benefits of 'six of the best'. Nursery rhymes, often chanted by children themselves, include the old woman who had so many children she did not know what to do, so she gave them some broth and bread and 'spanked them all soundly and sent them to bed'. Again, when Tom the piper's son stole a pig, 'The pig was eat and Tom was beat; And Tom went roaring down the street.' Beliefs in the value of 'a good clip round the ear', or the judicious use of the belt or cane are sustained in popular culture in the face of the professional consensus that such forms of punishment are abusive (Leach, n.d) and research evidence that far from being effective in modifying behaviour, they may be harmful (see Chapter 8).

In the second half of the twentieth century, debates in Western countries have tended to focus on the uses and abuses of corporal punishment in relation to children. Many view the terms 'physical punishment' and 'corporal punishment' as synonymous. In Britain, the narrower goal of abolishing corporal punishment in schools (Newell, 1972) was supplanted by the broader aspiration of abolishing physical punishment, as was illustrated by the closing of the organisation Society of Teachers Opposed to Physical Punishment (STOPP) and the founding in 1989 of the organisation End Physical Punishment of Children (EPOCH). Straus and Kantor (1994) define corporal punishment of a child as 'an act by parents intended to cause the child physical pain, but not injury, for purposes of correction or control of misbehaviour'· (Straus and Kantor, 1994, p. 543). Carey (1994), following Payne (1989), defines corporal punishment as 'any form of punishment used by a caregiver that is intended to inflict some measure of physical pain on a child'. Carey argues that typically, corporal punishment does not lead to a reduction in a given behaviour and that in such circumstances the continued use of the punishment may result in abuse of the person being punished. Carey goes so far as to suggest that under such conditions it is a misnomer to regard corporal punishment as a form of punishment (Carey, 1994, p. 1007). Alternatively, it could be argued that this demonstrates the intrinsically abusive nature of such punishments. Of course, this is even more confusing if one considers that corporal punishment in the classroom may include any form of physical assault, including throwing missiles, pulling hair, smacking and caning, excepting physical contact to prevent injury or self-injury. Of itself, corporal punishment is not a criminal offence; its banning simply removes the civil law defence of teaching or care staff that they have employed 'reasonable' corporal punishment to restrain a person or contain a situation.

The increasing concern of professionals about child abuse makes the use of corporal punishment more puzzling, since the boundary between these two is difficult to establish. Article 3 of the European Convention on Human Rights and Fundamental Freedoms in 1950 stated that 'No one shall be subjected to torture or to inhuman or degrading treatment or punishment' (Council of Europe, European Treaty Series, 4 November 1950, No. 5). It arose in the wake of the atrocities of the Nazis in the Second World War. Since 1950, its application has been extended to a range of areas, such as extradition, immigration, racial discrimination, the incarceration of mentally ill people and corporal punishment (Phillips, 1994, p. 154). Examples of litigation illustrate the need to clarify the nature of punishment in physical harm inflicted on one person by another, and the boundaries between torture, degrading treatment and inhuman treatment, these being terms commonly used in litigation. Unfortunately, such clarification is not easy to achieve.

Also, there are some disjunctions between the treatment of adults and children. Often, attitudes to corporal punishment inflicted on children are more tolerant of the punishment than if it were inflicted by an adult on another adult.

AN ABUSIVE TRADITION

The widespread use of corporal punishment throughout the world may be attributed on one hand to the attempted justification by some people of their inherent tendency towards treating others cruelly. On the other hand, it may be viewed as the most easily available form of punishment, whether applied with the slap of a hand, an everyday object such as a stick, or a specially made whip or cane. As indicated above, though, corporal punishment is all too often rooted in the history and culture of a country, as an accepted practice. Thus, in some countries such practices may continue despite widespread condemnation of them. Although in theory corporal punishment is now banned in many European countries, including Austria, Cyprus, Finland, Norway and Sweden, it is hard to legislate against, being such a widespread informal means of discipline and control. In Tolstoy's nineteenth-century novel *Resurrection* (1900) the Prince visits the prison at Moscow and finds that even though corporal punishment has been abolished in prisons, it is still used on the 700 or so people, including refugees, detained there not because of crimes but, for example, because of minor irregularities in their passports.

Abusive Nature of Traditional Corporal Punishments

It is possible to correlate positively the tendency for abuse and oppression of people generally in a society, the prominence of aggression and violence in the culture, the promotion of *macho* values, and the use of a range of psychological and physical punishments including corporal punishment (Adams, 1991, pp. 29–36). Corporal punishment of children

> seems to be a white tradition, exported to many parts of the world through slavery and colonialism, both of which used corporal punishment as a means of control. It appears that the only cultures where children are rarely or never physically punished are small, hunter-gatherer societies, now rapidly vanishing under the impact of urbanisation – but arguably among the most 'natural' of all human cultures.
> (EPOCH Worldwide and Rädda Barnen, 1996, p. 16)

Ancient Greece and Rome, where flogging was used for punishing criminals, were cultures which applauded the physical prowess of men, valued military might and relied on slaves to do the work for satisfying everyday needs. In the Roman Empire, the *ferula* – a flat leather strap – was used for minor offences; the *scutica* – two thongs of leather twisted together – was employed for more serious offences; the *flagellum* – three heavy leather thongs knotted at intervals – could be wielded so as to rip lumps of flesh off the offender's back (Van Yelyr, 1941, p. 77). Similar punishments have been inflicted traditionally in many other countries throughout the centuries, including France, Germany, Japan, China,

Russia, the USA and Britain. Whipping with knotted cords was a punishment used in Anglo-Saxon Britain.

In Britain, the Whipping Act 1530 first specified flogging as a penalty for some offences and marked a trend towards the increasing use of corporal punishment (Hibbert, 1966, p. 443). It provided for a vagrant to be taken to a market place 'and there tied to the end of a cart naked, and beaten with whips throughout each market town, or other place, till the body shall be bloody by reason of such whipping' (Van Yelyr, 1941, p. 89).

It has been asserted that corporal punishment traditionally has been the most common way of inflicting punishment (Van Yelyr, 1941, p. vi). Flagellation, in the form of the birch for juvenile offenders and the cat-o'-nine-tails for adult offenders, appears to have been unusually popular in Britain (Van Yelyr, 1941, p. vii). The general increase in harshness of the law which occurred in England from the late eighteenth century could scarcely compete with Scotland, where in the reign of James VI, children and minors were scourged for causing disturbances in churchyards. Scourging, or *fustigatio*, consisted of beating or whipping the offender, often in public.

Four boys who each threw a stone at a woman whom an older man was beating, were sentenced to be 'scourged through the city of Edinburgh, burnt in the face with a hot iron, and then ... sold as slaves to Barbadoes' (Cooper, 1869, p. 179). Vagabonds and absconding servants could be burnt in the ear and scourged for the first offence and executed for the second. For theft of bread worth a farthing a thief could be scourged, from one to four farthings scourged, for four farthings put in the jougs – an iron collar in two parts, locked round the offender's neck and often attached by a chain to a wall or post – and banished, from four to eight farthings lose an ear; and if subsequently apprehended with eight pennies, hanged (Cooper, 1869, p. 181).

The whip and the cane have been used by slave-drivers and the owners of labour to extract more work from their subjects, since time immemorial. Slaves were routinely beaten to death as they rowed, being punished for their increasing incapacity, and were replaced by a seemingly endless supply of fresh labour.

Biblical references to the use of corporal punishment are widespread. Calmet's *Dictionary of the Bible* apparently records 168 faults subject to corporal punishment. In the New Testament, Christ used a scourge, made of small cords bound together, to drive the money-lenders out of the temple. Paul and Silas were whipped, when 'the multitude rose up together against them: and the magistrates rent off their clothes, and commanded to beat them. And when they had laid many stripes upon them, they cast them into prison' (Van Yelyr, 1941, pp. 10–11).

After the Inquisition (see Chapter 2), corporal punishment continued to play a prominent part in religious persecution. The Society of Friends, or Quakers, were subjected to widespread religious persecution, from their foundation in the mid-seventeenth century, in many parts of Britain and, subsequently in the USA. Whipping was a common punishment employed to try to enforce their conformity (Van Yelyr, 1941, pp. 38–45). In the persecution of the Protestants in Southern France during the early nineteenth century, Wilks's history, quoted by Van Yelyr, highlighted the horrific use of a *fleur-de-lis*, a battledore covered in nails.

I have seen,' reported an eye-witness, 'them raise the garments of a female and apply with heavy blows to the bleeding body this *battoir* to which they gave a name that my pen refuses to inscribe. The cries of the sufferers – the streams of blood – the murmurs of indignation, which were suppressed by fear – nothing could move them.' Not even women who were big with child were spared – like other females, their petticoats were turned up and the gory battledore applied to their posteriors until the blood ran down in streams, and they screamed madly for mercy.

(Van Yelyr, 1941, pp. 37–8).

In the sixteenth and seventeenth centuries, men and women, including 'the mothers of illegitimate children, Scottish pedlars, beggars, drunkards, fortune tellers, sex offenders, and even lunatics' (Hibbert, 1966, p. 444), were whipped for many offences, following sentencing at Quarter Sessions. Often, children were flogged by their parents when executions were carried out 'to impress on their minds the awful lessons of the gallows' (Andrews, 1890, pp. 210–24, quoted in Hibbert, 1966, p. 444).

The criminal code of Tuscany, published by the Duke of Tuscany in 1786, was heavily dependent on the use of whipping as a sanction (Cooper, 1869, p. 147).

From the sixteenth to the eighteenth centuries, attitudes towards children were ambivalent, on one hand sympathetic towards rescuing them from hardship and harm through ignorance, whilst on the other hand being ready to administer the rod, if demanded by their youthful sinfulness (Wardle, 1974, p. 35). Flogging was still prevalent in seventeenth-century English schools and it was reported by Lord Taunton's Inquiry in 1868 that flogging was used as a punishment by 75 per cent of mixed schools (Freeman, 1979, p. 41).

In 1863, the attack by two men on a Member of Parliament in London was the spur to the passing of the Security from Violence Act which outlawed the flogging of those robbing with violence and attempting to garrotte victims (Hibbert, 1966, p. 443).

In the wake of the Whipping Act 1865, in 1878 in India 75 000 people were flogged and even in 1897, 54 078 (Sindall, 1990, p. 90). Such actions were widely supported. There was endorsement in Parliament and condemnation of critics in *The Times* when Governor Eyre suppressed the rising in Morant Bay in Jamaica in 1865 by massacring 600 people with troops, executing many hundreds more and 'by wide-spread flogging including the lashing of women on bare buttocks with piano wire' (Sindall, 1990, p. 90). Flogging was still used elsewhere in what remained of the British Empire, notably in the 1930s as part of the Australian penal code (Van Yelyr, 1941, p. 100).

Corporal punishment exemplifies the impossibility of distinguishing the abuses of punishment from what may be claimed as its proper uses. Despite the widespread use of corporal punishment in Britain informally and formally, to chastise adults and children, its use has aroused particular study and comment, at certain times more than others. From the late 1930s, the climate of professional opinion in Britain turned gradually but firmly against corporal punishment of children. An article in the *British Medical Journal* on 20 March 1939 states: 'A judicial birching, whatever may be the injury to the mind of a growing human being, might well confirm the offender in his potentially criminal ways ... . To tie him hand and foot to a tripod and flog him with a brine-soaked birch seems the best way to make a boy of 8 years look upon society as his natural enemy.'

A spate of publications in the late 1930s and early 1940s accompanied the work of the Committee established by the Home Office to examine the use of corporal punishment, which reported in 1938. This Committee encountered considerable pressure to maintain or even to extend the use of corporal punishment. Even campaigners opposed to the widespread use of corporal punishment and its abolition against adults, often argued for its continuance in schools, provided it was used immediately:

> The value of punishment, in the case of the child, is wholly concerned with its *immediate application*. The child, in many respects, is little removed from the domestic animal. Anyone with experience of domestic animals is well aware that the whipping of a dog, if it is to have any prohibitive or reformatory value, must be administered *immediately* after the offence has been committed.
>
> (Van Yelyr, 1941, pp. 229–30)

In 1938, the Committee on Corporal Punishment examined a study by the Howard League for Penal Reform, indicating that of 440 men convicted of robbery with violence between 1921 to 1930, of the 142 flogged well over half committed other serious crimes following their release from prison; less than 40 per cent of those not flogged committed serious crimes again. The recommended abolition of corporal punishment by this committee was passed in the Criminal Justice Act 1948, limiting this penalty to gross violence to prison officers, mutiny and incitement to mutiny committed by prisoners. Following the abolition of corporal punishment in the criminal justice system in England and Wales, the incidence of robbery with violence declined significantly from 87 451 offences on average per year between 1945 and 1948, to 768 in 1948 (Hibbert, 1966, p. 445).

Until its repeal in 1948, birching (up to six strokes) of young offenders and flogging adult offenders with the cat-o'-nine-tails were part of the penal code in Britain. Between 1931 and 1935 in Britain, flogging was given to eight men, for living on immoral earnings (Van Yelyr, 1941, p. 75). The *Manual of Correctional Standards* (1954) of the American Prison Association only disapproved of 'corporal punishments of the humiliating type' and reported that 'in several men's institutions where women are confined, women as well as men are flogged with a heavy leather strap as punishment for both minor and major infractions of the rules. The punishment is usually inflicted by a male employee.' (Taft, 1956, p. 559, quoted in Hibbert, 1966, p. 446). Prison flogging in England and Wales was abolished in practice only from 1967, though it had not been practised for many years before that (Gibson, 1978, p. 378). Birchings were no longer public in the 1930s.

The organisation STOPP was set up in the late 1960s, to campaign for the abolition of corporal punishment in schools (see Chapter 9). In Britain, corporal punishment for children was abolished finally in educational establishments and residential homes in 1986, yet a decade later, abuses of corporal punishment were still being discovered. In contrast, smacking was still allowed, though it was banned in at least five other European countries.

Whilst the Education Act 2 1986 banned corporal punishment in state schools, it was still allowed in independent schools, subject to certain conditions. It was not permitted in direct grant schools, schools maintained by the Ministry of Defence and city technology colleges; pupils occupying assisted places could not be subjected to corporal punishment; corporal punishment regarded as excessive or improperly motivated was to be treated as assault; the administration of corporal punishment where a pupil's parents were philosophically opposed to it was to be treated as a breach of the European Convention on Human Rights (Foot, 1996, p. 3).

Flagellation

The use of flagellation and self-flagellation has been closely associated with religious practices for many centuries. In some cultures, such customs have been justified with reference to the assumed vengeful instructions of one or more gods and goddesses. Herodotus records the self-flagellation of naked witnesses of human sacrifices to the goddess Isis (Van Yelyr, 1941, p. 15). The excuse for the annual Roman festival of *Lupercalia*, on 15 February, involving men with whips beating any women they encountered, was to increase their fertility (Van Yelyr, 1941, p. 15). Plutarch records the whipping of young boys before the altar of Diana, in the Feast of Flagellations among the *Lacedaemonians*. The harshness of such rituals can be judged by Cicero's account that whipping youths to death was not uncommon (Van Yelyr, 1941, p. 18). In the Christian tradition, notably in Italy, self-flagellation was seen traditionally as a response to the anger of God, visited upon people in the form of epidemics or disasters.

Self-flagellation, and sometimes group flagellation, figures significantly in monastic and other religious communities from medieval times, often as part of penance in response to sins (Scott, 1938, p. 121), the widespread belief in medicinal and other virtues of flagellation (Scott, 1938, p. 122) and the need for a physical means of suppressing physical cravings (Scott, 1938, p.122). Aldous Huxley's painstaking research (Huxley, 1952) into one example of an excessive zeal for mutilation and self-mutilation as a so-called punishment for nuns having consorted with devils, led to the adaptation of his shocking book in Ken Russell's film *The Devils*. Self-flagellation and flogging appear to have been the main means of punishment in early Christian monasteries and nunneries, according to Palladius' *Historia lausiaca*, being adopted as an alternative to excommunication (Van Yelyr, 1941, p. 19).

There is abundant evidence that until the early nineteenth century, at least, flagellation overlapped with sexual abuse and self-abuse (Van Yelyr, 1941, pp. 46–52) and with prostitution (Van Yelyr, 1941, p. 67–75), blurring the borderline between corporal punishment and sexual abuse and self-abuse (sado-masochism).

Flagellation did not die out in the Middle Ages. Self-flagellation among the Society of Jesuits, with a whip with a number of knotted thongs capable of inflicting major injuries, occurred until comparatively modern times (Van Yelyr, 1941, p. 30). Van Yelyr produces copies of bills of sale to give detailed evidence that as late as 1869, nuns in London still employed what were termed 'Articles of Piety' as instruments of corporal punishment and self-punishment. The *flagellum*, which sometimes had five tails to represent the five wounds of Christ, consisted of a wire instrument with spikes, designed to penetrate the flesh. Some versions had short rowels instead of spikes and these gouged out lumps of flesh. A variant, called 'Mother Superior's Wild Cat', had a series of pointed rowels along it, the seven-tailed cat representing the seven dolours of the Virgin Mary, and the nine-tailed *flagellum* symbolising the nine months during which 'the Word was made Flesh' (Van Yelyr, 1941, pp. 23–4).

Flagellation also is associated with the practices of a particular religious sect. Sometimes known as 'Brethren of the Cross', flagellants are regarded, according to one account, as originating in Hungary among a group of 'gigantic women' (Regan, 1994, p. 143). Flagellation could also be viewed as one response to the Armageddon people have feared was at hand at various historical moments, notably during the period of the Black Death which killed about a third of the population of Europe in the fourteenth century.

From the thirteenth century, flagellation as a mass phenomenon associated with religious practices, spread until its decline in the sixteenth century largely through a Brotherhood known as *Disciplinata di Gesu Cristo*, from Italy to France.

The growth of flagellant movements could be interpreted as a physical manifestation of social and political disease, equivalent to the plague itself. Camus used the coming of a plague to a city as a metaphor for the horrors of Nazi occupation, 600 years later (Camus, 1973). Sontag brilliantly illuminates the ways illnesses such as HIV/AIDS are used as vehicles for moralising and punishing people for their lifestyles (Sontag, 1991). Commentators allege that the Flagellants carried out their punitive rituals two or three times a day for each of the 33 years of Christ's life, but it is doubtful if many would have survived such mutilation, given that their movement forbade them to wash or change their clothing during this process (Regan, 1994, p. 145). The Flagellants carried out their rituals in public, often gathering in market-places,

forming wide circles before stripping to the waist and flinging their clothes into the middle of the circle, where they attracted the attentions of the local sick and afflicted who hoped to gain cures from handling the garments of such holy people. At a signal from the Master the Flagellants flung themselves down, usually with arms outstretched in imitation of the crucified Christ. Some, who had committed particular crimes, reacted in ways appropriate to their sins: adulterers face down in the dirt, perjurers on their sides holding up three fingers. The Master then walked round the circle whipping those who had committed crimes. This was immediately followed by the self-flagellation for which the movement was famous. Each flagellant carried a heavy scourge or whip, with three or four leather thongs tipped with metal studs or sharp spikes. With these they began furiously to whip their backs and breasts, while three of their number cheered them on with a rhythmic chant. Three times in total each Flagellant threw himself or herself to the ground and three times rose up to continue the beating, until their bodies were purple with blood and bruising. On the edge of the market place the townsfolk urged them on or wailed in horror at the dreadful sight.

(Regan, 1994, pp. 144–5)

The public ritual of self-flagellation reifies the body into a spectacle of penitence. However revelatory this spectacle of individual sorrow and pain is, it conceals a reality embedded in the power relationships which sustain the humiliation of the individual penitent, rather than the oppressive, male-dominated structure and power of the Church, evidenced in the conduct of the priests exorcising the devils in Loudun (Huxley, 1952).

Mass Flagellation

The mass flagellations of *Disciplinata di Gesu Cristo* took place at public services and meetings (Van Yelyr, 1941, pp. 54–65). As late as 1890, *Los Hermanos Penitentes*, a Flagellant sect descended from the original Spanish inhabitants of New Mexico and Colorado, still practised there. Van Yelyr draws from the *Catholic Encylopaedia* the observation that

before public celebrations were stopped in deference to American law, and as a result of the opposition of the Church, on the day appointed, the *Penitentes*, naked to the waist, and armed with scourges made of the leaf of the amole weed, marched through the streets to the temple, whipping themselves vigorously as they went. In the van of the procession were a few *Penitentes* with heavy crosses, which they dragged behind them, singing hymns lustily all the while. On arrival at the temple, prayers were offered, and then commenced an orgy of flagellation, the *Penitentes* whipping one another and themselves until their backs were masses of weals and blood. At the same time one of the men was bound to a cross, and the crucifixion, with all its grossly realistic features, was executed, in some instances going so far as to entail the death of the victim.

(Van Yelr, 1941, p. 66)

Van Yelr indicates that such rituals continued in secrecy into the twentieth century, in the face of opposition by the authorities, with the participants hooded, to avoid recognition (Van Yelr, 1941, p. 66).

DEPLOYMENT OF CORPORAL PUNISHMENT

Long-standing traditions of extremely harsh sentences of corporal punishment have characterised military, penal, domestic and schooling history in many Western countries. In Europe, such punishments were commonly deployed to buttress imperialist policies by explicitly racist means. At one level, the evidence supports Killingray's observation that

> modern society functioned through the law sustained by police, prisons, fines and social sanctions. To Victorian, and later, minds such institutions rarely existed in African societies, and if they did it was in a degraded form and to serve purposes vastly different from those required by modern capitalist society. Western notions of order and discipline, of that inter-related system of production and labour that constituted industrial time, were little known in African societies. Stick and whip would serve as teachers; at the same time humanity and economy dictated that their use be regulated. The problem was how to regulate.
>
> (Killingray, 1994, p. 204)

Thus, a sharp distinction was often made in the colonial era between what were viewed as the civilised mores, and means of disciplining misdemeanours, in the reputedly civilised society of the British mainland, and the anarchy which would overtake the British overlords in the colonies if firm discipline was not applied to the natives. However, as Stedman Jones shows, the dualist images of respectable society and the dangerous residuum which characterised and sustained the colonial structure were inverted in Victorian society, and served as a model of the emerging industrial city, of which London – 'the great Wen', as William Cobbett referred to it (Cobbett, 1957, p. 239) – was the archetype. The city remained an ambiguous symbol, both of Heaven and of Hell, the latter being the threat fulfilled if the mob of urban degenerates who formed the residuum broke loose from the East End and invaded the West End

(Stedman Jones, 1976, pp. 291–3). The pages of Doré's engravings of London (Doré and Jerrold, 1872), divided as their subject matter was between the slums of Whitechapel and the picnics of St James's, exemplify this dualism; it provided the rationale for means of curbing, controlling, disciplining and punishing pauper criminals and their children which were often as tough and authoritarian as those experienced by their colonial counterparts thousands of miles away. The great prisons of London – Pentonville, Holloway, Wandsworth, Wormwood Scrubs and Brixton – along with courts, police stations and, paradoxically, parks, theatres, zoological and botanical gardens, shopping streets for the leisure and entertainment of respectable and well-to-do people, were built in amongst the crowded houses of paupers and labourers.

Corporal Punishment by the State and in the Empire

The incidence of corporal punishment is surrounded with a certain coyness on the part of the authorities employing it as a penal sanction. Attempts by the author to obtain data from different governments as to the contemporary incidence of corporal punishment in particular, have been largely unsuccessful. Radzinowicz and King, 20 years previously, note a similar reluctance on the parts of the many countries to have their use of corporal punishment publicised (Radzinowicz and King, 1977, p. 159).

The widespread use of corporal punishment in schools, the household, the army, in the Colonies and at work, has been complemented by its deployment in penal institutions, in the form of flogging and the birch, although as Killingray notes, its use in adult prisons declined after the Whipping Act of 1861 as did the lash in the army, after its banning in the Army Act of 1881, though it was retained in military prisons until 1907 (Killingray, 1994, p. 203).

Flogging was recognised as the main penal sanction for soldiers in Europe, from Roman times (Scott, 1938, p. 81). 'In the English Army, for centuries, flogging seems to have been the customary mode of punishment for almost every offence' (Scott, 1938, p. 82). The Mutiny Act 1689 in Britain provided for the official use of flogging as a sanction, until the authorities began to discourage its use in the early nineteenth century. Deaths following military floggings were particularly common in tropical countries, fever being an ever-present risk (Scott, 1938, p. 85). Accounts of the severity of floggings in the army make it difficult to believe the assertion that those in the navy were even more severe (Scott, 1938, p. 92). Napier reports that towards the end of the eighteenth century, sentences of between 600 to 1000 lashes were common (Napier, 1837,

quoted in Scott, 1938, p. 91). Where the punishment had to be suspended
due to the injuries inflicted,

> I, then, often saw the unhappy victim ... brought out from the hospital
> *three* and *four* times to receive the remainder of his punishment, too severe
> to be borne, without danger of death, at one flogging; and, sometimes, I
> have witnessed this prolonged torture applied for the avowed purpose of
> adding to its severity. On these occasions it was terrible to see the new
> tender skin of the scarcely healed back again laid bare to receive the lash.'
>
> (Napier, 1837, quoted in Scott, 1938, p. 92)

Private Alexander Somerville describes the occasion when, on 29 May
1832 he was sentenced to 200 lashes with the 'cat'. Somerville says that at
the first stroke: 'I felt an astounding sensation between the shoulders under
my neck, which went to my toe-nails in one direction, my finger-nails in
another, and stung me to the heart as if a knife had gone through my body'
(Somerville, 1848, quoted in Scott, 1938, p. 89).

After the twenty-fifth stroke, the executioner changed and Somerville
almost bit his tongue in two with the pain:

> What with the blood from my tongue and my lips, which I had also
> bitten, and the blood from my lungs or some other internal part rup-
> tured by the writhing agony, I was almost choked and became black in
> the face. It now became Simpson's second turn to give twenty-five.
> Only fifty had been inflicted, and the time since they began was like a
> long period of life; I felt as if I had lived all the time of my real life in
> pain and torture, and that the time when existence had pleasure in it was
> a dream, long, long, gone by.
>
> (Somerville, 1848, quoted in Scott, 1938, p. 90)

The Mutiny Act of 1829 reduced the number of lashes which could be
given to 300. After Private White died at Hounslow in 1846 after 150
lashes with the 'cat', in 1847 the maximum was set at 50 lashes; in 1871,
the maximum was reduced to 25. At about that time, other Western countries were reforming their own responses to indiscipline in the armed
forces. An Act of Congress in the USA in1850 abolished flogging in the
US Navy. Nevertheless, extreme use of corporal punishment in prisons
continued well into the twentieth century. A prisoner was flogged to death
on a chain gang in North Carolina in 1925 (Van Yelyr, 1941, p. 105).

In the early twentieth century, many years after flogging had been abolished in the British Army, the use of physical violence, often excessive, by

Europeans against African 'subordinates' in labour, military and penal settings was not uncommon (Killingray, 1994, p. 201). Around 1900, soldiers in the Northern Territories of the Gold Coast could receive the maximum of 36 strokes with a whip or cane for stealing, 30 for looting, 25 for insubordination and sleeping on duty, and a minimum of 12 for a group of offences described as 'gross neglect' (Killingray, 1994, p. 208). After flogging with the cat-o'-nine-tails was abolished as a military punishment in 1908, the whip – a vicious instrument which 'could equally tear flesh and inflict long open wounds' – and the cane continued to be the official weapons for widespread use of flogging of rank and file soldiers in the African Colonial forces, until abolished in 1946 (Killingray, 1994, p. 202). Such punishment often involved 'publicly stretching a man on the ground and flogging his naked buttocks with whip or cane. An African NCO administered the flogging and a medical officer was meant to be present; a severe flogging might cause a man to bleed, vomit and defecate' (Killingray, 1994, p. 207).

In such circumstances, advocates of flogging as a form of corporal punishment found ready arguments embedded in racist attitudes reinforced by the compliance of Black inhabitants of Africa.

Along with the idea that child-like people needed to be schooled and disciplined with physical force, the stick or whip was convenient, instant and closely related with the offence. It was, so its advocates argued, readily understood by Africans; coming from societies that inflicted brutal punishments on offenders, Africans clearly recognised, and indeed expected, physical abuse as the reward for misdemeanours. And in any case, it was argued, they had an ability to bear pain, 'which the primitive African does not feel'. On the line of march, whether caravan or military column, on the farm or in the mine compound, labour and soldiers could only be discplined with the whip. Prisons rarely existed and incarceration only reduced a scarce labour force; fines were misunderstood and thus disliked, and, so it was argued by European overseers, Africans preferred flogging as a punishment.

(Killingray, 1994, p. 202)

During the Second World War, the War Office took over responsibility from the Colonial Office for the African colonial forces. The Army Act covered the newly expanded African forces who, whilst now subject to detention in military prisons, still were liable to corporal punishment whilst under active service. A British soldier, T. C. Watkins, noted in his diary on 22 June 1940 that West African troops were caned and lashed for gambling on a ship sailing to East Africa (Killingray, 1994, p. 211). Defaulters were forced to drill with sandbags or large stones on their heads and in 1940 in the Gold Coast 'a battalion commander forced soldiers to carry heavy rolls of barbed wire instead of sandbags on their heads' (Killingray, 1994, p. 211).

The abolition of corporal punishment in the African colonial forces was hastened by the social and political changes wrought by the Second World War, the reformist commitment of the Attlee Labour government in Britain (Killingray, 1994, p. 215), in the context of the increased sensitivity to the need to develop anti-racist policies in the aftermath of Nazi atrocities. However, Killingray (1994, pp. 215–16) notes how, whilst corporal punishment of juveniles declined in incidence and became milder, colonial officials and white settlers successfully resisted total abolition, for example, in penal institutions.

Corporal Punishment in the Household

The endorsement of the wholesale transplanting of the culture of corporal punishment into different sites, in Britain and abroad, was achieved by its place at the core of beliefs in 'good' family life. Round the hearth, in the living-room and the bedroom, the nurturing of virtue may have been sought through appeals to the values of hard work and respectability, but it was enforced by violence. On the whole, societal arrangements for formal punishment were complemented by culturally approved means of informal punishment in the household. Some of these were informally recognised and some were sanctioned by law. Thus, until the emancipation of women in Britain, the law regarded wives as the property of their husbands. In many countries, statutes, religious practices, common law and customs reinforced the subjection of women to physical abuse by their husbands, in the name of so-called legitimate punishment. King James II of England apparently justified regular beating of his wife with reference to Mohammed's advocacy in the *Koran* of the punishment of recalcitrant wives by their husbands (Van Yelyr, 1941, p. 162). Such attitudes were not out of place, since well until the nineteenth century, societies such as Britain and the USA were dependent on slave labour. According to Sutherland, Welsh law entitled a husband to strike his wife three times with a broomstick and French law legitimised the feudal practice of wife-beating, 'moderately and without causing death' (Sutherland, 1898, quoted in Van Yelyr, 1941, p. 163).

In some cultures and countries, decisions as to whether to administer corporal punishment are viewed as the prerogative of the state. In others, they are regarded as the preserve of household members, such as husbands or parents. Efforts to legislate corporal punishment out of existence tend to run foul of the persistence of the urge for people to use it informally, as a sanction and recourse to biblical sources such as Solomon for justification: 'He that spareth his rod hateth his son: but he that loveth him chasteneth him betimes' (Proverbs 13: 24).

In a minority of countries, corporal punishment of children by adults is forbidden by law. Sweden, in 1979, was the first country to pass legislation abolishing corporal punishment of children by parents or guardians, followed by Austria, Norway, Finland and Denmark. In other countries, where corporal punishment of children is not illegal, it is likely that the incidence of corporal punishment by adults in respect of children and young people is even higher than statistics suggest. In the USA, the National Family Violence Surveys indicate that more than 90 per cent of parents use corporal punishment (Straus and Kantor, 1994, p. 543). This high figure admittedly begs questions about the precise nature, and seriousness, of actions regarded as corporal punishment. In Bachman's survey, 61 per cent of tenth-graders had been slapped at least once by their parents (Straus and Donnelly, 1993, p. 419). A clear majority of at least 58 per cent of boys and nearly half, 44 per cent, of girls are estimated to have received corporal punishment in the USA (Straus and Kantor, 1994, p. 546). In this survey, 11.2 per cent of parents reported using one or more acts – kicking, biting, punching, beating up, scalding and attacking with a weapon such as a stick or belt – widely regarded as abusive and risking physical harm to the child (Straus and Kantor, 1994, p. 547).

Corporal Punishment in Schools

Corporal punishment appears to have been widespread in schools throughout the world, from the earliest times (Scott, 1938, p. 95). Girls were commonly birched as well as boys (Scott, 1938, p. 101). A letter describing life in a girls' boarding school at the end of the eighteenth century refers to two kinds of rod,

> one made of birchen twigs and the other of fine pieces of whalebone, wound round with waxed thread to keep them together. Either would give a stinging stroke, but the whalebone one, which we called "Soko" among ourselves, was especially dreaded. Its fangs were like a cat-o'-nine'tails, spreading over our unfortunate flesh.
>
> (Cooper, 1869, p. 456)

The first petition to Parliament aimed at abolishing beating pupils in school was in the seventeenth century (see below). In the nineteenth century, mutinies by pupils in many public schools were only suppressed temporarily by 'persistent and excessive flogging' (Adams, 1991, p. 31). Efforts were made in Britain to abolish corporal punishment in the criminal and juvenile justice systems in the 1930s and 1940s. This was in marked contrast with the situation in other countries, some of which had abolished corporal punishment many years previously. In Poland, for instance, corporal punishment in schools had been abolished in 1783 (Benthall, 1991, p. 377). This was not the case in Germany. Goethe experienced the verbal and physical oppressiveness of a German school in the mid-eighteenth century (Goethe, 1904, pp. 58–9).

The different kinds of corporal punishment employed in public schools typify its variety in other settings. Thrashings by other boys were part of the everyday culture of mid-Victorian English public-school life depicted in *Tom Brown's Schooldays* (Hughes, 1939, pp. 264–5). Huckleberry Finn, in the novel first published in 1884 in the USA, accepts that after 'playing hookey' from school 'the hiding I got next day done me good and cheered me up' (Twain, 1942, pp. 28–9). James Hilton's autobiographical sequel to *Goodbye Mr Chips* refers to corporal punishment, bullying and fighting at 'Brookfield' school, though not from that author's personal experience of these (Hilton, 1938, p. 41). Beating by other boys – in this case with a hairbrush across the bare buttocks – was still a feature of boarding-school life in the novel by Roy Fuller published in 1959 (Fuller, 1959). James Joyce describes with sensitivity the pain and indignity of a beating by the prefect of studies in a Jesuit school in Edwardian Ireland (Joyce, 1936, p. 55).

According to Jonathan Benthall, the then Director of the Royal Anthropological Institute for Great Britain and Ireland, informal punishments apart, a pupil at Eton public school in the 1950s might expect to encounter at least six forms of corporal punishment during his school career: *siphoning*, a relatively mild beating by the captain of chamber, or head of the first-year boys' dormitory; a more serious *beating* with a cane, by the captain of the school or a deputy; *birching* or *flogging* by the headmaster or the lower master for the junior part of the school; *pop-tanning*, a much-feared caning by an athletic, senior boy; *eight-tanning*, carried out by the captain of the boats for offences committed on the river and *screwing*, involving a caning on the bottom by the housemaster without witnesses (Benthall, 1991, pp. 378–82). Bradley's history of Marlborough College – a public school in southern England – gives a similar picture, in which mass flogging was not unkown (Bradley, Champneys and Baines, and others, 1927, p. 162).

The sparing references by Evelyn Waugh, in his diaries of the years 1919 to 1921 when he was a pupil at Lancing College, indicate a culture in which corporal punishment was the norm rather than the exception (Davie, 1976, pp. 60, 83).

It is difficult to accept Scott's statement in the mid-1930s that 'to-day there is little corporal punishment of any kind in schools' (Scott, 1938, p. 105). The use of corporal punishment in schools run by religious orders, such as the Salesians of Don Bosco, ensured the continuance of its many forms – from classroom canings to full-scale beatings by the headmaster – into the second half of the twentieth century (personal account to the author from former pupil at a Salesian College in the 1950s). Attempts were made in the latter decades of the twentieth century to abolish these practices in many boarding schools, including public schools. But many informal punishments remain, a testament to the functionality of corporal punishment, as a 'ritual of transition', 'erotic flagellation', and as a 'ritual of authority' (Benthall, 1991, pp. 382–6). Regarding the first, Benthall refers to Gathorne-Hardy's (1977) argument that corporal punishment is one physical ordeal to be undergone by the male children of the upper classes, in their rites of passage from adolescence to adulthood (Benthall, 1991, p. 382). Second, Benthall draws on the work of Gibson (1978) in his discussion of the close relationship between erotic flagellation – probably known as *le vice anglais* largely because of the amount of masochistic verse the poet Swinburne wrote about birching at Eton – and punitive beating. Benthall and Gibson refer to Desmond Morris (1967), who argues that the presentation of their rumps is one way in which both male and female primates may try to appease an attacker.

> Therefore beating is a form of pseudo copulation, the cane representing the erect phallus. Gibson also argues for a close association between flagellation and homosexuality, for both involve sexual excitation of the anal area … . Our own largely first-hand accounts of Eton beating in the 1950s bear Gibson out … . Screwing, the school slang for beating by a housemaster, is explicit enough. Bending over chairs with maximum rump display, under the guillotinelike sash window, or on a block which recalls the traditional executioner, provides the posture and the props to complement the surrogate orgasm of the act of flagellation itself.
>
> (Benthall, 1991, p. 384).

Third, the ritual of authority, often carried out in private, is redolent of membership of hierarchical, often secret, societies: 'The analogy between public schools and prison camps or totalitarian states should not be over-done, but it is one that has often occurred to the schoolboys themselves, and is given some support by the work of Goffman (1967) and others on institutionalization' (Benthall, 1991, p. 386).

The traditions of secrecy and solidarity which surround such institu-tions as public schools militate against the exposure of such practices. Paul Foot writes of the hypocrisy and defensive solidarity which pre-vented the public exposure of Anthony Chenevix-Trench, who rose to be headmaster of Eton public school, as a persistent flogger of young boys, in an independent school system where housemasters and senior boys usually administered the corporal punishments (Foot, 1996, pp. 2–3). The tensions between openness and suppression are well illustrated by the fact that the footnote to Foot's article contains testimony from other ex-pupils of Chenevix-Trench both corroborating and contradicting Foot's assertions (footnote to Foot, 1996, p. 3). The socialisation of upper middle-class children through the calculated emotional depriva-tions of the public boarding-school system, and the practice of encourag-ing suppression of emotions at times of separation from parents, combined with the incidence of physical and emotional punishment, abuse and bullying which occurred. This created a self-perpetuating culture of violence, expressed in the succeeding generation through similar patterns of acted-out aggression and suppression of feelings reflecting dominant versions of acceptable masculine behaviour (Gathorne-Hardy, 1977).

Fortunately, a growing consensus allows the redefinition of much so-called corporal punishment as straightforward criminal violence. In Greybrook School, Newbiggin, Northumberland in the early 1990s,

> girls and boys at a private boarding school were systematically thrashed across their bottoms with a horse whip, cane and ruler to 'promote and safeguard their welfare'. The offences emerged when a 12-year-old girl complained to police in Islington that she had been beaten normally across her clothing but once on her bare bottom. In her case a bamboo cane was used.

Police and social services staff interviewing pupils at the school uncov-ered a picture of 'the regular and systematic course of punishment by this man'. When charged with assault occasioning actual bodily harm, the headmaster accepted that such punishments were 'in excess of what in this country is regarded as proper physical correction of a child' (*Guardian*, 7 September 1994).

Corporal Punishment in Residential Child Care

There were many reported, and in all likelihood many more unrecorded, incidents of long-standing physical, and sometimes sexual, abuse of children and adults, domestically and in institutional settings, sometimes by peers, sometimes by professionals in care roles, misusing their power over them. There is a question as to how these activities have been so persistent, despite many revelations and inquiry reports, sometimes repeatedly in the same setting. One explanation is that the culture of abusive violence towards children is so ingrained in socialisation practices as to be virtually ineradicable from such institutions.

The severe regime to which priests and nuns were subjected has been mirrored in many accounts of the harsh punishments they meted out to children. The following example is typical of long-standing abuse in many child-care settings, where a combination of religious repression of staff, institutional isolation and lack of independent inspection or advocacy for the children, contributed to excessive abuses in the regime not coming to light for many years. Former inmates of St Joseph's Orphanage in Cavan, Ireland, recall their treatment by nuns in the 1950s:

> The poor diet, poor hygiene and lack of care took their toll in health and in life. Hannah remembers two of her friends dying from TB. 'I used to get boils on my head. My mother cried when she saw me. A nun burst one by hitting me on the head with a stick and the stuff ran down the side of my face. One morning Lizzie Brophy said she could not get up but Mother Carmel ordered her out although we kept saying she wasn't well. Lizzie kept crying that she had terrible pains, but Mother Carmel hit her with a black strap. When she did get up she fell on the floor and was taken to the Infirmary. They said she had rheumatic fever. The poor thing died a few weeks later. She was fourteen. God forgive me, but when I read about Belsen, I thought it was not much different.'
>
> (Arnold and Laskey, 1985, p. 58)

Frances, born in 1950, went to the orphanage when she was four. After describing how one visiting priest had sexually abused her, she added:

> The nuns had beaten Tina Martin terribly on the legs once – she used to get it a lot – and she came into school all black and blue, and the teacher said, 'Tina, what happened to you?' and she said, 'I fell over a chair, Miss.' The teacher knew well she'd been hit but nobody would ever say anything to the nuns. They were bad, bad women when I think of it

now. They ruined all our lives. I remember some priest coming to give a lecture to them and we were forbidden to go out in the yard in case we got a glimpse of him. But I went out and of course someone told on me and Mother Catherine got a branch off a tree and beat me till white lumps came up. One of the girls was beaten black and blue for chewing the Communion bread instead of swallowing it. Why did they hit us so much? It seemed to be for such little things. Catherine was the worst. She had real tight lips and every time she came back from holidays she'd have a big boil at the end of her nose. Once in secondary school I lost my knitting needles. Actually someone had nicked them – we were always nicking things on each other – and I was told to go back to the orphanage and find them. I was wandering round not knowing what to do when Catherine found me. 'Go upstairs into the shoe room!' she said, 'and take off your clothes.' When she came up she just sat on a little box and stared at me naked and I stood there holding myself. In the end she beat me. Would you believe she did a Child Care course somewhere after she left Cavan?

(Arnold and Laskey, 1985, p. 113)

Even before corporal punishment in schools was abolished, the power of teachers and other people with responsibility for control and care of children or young people under Section 1 of the Children and Young Persons Act 1933 to punish children was limited in common law to that which was not unreasonable or excessive. The regulations for voluntary homes (the Administration of Children's Homes Regulations 1952), the only existing regulations referring specifically to corporal punishment, forbade its use for girls aged ten or over, and boys over school-leaving age. Children under ten could only be physically punished by smacking the hands with bare hands. Boys aged between 10 and 16 could only be caned six times or less on the backside with a cane approved by the Secretary of State. No punishment could be given with another child present and no punishment of any child with a known physical or mental disability could be given without the approval of a medical professional.

There was a marked decline in the use of corporal punishment in all types of schools in Britain in the 1970s and 1980s. Among local authorities in England and Wales which still used corporal punishment, Cleveland recorded the highest incidence, with 5326 canings in its secondary schools in 1980–81. Of these, 819 children received no less than 2550 beatings, 47.9 per cent of the total (Anon., 1984, p. 5). A survey by STOPP estimated in 1981 that a total of nearly a quarter of a million beatings a year were still being administered in English schools, using 'fists, gymshoes, lumps of wood, bunsen-burning tubing, rulers, pointers, blackboard rubbers' (Anon., 1981, p. 5). The situation in Scotland was worse, with almost two and a half beatings per child every year, an average of nearly seven beatings a year for children under 16 in Scottish secondary schools (Anon., 1981, p. 5). In its submission in the late 1970s for the abolition of corporal punishment in schools, STOPP recorded that in Edinburgh, as late as 1973/74, there were an average of 10 000 uses of the tawse – the Scottish equivalent of the cane – in each of two terms (STOPP, n.d., p. 1).

In a briefing paper, STOPP pointed out the wider context that whilst many Third World countries resorted to corporal punishment, in most Western European countries, save Germany during the Nazi period, there was no record of corporal punishment ever having been used (STOPP, 1982, p. 9). In contrast, although six states in the USA recorded no beatings at all in 1982, 792 556 beatings were recorded in schools in other states, itself a reduction on the total of 1 027 918 for 1980 (Anon., 1983, p. 9). In July 1978, the then Secretary of State of Social Services David Ennals said that he believed corporal punishment in children's homes was 'neither desirable nor proper', and the chief social work officer of the DHSS sent a letter to all social services departments to that effect. In January 1981, a DHSS working party on Control and Discipline in Community Homes condemned corporal punishment (para. 355):

> The use of corporal punishment may damage or destroy the growth of relationships between adults and children and may also reinforce the inability of the adult to demonstrate his or her domination by other than physical means ... corporal punishment is not compatible with the principles on which control and discipline in community homes should be based and we recommend that the use of any form of corporal punishment in community homes should therefore be prohibited.

By 1982, opposition to corporal punishment from the British Association of Social Workers, the Residential Care Association, the National Association of Probation Officers, the Association of Directors of Social Services and Royal College of Psychiatrists added momentum to the rapid movement away from corporal punishment in the education system: 10 per cent of 125 local education authorities in Britain had banned corporal punishment in all their maintained schools and a third were seriously considering abolition. By 1983, a survey by the Children's Legal Centre indicated the small but growing trend towards the banning by local authorities of hitting children, in foster homes and children's homes (Hodgkin, 1986, p. 47). By the late 1980s, corporal punishment was formally abandoned in child care in Britain (see Chapter 9).

CONTROVERSIES OVER THE USE OF CORPORAL PUNISHMENT

Unsurprisingly perhaps, research into the widespread use of corporal punishment tends to be advanced by its abolitionists, with some notable exceptions in the area of behavioural therapy. Murray Straus, for example, in the USA, has devoted much of his career to researching, and campaigning against, corporal punishment, at the Family Research Laboratory of the University of New Hampshire. Both examination of the nature of corporal punishment, and the cause of its abolition, were advanced by the 1978 case of the 15-year-old schoolboy birched on the Isle of Man (*Tyrer* v. *United Kingdom*) and the 1982 cases of Jeffrey Cosans, withdrawn by his parents because he faced corporal punishment on his return for breaking a school rule, and Gordon Campbell, whose parents withdrew him because he faced the tawse (Phillips, 1994, p. 155). The Education (No. 2) Act 1986 followed the Campbell case and to all intents and purposes led to the abolition of corporal punishment in state schools in Britain, leaving the possibility of petitions from pupils in private schools, where corporal punishment was still allowed (Phillips, 1994, p. 156).

Subsequently, there were judgements on two UK cases in the private-school sector – *Costello-Roberts* v. *United Kingdom*, where the claim was that a seven year-old being 'whacked' three times with a slipper violated Article 3, and *Y.* v. *United Kingdom*, where the Commission had to consider whether Article 3 was violated by a boy being caned four times through his trousers, so hard that it raised painful weals and bruises on his buttocks. In the former case, the Commission did not view the punishment as degrading (Phillips, 1994, p. 156), thus confirming a view that it is the severity of the punishment and not the punishment *per se* which is degrading and violates Article 3 (Phillips, 1994, p. 157). A further claim by opponents was that corporal punishment violated Article 8(1): 'Everyone has the right to respect for his private and family life, his home and his correspondence.' The Commission supported this, rejecting the UK submission that the parents implicitly consented to the boy's treatment because they should have known that corporal punishment was used at the school to which they chose to send him. *Y.* v. *United Kingdom* was settled soon after by a £8000 compensation payment, plus legal costs, by the UK (Phillips, 1994, p. 157).

Such judgements at the time failed to distinguish precisely between what constituted inhuman or degrading treatment, and torture (Phillips, 1994, p. 159), or to clarify the weight to be given to the rehabilitative, retributive or deterrent nature of corporal punishment (Phillips, 1994, p. 160). Phillips suggests that, whilst this would not necessarily have led to different judgements, the reasoning wold have been more comprehensive and satisfactory if the clarification had been undertaken (Phillips, 1994, p. 161). The inclusion of the need to prove the deterrent value of punishment would have clarified a query by Eleanor Roosevelt, chairperson of the Committee drafting the Universal Declaration of Human Rights, who in 1947 expresssed concern that the condemnation of torture and ill-treatment could prohibit the practice of compulsory vaccination (Phillips, 1994, p. 162). The distinction between those who administer corporal punishment and those against whose violence corporal punishment may be directed, is difficult to maintain. A review of the use of corporal punishment by STOPP (STOPP, 1980) points out that ironically, many teachers using corporal punishment for bullying acted as bullies themselves.

Arguments for and against corporal punishment may be illustrated with reference to the controversy about spanking children, as illustrated in the debate in the USA, between Oosterhuis (1993) and Larzelere (1993) and debates about the desirability and efficacy of smacking young children, which came to a head in Britain in the early 1990s.

Whilst culturally many societies idealise the family as a setting where love, nurture and care flourish, in practice, research suggests that just as many marriages are a 'licence to hit'; as Patterson puts it, 'in the family, hate is more likely than love' (Patterson, 1982, p. 113). In the late 1980s, one estimate was that in the USA between 2 and 3 million daily acts of corporal punishment were still carried out (Benthall, 1991, p. 377).

The Department of Health in Britain argues that parents have the right to administer corporal punishment, in the form of reasonable chastisement, in contrast with the fact that corporal punishment is banned in state schools. Ann Bradley argues that it is misguided to take parents to court for minor physical punishments of their children (Bradley, 1993, p. 12) and James Heartfield points out that extensions of children's rights invade parents' necessary freedom to bring up their children the way they wish (Heartfield, 1993, p. 13). But the justification of abusive punishment of children as 'necessary' in the view of a 'responsible adult', parent or guardian, can only be prevented by banning completely the physical punishment of children.

There is a blurred boundary between corporal punishment in the household and physical abuse. The hitting of children is widespread. Research supported by the Department of Health into 400 families indicates that 91 per cent of all children were hit and 77 per cent in the previous year, including the finding that a third of four-year-olds and more than a quarter of seven-year-olds were hit more frequently than once a week (Department of Health, 1995, pp. 83–5; Dyer, 1996).

The granting of permission by the European Commission of Human Rights in Strasbourg on 9 September 1996, for a 12-year-old boy to pursue his case against his beating by his stepfather, led to widespread media speculation in the UK about the possibility of the introduction of curbs on smacking children in the home (Dyer, 1996). The boy's stepfather was charged with assault occasioning actual bodily harm but was acquitted by the jury. This case was significant not only in itself, but because through it the arguments for and against corporal punishment were rehearsed in the mass media.

Organisations such as Families for Discipline support the use of corporal punishment. Arguments for corporal punishment emphasise selected research which concludes that the end justifies the means. It has been alleged that severe punishment can effectively eliminate certain behaviours (Azrin and Holz, 1966; Larzelere, 1993) concludes that sociopathic children can only be dealt with effectively by teaching their parents how to socialise them, including the use of physical punishment.

Arguments against corporal punishment are both comparative and absolute: comparative arguments point out that if adults punished each other by administering the kinds of canings they give children, they would be liable to be charged with actual or grievous bodily harm; absolute arguments include the view that corporal punishment is a form of abuse and is wrong in principle. Additional arguments against corporal punishment are fuelled by the belief that even if not immediately, in the longer term, corporal punishment of children increases their aggressive and violent behaviour. Opponents of corporal punishment concede that if the threat or actuality of severe physical pain is great enough, certain actions by a person may be curtailed or prevented, but that the negative consequences of this punishment far outweigh this short-term consequence, in what Peter Newell of EPOCH describes as 'a spiral of violent attitudes and actions which can be confidently predicted to breed more violence, more depression, more unconstructive punitive attitudes' (Newell and Lynn, 1996, p. 4). By the mid-1990s, at least 68 organisations, including the Association of Directors of Social Services, Barnardo's, Family Service Units, the National Children's Bureau and Save the Children Fund, supported the aim of EPOCH to end all physical punishment, by education and legal reform.

Spanking Children: The Debate in the USA

Larzelere's argument for discriminating between appropriate and inappropriate punishment is based on an interpretation of some research: that in certain circumstances spanking benefts children in particular settings, namely the treatment of autistic children, parental training of young children's behaviour and reduction of toddlers' recurrent misbehaviour.

But the evidence is thin and there are concerns about how the use of spanking could be kept within non-abusive bounds. In the first of these areas, Larzelere quotes Lovaas, who claims that intensive parental involvement is effective, including 'responding to self-stimulatory, aggressive and noncompliant behaviour with a loud "No!" and an occasional slap on the thigh' in work with autistic children (Larzelere, 1993, p. 143); in the second area, the compliance of the child is enforced after a warning ' "If you get off the chair again, I will spank you." If the child disobeys, the adult smacks the child's bottom with an open hand' (Larzelere, 1993, p. 143). Larzelere goes to some length to explain how use of the open hand to smack no more than twice 'minimizes the danger of an escalation to abusive punishment' (Larzelere, 1993, p. 144); in the third area, Larzelere argues that the use of a combination of reasoning and punishment as a means of dealing with fighting or disobedience among toddlers delays the next misbehaviour significantly longer than either punishment alone, reasoning alone or other discipline responses (Larzelere and Schneider, 1991a; 1991b; referred to in Larzelere, 1993, p. 143). However, Larzelere admits that 'this held true whether the punishment was corporal or noncorporal' and 'the only response that was as effective as a combination of reasoning and corporal punishment was a combination of noncorporal punishment and reasoning. The latter combination was equally effective for fighting incidents and slightly but not significantly more effective for disobedience incidents' (Larzelere and Schneider, 1991b).

Larzelere's entire case seems to rest on somewhat shaky empirical data in support of his attempt to distinguish 'appropriate spanking' and 'inappropriate corporal punishment' (Larzelere, 1993, p. 146). By Larzelere's own admission, the evidence does not support him going beyond the cautious conclusion that 'psychological research has made it very clear that negative consequences in general (i.e. punishers) are very effective at suppressing target misbehaviour, with minimal risk of negative side effects' (Aronfreed, 1968; Axelrod and Apsche, 1983; Azrin and Holz, 1966; Parke, 1974; Patterson, 1982; Walters and Grusec, 1977).

It is not as well established that certain uses of spanking may have the same beneficial effect. Nonetheless, the available evidence suggests that some moderate spanking of children from 2 to 6 years of age is effective, particularly as a backup to less aversive discipline responses such as reasoning or time-out. We need more research to further distinguish appropriate from inappropriate uses of corporal punishment.

(Larzelere, 1993, p. 146)

Also, significantly, Larzelere admits that

although I am arguing against a complete prohibition of all corporal punishment, I agree with Oosterhuis that many parents use corporal punishment inappropriately, and that this tends to be true of conservative Christian parents. Some inappropriate uses ... include spanking older children or children under 2 years of age, spanking too harshly, spanking in anger, spanking without developing less aversive discipline responses, and spanking in place of positive parenting. Delinquency and criminality are predicted by parental punishment that is overly harsh, overly negligent, or inconsistently vacillating between strictness and laxity.

(Larzelere, 1993, p. 145).

Moral arguments – which tend to be absolute – apart, if Larzelere, the advocate of corporal punishment, feels bound to add all the above caveats, the opponents of corporal punishment have even less of a necessity to make their case. Not surprisingly, research into the practice of spanking young children often points towards more complex relationships between adults' actions and the behaviour of children, as is illustrated by the findings of Socolar and Stein (1995). The high correlation between beliefs about child-rearing and spanking suggests the possibility that a negative approach to the child may form part of the context in which the child receives physical punishment, a context which should be taken into account in any attempt to interpret the data, yet one which often is missing from positivist, behavioural research.

The harmful effects of corporal punishment in many circumstances on young children are well-documented (Straus and Donnelly, 1994; Straus and Gimpel, 1992). But questions have been raised about whether the high correlation between beliefs and spanking of young children incidates that the negative impact of spanking results from spanking *per se*, the negative approach towards the child, or both (Socolar and Stein, 1995, p. 105). The psychological impact of corporal punishment includes introducing feelings of helplessness and powerlessness (Straus and Gimpel, 1992, quoted in Straus and Kantor, 1994, p. 558). Straus and Kantor's research indicates that the use of corporal punishment by parents of adolescents carries the risk in later life of depression, alcohol abuse, physical abuse of children, physical assault on female partners and suicide (Straus and Kantor, 1994, p. 558). Carey (1994) reviews research on the effectiveness of punishment in general, and corporal punishment in particular, in child-rearing, and concludes that the maxim 'Spare the rod and spoil the child' would be better rephrased 'Use the rod and spoil the child.'

Smacking by Parents and Childminders: Controversy in the UK

The Children Act 1989 replaced former descriptions of parental 'rights', 'powers' and 'duties' with the term 'parental responsibility'. Parental responsibility involves the complex interaction between children, their parents and other people outside the family. The needs, wants and rights of children will change as they grow older and parental duties, powers and responsibilities will change also. The law, and professionals who exercise the law, may intervene to decide the extent to which a child should be allowed to make decisions and the extent to which such decisions are in the best interests of the child.

Parents have a right to administer 'lawful chastisement' but this must be moderate and reasonable. It must also be in proportion to the offence the child has committed, taking into account age, understanding and physique, and it should not be imposed for an ulterior motive such as gratifying emotions or perverted sexuality. A degree of physical restraint is also lawful if it is required to protect a young or disabled child from danger or to teach the child to protect himself or herself (Hoggett, 1993, p. 15).

The Scottish Law Commission (1992) considered that 'it would be going too far to criminalise ordinary safe smacks of the sort occasionally resorted to by many thousands of affectionate parents' (para. 2.95) but recommended that 'it should be unlawful to strike a child with a stick, belt or other object or in such a way as to cause, or to risk causing, injury, or such a way to cause, or to risk causing, pain or discomfort lasting more than a very short time' (Hoggett, 1993, p. 15). Not all corporal punishment is considered 'degrading punishment' and therefore condemned under Article 3 of the European Convention on Human Rights (*The Times*, 26 March 1993). But judicially ordered corporal punishment is defined as degrading and corporal punishment is banned in all state schools (Education (No. 2) Act 1986, S.47), in all residential homes for children and local authority foster placements (Hoggett, 1993, p. 15).

The controversy in the mid-1990s over corporal punishment by child-minders arose when Sutton Borough Council decided to strike Anne Davis off its register of childminders, after she had refused to sign an undertaking that she would never use physical punishment in her work. In March 1994, the high-court ruling by Mr Justice Wilson that the council was wrong to adopt a blanket policy of refusing to register childminders who smacked children, and that a childminder can smack a child, was endorsed by John Bowatt, in 1994 Health Minister in the Conservative government responsible for childminding (*Guardian*, 16 March 1994)

The debate in the letter pages of the press over the judgement in the case brought by Sutton Council is indicative of the controversial nature of the issues it raises. On one hand, there is the common-sense view that it does not harm for an adult to discipline a child by mild physical punishment. On the other hand, there is the view that physical coercion is not consistent with inculcating in children the view that relationships between adults and children are based on higher values than physical coercion. (See, for instance, arguments against childminding smacking, *Guardian* letters, 21 March 1995.) Joan Lestor introduced a Bill in July 1994, aiming to ensure that corporal punishment is no longer used in childminding and daycare for young children. Joan Lestor wrote, in a letter to the *Guardian* on 1 October 1994, that 'it is a shameful anomaly that childminders can smack children in their care when we have abolished corporal punishment in schools and day nurseries'. She called for the Secretary of State 'to issue guidelines on the use of corporal punishment by childminders. She must clearly state the age at which it will be acceptable to smack a child and give guidance on the type of corporal punishment which will be acceptable.'

In the autumn of 1994, Virginia Bottomley, then Secretary of State for Health, became involved in a heated debate about the smacking of children at a National Children's Bureau conference, during which she said that she had smacked her own children and would not object to her children's grand-parents (who were equivalent to childminders, she maintained) smacking her children.The director of the National Childminding Association said it was a 'strange state of affairs when government policy appears to be made according to the personal practice of ministers, and very peculiar indeed for a minister to admit that fact in public. Because she smacked her own children doesn't make it right for child minders to smack other people's.' In a later statement issued from the Department of Health, aimed at cooling the controversy, Virginia Bottomley said that many parents felt there were occasions when 'it is appropriate to use a mild form of physical punishment to rebuke their child' (*Guardian*, 28 September 1994).

In response to Virginia Bottomley's remarks, Chris Brown from the NSPCC called for the Government to issue 'clear regulations to prevent childminders physically punishing children, and introduce measures to promote forms of positive discipline and provide a better range of family support services'. He gave six reasons for this, paraphrased here: (1) Physical punishment can escalate into more serious forms of abuse; (2) physical punishment seldom, if ever, improves a child's behaviour; (3) it is ludicrous and unjust that children are denied the same protection in law as adults when wife beating and other forms of domestic violence are considered totally unacceptable; (4) the use of physical punishment on children legitimates violence as acceptable and makes it likely that it will be handed down through the generations; (5) the stresses faced by carers, including parents, need to be recognised and work should be done along-side them to address these; (6) the UN Convention on the Rights of the Child, which includes the requirement that parties take legal, social and educational measures to protect children from physical and mental abuse, has been ratified by the UK (*Guardian*, 12 October 1994) .

In December 1994, the Department of Health issued guidelines on the smacking of children by childminders. These stated that a childminder could smack a child, with the consent of the parent. The National Childminding Association, the National Children's Bureau and End Physical Punishment of Children (EPOCH) commented that the guidelines were confusing (and see Chapter 4 for more detail on physical punishment in child care). The guidelines stated that a childminder could not shake a child and the Association of Directors of Social Services criticised the fact that the guidance did not put the interests of the child first, and also the fact that 'the distinctions between smacking, gently smacking and shaking will lead to inevitable conflicts of interpretations' (*Guardian*, 3 December 1994).

7 Capital Punishment

The world itself is but a large prison, out of which some are daily led to execution.
(Sir Walter Raleigh, returning to prison from his trial, quoted in
Cohen and Cohen, 1992, p. 325)

INTRODUCTION

This chapter examines the ultimate penal deterrent – the taking of an offender's life, by the state or by its agents. It deals with different types of capital punishments; it examines arguments for and against capital punishment; it illustrates the process of capital punishment and its impact on relatives, friends, officials and others closely involved. Execution, of course, may also be viewed as the ultimate act of power, in keeping with dominant images of masculinity. The intersection between issues of dominant masculinities, political authoritarianism and aggression and the deployment of capital punishment by a government in power, is indicated in this chapter. There is not space to fill out these connections in further detail.

The Ultimate Sanction

P. D. James stated in a radio interview that the murder mystery is the archetypal detective novel to write in that it is most likely to provide abiding fascination, because it deals with the ultimate crime – one person's death at the hands of another.

Undeniably, capital punishment acts to prevent the executed person from repeating the offence. However, there is a sense in which execution is the most painful and extreme sanction to be employed as a punishment, although some would argue that uncertainty and various lesser psychological and physical punishments impose more hurt. But the general consensus among researchers, commentators and professionals in criminal justice is that capital punishment is an inherently abusive and degrading punishment, ineffective as a means of deterring others; many methods are anything but quick and painless methods of inflicting death. In short, even aside from the moral opposition to capital punishment, there is nothing to commend this widespread practice, which is declining in many parts of the world, though notably not in that most punitive of Western democracies – the USA.

GLOBAL INCIDENCE OF CAPITAL PUNISHMENT

Capital punishment plays a crucial role in the politics of many states, not least in the intentions of those in power, at any rate, in the furtherance of the goal of maintaining order and heading off challenges to the political status quo. It is a favoured instrument of repression by right-wing governments. It is deeply rooted in the culture and politics of many countries, but the search for the perpetrator, strengthened by the mass media, may be closer to a witch-hunt reinforcing popular stereotypes of offenders and victims rather than a search for justice (Caputi, 1987). In Western Europe, for example, where Celtic stories are as diverse and numerous as any other traditions, Jacob's collection contains the story of Munachar the elf, who spends the entire story trying to obtain the materials to hang Manachar for eating all the raspberries Munachar has picked (Jacobs, 1968, pp. 83–7).

However, Amnesty International notes the slow trend, evident for much of the twentieth century, towards countries abolishing the death penalty, at the rate of about two countries a year. The arguments of abolitionists gradually gained ground from the mid-nineteenth century. Capital punishment was abolished by the end of the nineteenth century in Belgium, Finland, The Netherlands, Luxembourg, Portugal, Romania and Italy. It was abolished in Norway in 1905, Sweden in 1921, Denmark in 1930, Switzerland in 1942, and Italy again in 1948, after the Fascists had reintroduced it in 1931. No executions have been carried out in Eire since 1950, nor in Belgium (war criminals excepted) since 1918, nor in Greece since 1972, nor in Northern Ireland since that in 1961 for a non-sectarian incident when a man was hanged for murdering a girl (*Observer*, 3 July 1983). In France, the last public guillotining was carried out in 1977 and capital punishment was abolished in 1981. Hitler had reintroduced beheading in West Germany and this was abolished in 1949 (Hibbert, 1966, p. 407).

By the end of 1995, 93 countries retained capital punishment and still carried out judicial executions; 101 had abolished it for all but very exceptional instances, such as war crimes. South Africa has abolished the death penalty and it has not been used for a decade in Turkey. Romania, Hungary and the Czech and Slovak republics have abolished it, so, in practice, no countries in Western Europe use the death penalty.

In South Africa, corporal punishment and capital punishment were used for many decades as part of a policy of retribution, in a penal system designed to quell political unrest and reinforce the role of the indigenous black population as little more than serfs or slaves. Fundamentalist Christianity, with strong links with Calvinism as interpreted by the Dutch Reformed Churches and the majority of the dominant Afrikaner group, provided them with the moral justification for the harshness of the criminal justice system and the severity of punishments of criminals within it. As David Welsh, a specialist in African Studies at the University of Cape Town, notes:

> Traditionally, Calvinism emphasizes personal responsibility, disipline and asceticism among its followers. The doctrine entails a built-in resistance to any theories of crime causation which might appear to undermine the notions of free will ... . Where it is the religion of the dominant group, Calvinism reinforces authoritarian patterns of government and provides moral justification for severe measures against criminals who are viewed as threats to law and order and, therefore, enemies of the state.
>
> (Welsh, 1969, p. 421)

Amnesty International estimates that worldwide more than 2000 prisoners were executed and 4000 sentenced to death in 1994, the incidence being highest in China, Iran and Nigeria (Jones, 1996, p. 16). In Saudi Arabia, in 1994 alone 192 offenders were beheaded. In the USA, since the death penalty was reinstated in 1976, nearly 300 offenders have been executed. The rate of executions in the USA is increasing, from 5 in 1983 to 38 in 1993 and 14 in the first three months of 1995 (*The Times,* 7 April 1995). Texas has possibly the highest number of executions per year of any country or state in the world.

Although it is unlikely that the death penalty will be restored in Western European countries, there are constant debates about its reintroduction. A poll by Public Opinion Surveys published in June 1983 found that less than a third of those interviewed felt that hanging should be reintroduced in Britain, whilst the largest group – 42 per cent – supported death by lethal injection (*Guardian,* 20 June 1983). A shootout in Paris in which four people, including three policemen, died and half a dozen were injured, by a young couple reminiscent of characters in the cult films *Killing Zoe, Natural Born Killers* and *Leon,* showing at the time, led to calls early in October 1994 for the return of the guillotine in France. In Northern Ireland, it was suggested that the restoration of capital punishment would mean that the Diplock courts, much criticised bodies which had sat without juries, under the Northern Ireland Emergency Provisions Act 1973, would need the added safeguard of a judge sitting alongside the two assessors (*Guardian*, 27 June 1983).

Sometimes the political pressures against executions are outpaced by other forces pressuring for them. In February 1995, the Privy Council in London asked British colonies and former colonies not to keep convicted and sentenced offenders on death row for more than five years. The government of St Vincent announced that it would be ignoring this advice. On 13 February 1995, the same day, three men were executed there. But more than 200 death sentences were commuted to life imprisonment. Behind the scenes, Commonwealth countries such as Bahamas, Barbados, Belize, Jamaica and Trinidad have agitated in the 1990s to throw off the power of the Privy Council as the court of final appeal for about 100 prisoners sentenced to death. A London solicitor acting for more than 80 appellants on death row in the Caribbean instanced the flimsy evidence on which many prosecutions were alleged to be based. 'In one pending appeal, Ellis Taibo was convicted of killing a British aid worker, Gill Oborn. The Belize police flew in forensic experts from Scotland Yard, yet the only evidence against Taibo was a claim that he was seen wearing a shirt later found near the scene of the crime' (*Observer*, 4 February 1996).

War Crimes and Punishment

Execution tends to feature in tariffs of wartime punishments, even where the death penalty has been abolished in all other circumstances. The extreme conditions often generated in criminal justice systems during wartime often produce contradictory outcomes. Bettelheim writes of punishment in the dehumanised environment of the German concentration camp in the Second World War. A prisoner due to receive a flogging was discharged; a newcomer given his number received the punishment a few days later, because punishments were recorded by number and not by person (Bettelheim, 1970, p. 218). Many thousands of even more harrowing accounts involving executions exist in relation to the arbitrariness of death sentences in concentration camps (Gilbert, 1986). Subsequent to executions, the executioners themselves may be liable to trial, and possibly execution, where found guilty of war crimes. Massacres and ethnic cleansing, such as in Rwanda and former Yugoslavia in the 1990s have revived debates about whether too many Nazi war criminals escaped after the Second World War. The War Crimes Act 1991 in Britain, a deeply controversial measure at the time of its passing, aroused strong opposition. Arguments against charging war criminals years after a war, include their extreme age and doubts about the validity of the memories of witnesses against them and therefore the difficulty of proving their guilt. Behind opposition to investigating war crimes may lie collective embarrassment and guilt about the skeletons in the cupboards of ex-service personnel, politicians and civil servants concerning wartime activities. Trials of war criminals provide an opportunity for people, individually and collectively, to come to terms with the past. But in Rwanda, for example, the arrest of alleged murderers is no guarantee that the judicial process will be completed speedily and effectively. Upwards of half a million people died in the genocide of Rwanda in 1994. Of those accused of their murder, 7000 were incarcerated in Gitarama, a prison built for 400, and described by an eye-witness as 'the most crowded penitentiary in the world, and probably the most horrific'. Lack of cash and logistical resources were said to be responsible for the fact that a year and a quarter after the start of the massacres not a single genocide case had been completed, either by the international war crimes tribunal or by the tribunal in Rwanda itself (Orr, 1995).

Politics and Capital Punishment

One index of punitiveness by the state is the adherence to capital punishment. Another is the correlation between crimes of varying degrees of seriousness and custodial sentences. In countries where military and paramilitary, as well as dissident, groups are less moderate, the murder rate escalates. Thus, in Columbia, according to the Andean Commission of Jurists, about 14 per cent of the 25 000 murders committed in 1995 were 'political' killings by the police and the army. Meanwhile, guerrilla forces contribute their share of the anarchic killings. The fifth front of the Revolutionary Armed Forces of Colombia (Farc – the longest established and largest group) carries out mass killings; for instance, in an incident in the so-called killing fields of Urabá, pulling a dozen banana labourers from a bus and shooting them (*Guardian*, 23 February 1996).

Whether or not death squads – which could be viewed as an informal, punitive and controlling mechanism employed by powerful groups against others in a society – are a twentieth-century phenomenon, there is an increasing tendency towards documenting their activities, particularly in some countries of Central America and evidenced in the 'citizen force' army in South Africa (Catholic Institute for International Relations, 1989).

In the USA, the development of right-wing groups, some associated with fundamentalist religion, correlates since the mid-1970s with increasing punitiveness in the penal system. The death penalty was restored in 1976 and the incarceration rate rose steadily through the 1980s and early 1990s, to maintain the position of the USA as, by this measure alone, one of the most punitive countries in the world. Capital punishment is advocated by groups such as the New Puritans of Chicago. They espouse pro-family and traditional values, are almost exclusively white, middle-class, anti-black and other ethnic groups; they advocate longer sentences for offenders and the increasing use of capital punishment.

Notable exceptions to the trend towards individualised executions sequestered behind prison walls include Iraq, China and Nigeria, where exemplary mass executions have still taken place since the 1980s. The execution in August 1996 was ordered by Saddam Hussein of more than 120 Iraqi officers who planned a coup against him (*Sunday Times*, 8 September 1996). However, such mass shootings are not only a feature of wartime history. In the face of pressure to curb street robberies, the military government of Nigeria took exemplary action, in the execution by firing squad of about more than 50 convicted armed robbers on 22 July (*BBC World Service News*, 22 July 1995). The adoption of methods of mass execution in China, seems to have provided public demonstration of the commitment to punish offenders in the face of a crime wave, in the 1980s and 1990s. In 1993, official statistics admitted to 1400 people having been executed, the actual figure very likely being higher than this. The witnessing by Billy Bailey's two children, of his execution in January 1996 – he was sentenced to death in Delaware in 1979 – was criticised as a retrograde move towards public execution (*Guardian*, 26 January 1996).

In Russia, for his first three years in power, President Yeltsin granted appeals for clemency in about 300 cases where prisoners were under sentence of death and only a handful of prisoners was executed. In 1995, this policy appeared to have been reversed, with 86 executions and only five appeals for clemency granted. Under the Russian Constitution, the death penalty only applies to more serious cases of murder with aggravation and the currently rare case of high treason – equivalent to spying. Now that Russia has joined the Council of Europe, there is increasing pressure on President Yeltsin to declare an immediate moratorium on the use of the death penalty and its phasing-out over three years. However, the counter-argument – of rising crime and the consequent need to build a new prison every year to house reprieved prisoners – appears based on the dubious grounds that it is cheaper to execute people (*Guardian*, 2 May 1996).

The interests of criminal justice systems and commerce converge in the lucrative trade in body organs which exists alongside the execution industry. This is particularly well-established in countries which practise mass executions. For example, accounts from human rights activists relate how

> the corpses of the executed are thrown into waiting vans for surgeons to extract organs, which are then sold on for medical transplants. When a top Chinese official needs a kidney, the prisoner is forced to kneel and is shot in the head. If, say, corneas are in particular demand at the time, he will be shot in the back.
>
> (Jones, 1996, p. 16)

TRENDS IN THE USE OF CAPITAL PUNISHMENT

According to Wilkinson in the Newgate Calendar (1991, p. 9), the gibbet – a hook on which offenders were hung in public, either before or after execution – was first used in England in AD 1236. The gibbet was recorded also as a penance, among the Gentoos of India, reportedly used on three volunteers, as witnessed by officers of the East India Company:

> According to the custom of Indian festivals, they were adorned with flowers, cloathed (*sic*) in their best apparel, and attended by their relations. They marched, or rather ran, round the apparatus several times, flowers being in the mean time strewed before them. The engine of torture used upon this occasion was a stout upright post, thirty feet in height. At the bottom was a stage, and about half way towards the top another, on which two priests, or rather executioners, were mounted with drawn sabres, in place of books of religion, in their hands. Across the top of the post, or pole, was another, of about half the length and circumference, strongly lashed thereto with ropes. At each extremity were hooks of iron, somewhat resembling, but larger than, those used by butchers in England, to hang up their meat in the shambles. The sufferer was hoisted up to the executioners. They immediately proceeded to strip their prey of his robes, and then fixed the hooks into the fleshy part of his back, near the shoulder blades. The ropes affixed to these hooks, and tied to the transverse beam. Behind him two smaller ropes depended from the beam which received his great toes in separate loops. Over the penitent's head was suspended a kind of flat muslin canopy, with a narrow flounce, just sufficient to shade his face from the sun, but

not conceal him from view. Thus prepared he is slung into the air, by means of ropes tied at the opposite end of the pole, and hanged round to give full views to the surrounding crowd. The air was now rent with shouts of applause, almost to adoration. The trumpets sounded, the drums beat, and pateraroes fired. The traverse beam, turning on a pivot, was slowly moved round, over the head of the multitude. Notwithstanding the torture which the victims must feel, they supported it generally with patient firmness.

(Wilkinson, 1991, pp. 10–11)

The ritual of execution traditionally has far exceeded the pragmatic accomplishment of killing the criminal. The practice of trying and sentencing the bodies of the victims of the Inquisition after death was not unknown in other countries. In Scotland in 1600, the body of the Earl of Gowrie and his brother were brought to court and sentenced to be hanged, quartered and gibbeted, and Logan of Restalrig was tried three years after his death and had his property confiscated after being found guilty of conspiracy (Griffiths, 1991, p. 75). From the late eighteenth century, less gory methods of execution were sought than hanging, drawing and quartering, for example, as the emphasis shifted from inflicting injury on the body and demonstrating the power of the state, to ending life as efficaciously as possible.

In 1827, the bloody code was repealed in Britain. Between then and 1868 some 400 to 500 people were executed, but whereas before felonious crimes had been punishable by death, now only murderers were executed. So, execution became more of a spectacle, because it was less common. However, at the same time the actual site of execution in many Western countries was shifted out of the casual gaze of the public and into the more regulated theatre of the execution chamber in the prison.

Changing patterns of capital punishment for offenders in Western countries are rooted in social and cultural features specific to different countries. Thus, in Britain, a long tradition of public executions, using a range of horrific means to desecrate and often dismember the offender, was gradually replaced in the nineteenth century by hanging in the relative seclusion of a purpose-built hanging-shed in the prison. Again, as an authoritative study of the use of executions in Texas notes, 'slavery, criminal justice, lynchings and capital punishment are historically closely intertwined in the United States' (Marquart, Ekland-Olson and Sorensen, 1994, p. 185). In the USA, the tradition of public hangings and lynchings increasingly has been taken out of local communities during the twentieth century and put in the hands of the federal and state authorities, relying heavily on the use of gas, lethal injection and electrocution, behind the walls of the prison. In Texas in 1923, the Statute Providing for the Electrocution of Convicts Condemned to Death ([SB No. 53], ch. 51) replaced local hangings and lynchings with the use of the electric chair at Huntsville state penitentiary (Marquart, Ekland-Olson and Sorensen, 1994, p. 1).

From Lynching to Formal Execution

Executions are by no means the sole preserve of formal criminal justice procedures. A continuum of activities can be identified, from the lynch mob through to the militia, secret police or death squads of some political regimes – both of the political Left and the Right. The word 'lynch' as described by the Compact Edition of the *Oxford English Dictionary* (1979), originally meant punishing by tarring and feathering or whipping and later was used to describe executions by a mob of people. What is less clear is whether this reflects simply a semantic change, or whether at the time 'lynch' found its way into the thirteenth edition of the dictionary of the Spanish Academy (Borges, 1975), it only referred to scourging people, in contrast with its usage in the USA in the late nineteenth century, when it referred to killings. Lynching constitutes a traditional form of execution condoned, or at least colluded in, by the authorities in some countries. Thus, in the USA, the lynching of prisoners was not uncommon into the early years of the twentieth century. It could be argued that, whilst the lynch mob is not legal, nor justifiable, like the use of the stocks, it is an aspect of the community's direct stake in the processes of punishment.

Lynchings were a traditional aspect of vigilante justice often assumed to contribute to maintaining somewhat precarious social order, but in reality, used disproportionately, in the USA at any rate, on marginal, including immigrant and non-white, groups (Marquart, Ekland-Olson and Sorensen, 1994, p. 5). Lucas Beauchamp, in William Faulkner's novel *Intruder in the Dust* (Faulkner, 1960), a black man accused of murder in a southern state of the USA, manages to escape the lynch mob, partly because he behaves as though he has a white ancestor. Research demonstrates that more than 90 per cent of recorded lynchings in the former states of the Confederacy – South Carolina, Mississippi, Georgia and Florida – were of African origin and over 95 per cent were black. They tended to occur in localities where plantation slavery was most strongly established (Marquart, Ekland-Olson and Sorensen, 1994, p. 6). A total of 4951 people were lynched in the USA between 1882 and 1927 (Lane, 1993, p. 322). For example, in 1893, a mob of upwards of up to 10,000 spectators gathered in Paris, Texas, many travelling from miles around to witness the lynching of a retarded black man accused of killing a small child. First red-hot pokers were pushed into his body; then his eyes were burned out, and flaming brands forced down his throat. After almost an hour of this torture, the unfortunate man was burned alive ... . In 1918, in a five-day orgy of mob violence in Georgia, eight blacks were murdered, one of them a pregnant woman who was slowly roasted alive and her baby cut from her womb and trampled by the crowd; two others were burned to death for no greater crime than allegedly 'talking back' to whites

(Lane, 1993, pp. 322–3).

The change from informal lynchings to formal state-administered executions did not necessarily imply enhanced social and criminal justice. First, traditions of local intimidation and racism die hard and in the USA persisted to the 1980s. For example, in February 1987, the mother of a 19-year-old Black, beaten, strangled and hanged from a tree by the local members of the Klu Klux Klan, was awarded $7 million in damages (Lane, 1993, p. 323). But more significant, 'the line between legal hangings and illegal lynchings was often very thin. Both often appeared to be administered as much to maintain the caste-like system of domination as to even the scales of justice' (Marquart, Ekland-Olson and Sorensen, 1994, p. 13). Subsequently, the institution of formal executions accompanied a struggle between local and federal authorities, the latter representing the potentially greater protection for oppressed groups, including black people in former slave plantation localities, through a more centralised, rational, due process of law and capital punishment, which at least blurred, if not removing, the sharp contours of racial discrimination (Marquart, Ekland-Olson and Sorensen, 1994, pp. 16–7).

In the period 1900 to 1949, of the 1080 men and 130 women convicted in Britain of capital offences, about 40 per cent of the men and 90 per cent of the women were reprieved. This could be explained in the ways inequalities of treatment by the criminal justice system, which in some respects disadvantaged women, in the most serious crime of murder, as Ignatieff notes, could work to their advantage:

In the nineteenth century, the Victorian murderess could often secure clemency by playing on the patriarchal image of women as the weaker sex. Since they were though to be unusually vulnerable to the the onslaughts of passion, women benefited disproportionately from patriarchal interpretations of the McNaughten rules on criminal insanity.

Those who were sent to the gallows tended to be those whose crimes contradicted male expectations of female passivity.

(Ignatieff, 1983, p. 25)

The Infanticide Act 1938 allowed women to escape execution if they could prove they were still suffering the effects of childbirth or lactation.

After the Second World War, the Nuremberg Trials and retribution through executions of Nazi war criminals by firing squad, in Western Europe various countries turned away from capital punishment. In Britain, the last hanging before capital punishment was abolished was in 1964. The abolition of capital punishment took place in England, Scotland and Wales for most offences, save crimes against the monarch such as murder or violation of the Queen, in 1969 and Northern Ireland in 1973 (Potter, 1993). Despite the abolition of capital punishment in Britain for most murders in the 1960s, the gallows at HM prison Wandsworth were retained, as execution was still the ultimate penalty for treason, violent piracy and arson in HM dockyards (*The Times*, 13 July 1983).

This was informed by general doubts about the fear of executing the wrong person, informed perhaps by the controversy about whether Derek Bentley, executed in 1952, had been guilty, and lack of firm evidence that execution acted as a deterrent to potential murderers.

Towards Reintroduction of the Death Penalty

In some countries the trend has been reversed. In the Philippines, the death penalty was reinstated in 1993, after six years without it. In July 1994, in Trinidad, Glen Ashby was executed during the hearing of his appeal by the Privy Council in Britain. In 1967, all executions were suspended in the USA, while the Supreme Court considered the constitutional appropriateness of the existing laws on capital punishment. In the meantime, all prisoners on death row were reprieved. The anti-Vietnam War protests and community action movements contributed to the declaration on 29 June 1972 that the death penalty was unlawful because, as 'cruel and unusual punishment', it violated the Eight and Fourteenth Amendments to the Constitution. When the Supreme Court ruled in 1972 that the existing laws should be abolished, it did not deny the principle of capital punishment, so the way was left open for executions to recommence in the future. Subsequently, Gary Gilmour's execution in 1976 by firing squad at his own request, broke the stay of executions in the USA.

Following the request of Gary Gilmour to be executed, most states immediately began to reintroduce capital punishment. Only six people were executed in the USA between 1967 and 1982. From the 1980s, the number of prisoners on death row increased rapidly and the number of executions rose (Chesshyre, 1983, p. 7). Twenty-seven states of the USA retain the death penalty in the mid-1990s. By 1996, executions in the USA proceeded at the rate of about five per month, supported by a widespread political and public consensus about their desirability and appropriateness (*Guardian*, 26 January 1996). In the mid-1990s, there are about 3000 people on death row in the USA, 50 of these being women. About half of these offenders have been found guilty of killing their spouse, lover or child (Jones, 1996, p. 16).

METHODS OF EXECUTION

Among the great range of execution methods employed over the centuries, for carrying out the death sentence on offenders in different parts of the world, none has been found which does justice to the person executed – in terms of providing the certainty of instantaneous, painless and dignified death – and does not demean the humanity of the executioner and the society in which the execution takes place. Methods used traditionally (unless otherwise mentioned, in Britain) – following the sentence of a court or its equivalent – include beheading, last recorded in Germany in 1924 on Fritz Haarmann; boiling alive, in the reign of Henry VIII; burning, in sixteenth-century Russia and in Britain about 1790; covering runaway slaves with molasses and hanging them from tree branches or tying them down as food for ants; crucifixion, abolished by the Roman Emperor in the fourth century AD but still used in France in the twelfth century AD; drawing and quartering (cutting out innards while still alive) until the late eighteenth century; garrotting (slow choking), used in Spain in the seventeenth century and finally abolished in December 1979; firing squad, still used in Indonesia, Iran, Iraq, Nigeria, Taiwan and in two states of the USA; the gibbet (hanging on a hook), used in medieval times; hanging in chains, used on James Cook in Leicester in 1834; impaling, used in Turkey in the late nineteenth century; the mazzatello (mallet blows to the skull and then death by knife), used in Italy until unification in the nineteenth century; pressing (putting weights on the outstretched body), used on Margaret Clitheroe in York in 1586 and abolished in 1772; and stoning, a traditional Middle Eastern method referred to in Biblical sources and still used in Iran.

In some countries, execution procedures may be determined by political rather than criminal justice considerations (Ghazi, 1995). Thus, in Japan, the execution of two prisoners in December 1994 appears to have been a sequel to the publication by the Government two days previously of an opinion poll in support of the death penalty (Anon., 1995, p. 12). Exemplary executions in Iraq and China (see above) serve to support attempts by governments to implement tough criminal justice policies.

Failures and Accidents

It goes without saying that cases where executions have not gone smoothly, embarrassingly for the authorities, contradict all attempts to present them cosmetically as an acceptable, humane penal sanction. Execution, unsurprisingly, may induce bizarre behaviour in the offender and in the past methods have been by no means equally reliable. Many executions, despite the efforts of the authorities, have involved the sentenced person in a slow, painful death, some leading to maiming and the defilement of the body before death ensued. In some cases, more than one attempt has been made to execute a person, whilst in others people have recovered, for example, after being hanged. The Amnesty International report (Amnesty International, 1989) describes accidents when attempts were made to execute by lethal injection and other methods.

The remainder of this section selects for further discussion the use of the guillotine in France, hanging and the use of 'newer' technologies of execution in the USA, including electrocution, lethal gas and lethal injection.

Guillotining

The guillotine is the ultimate symbol of efficiency in the machine age. In France, the invention of the guillotine made possible what would have been physically unmanageable – the carrying out of multiple executions, sometimes as many as forty or fifty by one executioner in a single day. Guillotining represents an ultimate equation between the necessity of a particular group to inflict hurt and the aspiration to achieve public, instant and multiple executions. The powerful imagery evoked by guillotining and the fascination it has held traditionally for politicians, reformers, advocates and critics alike, indicate that it occupies a similarly archetypal position in French society as other forms of execution in other countries (Camus, 1961; Arasse, 1991). Guillotining makes a mockery of a person by reducing him or her to an undignified horizontal position – a frozen posture of two portions of lifeless meat, an unspoken challenge to whoever would guess in which life resides the longer, the head or the trunk. The question as to whether life and the personality resides in the head, the heart or is distributed throughout the body as a whole, is a metaphysical issue made possible by the instantaneous action of the guillotine (Arasse, 1991, pp. 40–2).

The recollections of Marie-Victoire Monnard, aged 13, an apprentice seamstress, are a reminder that the horrors of the guillotine during the French Revolution were less protracted than death by mutilation. She recalled that

> Assassins cut off the nose and ears of the Duke de Brissac, leaving him like this for an entire day before despatching him. One of his legs they posted to Madame Dubarry. The Princesse de Lamballe was most fearfully tortured for four hours. My pen jibs at giving details. They tore off her breasts with their teeth and then did all possible, for two whole hours, to force her back to consciousness, to make her death the more agonising.

> (Vansittart, 1989, p. 178)

Hanging

Traditionally the offender was often hanged at the location of the murder and subsequently left there, thus marking society's response to the crime in a less ephemeral way than some other punishments. Archie, aged 19, in Stevenson's novel *The Weir of Hermiston*, set in Scotland in 1813, watches the hanging of Duncan Jopp throughout 'the brutal instant of execution, and the paltry dangling of the remains like a broken jumping-jack. He had been prepared for something terrible, not for this tragic meanness. He stood a moment silent, and then – I denounce this God-defying murder, he shouts' (Stevenson, 1909, p. 34). A turning point in informed sensibilities in Britain could have been the public execution of François Courvoisier, which Thackeray witnessed in July 1840 and wrote about, in great shock, in his essay 'Going to See a Man Hanged' (Thackeray, 1898).

Hanging is still used in Afghanistan, four states in the USA, Iran, Iraq, Jamaica, Japan and Malaysia. It involves causing death by tying a noose round the neck and opening a trap-door under the feet. This causes a very violent physical shock to the body, as well as dislocations to the upper vertebrae of the neck. Sometimes officials used to pull on the legs of victims to hasten the process of strangulation. The use of a more primitive noose in the nineteenth century led to botched hangings, as in the last public hangings in Britain, of Fenians in Manchester in 1868. In Britain, hanging was improved, with the introduction of 'the drop' in 1888, which broke the neck of the victim, rather than achieving only slow strangulation as formerly. The noose used in British executions until the 1960s was leather-lined with a metal eye spliced into it through which ran the rest of the rope. This metal eye, placed on the collar-bone below the left ear, was designed to break the neck rather than strangle the offender. Increasingly, subsequent executions became subject to a gruesome mechanics, in which the calculation of the weight of the offender and the length of the rope had to be measured against the achievement of a proper dislocation of the vertebrae, rather than, in effect, suffocating people.

After the hanging, the body may be handed over to relatives with mutilations suggesting pain in the prisoner's last moments, particularly in the contortions of the face, such as bulging eyes, and in the elongation of the neck.

'Newer' Technologies of Execution in the USA

In the USA, lynching – generally by hanging – has been gradually replaced by three methods probably unique to the USA: the electric chair, lethal gassing and lethal injection; shooting by firing squad continues to be used in a tiny minority of cases. Lethal injection is the most used method of execution in the USA in the late twentieth century. Bearing in mind that some states use more than one method, the methods used in executions since 1976 are as shown in Table 7.1.

Table 7.1   Methods of Execution in the USA since 1976

Method	No. of states	No. of executions
Lethal injection	31	155
Electrocution	11	119
Gas chamber	7	9
Hanging	4	2
Firing squad	1	
Total	54	285

Source: Death Penalty Information Center, 1995, *Facts About the Death Penalty*, 21 June.

Electrocution

Albert French's novel (French, 1994) highlights the racist attitudes which led to the execution by electrocution in Mississippi State in 1937 of the ten-year-old Black boy Billy Lee Turner for the murder of Lori Pasko. In 1890, the *New York Times* described the electric chair as 'euthanasia by electricity' providing 'instantaneous and painless death'. Electrocution involves the prisoner being forcibly shaved and fed, before being strapped into a chair, having electrodes attached to the body and being given a shock of between 1500 and 2000 volts. Medical accounts of the signs and symptoms of execution by electrocution indicate that the prisoner dies in distress and pain, by asphyxia and cardiac arrest. The heat generated by passing an electric current through the body for several minutes at varying strengths leads to the blood boiling and the major organs such as the brain being cooked. The person drools and vomits, defecates and urinates. There are third-degree flesh burns, convulsions, grimaces and dilated pupils. Smoke, sparks and flames may issue from the head during the administration of the electric current.

The electric chair was canvassed in the latter years of the nineteenth century as a means of execution in the USA and is currently used in a dozen states. Its use partly came about because of concerns over the problems of execution by hanging. In the USA, the bringing of electric power to the streets of major cities – notably New York in the late 1880s – and the death of a man who fell from a building on to high voltage cables, inspired David Hill the governor of New York in 1886 to set up a commission to examine the feasibility of using electrocution to execute offenders. In the event, the electric chair was actually invented by a dentist. The first man executed by electrocution, William Kemmler, was partly cooked in a botched application of the current, which needed repeating before he was pronounced dead.

Such difficulties in the use of the electric chair have led to the consideration of alternative methods such as lethal gas and lethal injection. Subsequently, the gas chamber was introduced on the dubious grounds that it provided a more seemly method of execution; in fact, it was slower and apparently more painful for the person executed, but it could cause less unease among those watching since it brought about less visible trauma to the body. Later, lethal injection was invented, to remove still further the staff carrying out and witnessing the execution from direct interaction with the body at the point of execution and make the entire process more sanitised, less bloody, and, thereby it was hoped, even more palatable to participants and to the public. However, there were three botched executions by lethal injection, two in Illinois and one in

Missouri, and measures were introduced to render the procedures more automatic.

At each stage, the adoption of more advanced technology in the USA rendered more cosmetic and distanced the actual process of killing a person, in much the same way that the guillotine linked the mechanism of a lever and the impersonal, automatic force of gravity, to remove the executioner one step from the act of using a weapon, such as an axe, to kill a person. The trappings of medical and technological science thus enveloped with the veneer of civilisation the act by one human being of ending the life of another.

Lethal gas

Execution by lethal gas was approved in Nevada in 1921 and first used in that state in 1924; ten more states had installed gas chambers by 1960 (Lane, 1993, p. 212). Currently, five states in the USA use lethal gas. Lethal gassing involves dropping a pellet of cyanide into a bowl of sulphuric acid placed under the chair into which the offender is strapped. The observers from outside the execution chamber watch the person convulse and become unconscious; the trauma of this process is illustrated in the description of the death of David Lawson in 1994 (see below). Prior to execution, the person has submitted to the inhumane shaming of having all outer clothes removed so that pockets of gas will not persist in them. This method is unavoidably linked with the use of gassing in the Holocaust.

Lethal injection

Lethal injection was first used in the USA in December in 1982, having been approved as a method of execution in 1977 by Oklahoma State and Texas State and is now a possible method of execution in more than 30 states. This method involves injecting lethal drugs into a vein of the arm. A sequence of three drugs is commonly used: sodium penathol to induce torpor, panpruim bromide to stop involuntary muscle movement and potassium choloride to stop the heart. The use of complex technology involves remote control over a series of rods and syringes which may administer a cocktail of drugs in succession – an anasthetic, a muscle relaxant to stop the lungs working and then a chemical which stops the heart beating. Reportedly, when a lethal injection is given, a person can take 5 to 15 minutes to die. In Texas in 1985, 40 minutes were occupied making 23 attempts to find a suitable vein, whilst the condemned man was strapped to the trolley (Lane, 1993, p. 319). In January 1996, the search by staff for a usable vein into which to insert the tube to execute convicted murderer Richard Townes, on death row since 1976, after 20 minutes led to it being inserted in his right foot (*Guardian*, 26 January 1996).

Firing squad

In theory, two states of the USA use the firing squad as a method of execution, as well as Indonesia, Iraq, Iran, Nigeria and Taiwan. Typically, as movingly portrayed in the film of Norman Mailer's book about the murderer Gary Gilmour, the person is strapped into a chair and a hood with blindfold is put over the head, before the firing squad, only a small proportion (perhaps as few as one) of whom have a live bullet, fire at the target pinned to the chest.

CONTESTED USE OF CAPITAL PUNISHMENT

The policy and practice of capital punishment is frequently challenged on several grounds: its discriminatory use; its use against those who offend as juveniles and arguments against its use *per se*.

Discriminatory Use of Capital Punishment

Critics of criminal justice processes indicate the ways in which broader inequalities in the system are reflected in the selection of offenders for execution. Sorensen and Wallace note that in the USA

> the criminal justice system has been likened to a funnel, narrowing the stream of offenders from arrest to ultimate disposition. This is not only true of less serious crimes, but also true of homicide. Prosecutors may not charge offenders with a crime due to lack of evidence, or because a justification or defense exists. Plea bargains are also commonplace in the processing of homicide cases. Deals are struck with offenders who testify against their partners in crime, often in exchange for leniency. Prosecutors are allowed broad discretion in choosing those they will charge with capital murder. In addition, defense attorneys are often ineffective, jury selection procedures biased, juries improperly instructed, and post-conviction relief inadequate ... . The result is a system of capital punishment in which a few persons, often similar in every other respect to those not selected for capital punishment, are sentenced to death.

> (Sorensen and Wallace, 1995, p. 61)

In a detailed examination of litigation and research in this area, Sorensen and Wallace conclude that whilst there is less conclusive evidence of racial discrimination against black people in sentencing decisions among those convicted of capital murder (Arkin, 1980), great disparities – and hence unjust justice – exist at the stage of indictment and charging, for example, in Florida (Radelet and Pierce, 1985), Kentucky, New Jersey (Bienen, Weiner, Denno, Allison and Hills, 1988) and South Carolina (Paternoster, 1984). One possible explanation is that prosecutors, not consciously motivated by racism, pursue those cases most likely to lead to conviction (Radelet and Pierce, 1985). Thus, murders of white people by black people receive priority attention, rather than vice versa. Later in the trial, research examining which legally relevant factors influence the death penalty decision, indicates that where the case involves a white victim prosecutors are 2.7 times more likely to move to the penalty stage of the trial without plea bargaining, and the probability of a death sentence decision once put before the jury is 8 per cent greater, if the victim was white rather than black (Baldus, Pulaki and Woodworth, 1990). According to research by Baldus and colleagues, 'the overall odds of receiving a death sentence were increased by a factor of 4.3 if the victim was white' (Sorensen and Wallace, 1995, p. 64).

Execution of Those who Offended as Juveniles

The execution of offenders who were juveniles when the offence was committed contravenes Article 6 of UN law dealing with the human rights of children. International treaties and conventions on human rights forbid the passing of death sentences on people with learning disabilities, who are ill, awaiting appeals or under 18 at the time of committal. No more than seven countries in 1995 – Bangladesh, Barbados, Iran, Iraq, China, Pakistan and the USA – allow offenders who were juveniles when they committed a crime for which they are found guilty of murder to be executed by the state. The USA is one of four countries where executions in such circumstances currently take place. In contrast, in the USA a young person of 17 cannot buy liquor, go to a club or vote, but can be imprisoned with adults. Execution has been a traditional punishment for juveniles in the USA for more than 350 years. Since the reintroduction of the death penalty in 1976, 137 offenders who committed the crime whilst juveniles, have been sentenced to death in the USA. More than 30 of these are in death cells in 1995 (Linebaugh, 1995a, p. 29).

In the UK, a report by Justice alleged that the system for dealing with children committing murders in England and Wales fell short of meeting international standards of human rights. The report criticises the 'political' setting of a minimum sentence by the Home Secretary, for instance, in the case of the two boys who killed two-year-old James Bulger in February 1993, who were sentenced to be detained at Her Majesty's pleasure – the juvenile equivalent of a mandatory life sentence for murder. The report recommended the abolition of the mandatory sentence of detention at Her Majesty's pleasure, with discretion to impose an appropriate sentence.

Arguments for Capital Punishment

Arguments for the use of the death penalty include its use as an effective prevention of the offender reoffending; its function as a deterrent to others; its use as a way of the community showing its rejection of the offender; its doubtful but nevertheless claimed deterrent value through the high probability of apprehension and conviction and execution; and the claim that death is far less likely to occur because of a miscarriage of justice than for other causes.

Cesare Lombroso (1918, p. 427) argued that capital punishment should be retained for criminals who in his view were born constitutionally unable to be reformed. This argument was to fuel not only eugenic theories in the twentieth century, leading to the discouragement of some people from having children, but also the social hygiene theories on which the German Nazi party drew.

The Police Federation of England and Wales argued in 1983 for a return to capital punishment, not for particular crimes such as the murder of police officers, but as an option available for all kinds of murder. A Home Office Research Study showed that in such circumstance where, as before 1957, the distinction between capital and non-capital murders was abolished, more than 60 per cent of convicted murderers would have been hanged, a rate of more than one hanging a week, and possibly as many as 90 per year (Smith, 1979). The Police Federation maintained that the abolition of the death penalty had not made criminals more humane; in fact, they were more willing than hitherto to use firearms (*Guardian*, 5 July 1983, p. 28).

The philosopher Roger Scruton makes the case of the moral retributivist.

Punishment is justified not by its effects but by the crime itself. There is only one measure of the rightness of a punishment, and that is whether it is a just retribution for the crime. that is why we need the death penalty. That is not to say that punishment is not *also* a useful deterrent:

but deterrence should be seen as one of the side-effects of punishment, rather than its essence.

(Scruton, 1995).

Arguments against Capital Punishment

Compared with the arguments for capital punishment, the practical and moral arguments against are overwhelming.

Practical arguments against
First, it may be argued that execution has a damaging effect on society and specifically on institutions and professionals directly involved. For example, when the possibility of reintroducing capital punishment was being debated in parliaments and in the press in Britain in 1983, a letter to the *Guardian* by several forensic psychiatrists argued that recruitment of prison doctors would suffer if they had to certify prisoners as fit to be hanged and attend their executions; executions would further demoralise staff and prisoners and 'dehumanise prisons' (*Guardian*, 5 July 1983, p. 28).

Second, there is the impact on the prison and other nearby communities. The prison governors' branch of the Society of Civil and Public Servants, in a letter before the Parliamentary debate on the restoration of capital punishment, to Leon Brittan, then Home Secretary, justified their opposition on the following largely pragmatic grounds: the effect on the rest of the prison of holding a condemned prisoner, especially in terms of increasing verbal and physical aggression 'rising to a crescendo the night before the execution'; the incompatibility of execution with the aims of the prison service; the danger that agitators would 'use executions as a convenient and very potent focus for discontent'; the increased risk of fractured relationships between staff and prisoners, necessitating increased use of force; staff facing reprisals; demonstrations outside prisons would be larger and more active than in the former days of hanging and so there would be a need for actual executions to be excluded from prisons (*Guardian*, 11 July 1983, p. 2).

The six Roman Catholic Northern Ireland bishops stated that, moral justifications apart, the reintroduction of capital punishment 'would be disastrous. It would gravely exacerbate an already dangerous and explosive situation' (*Guardian*, 5 July 1983, p. 28).

Third, there is no evidence that executing offenders deters others. It could even lead to further offences as reprisals and it could create political martyrs. At a practical level, Enrico Ferri (1917) stated that for the death penalty to deter through terror, and to prevent future generations becoming criminal through, in effect, artificial selection, 'in Italy, for example, it would be necessary to execute at least one thousand people every year' (Ferri, 1971, p. 242). His opposition to the death penalty, therefore, was on the grounds that no country would apply it unswervingly in this way to the great number of born criminals who committed the most serious crimes of violence (Ferri, 1917, p. 243). Bishop Augustine Harris, president of the Roman Catholic Social Welfare Commission, said that 'legalised and retaliatory killing' had not proved effective at controlling crime (*Guardian*, 5 July 1983, p. 28).

Fourth, the ultimate arbitrariness of the protracted process of appeal by inmates on death row in the USA is epitomised in cases where the latest of many stays of execution is granted minutes too late to save a person from death. Thus, it seems likely that Caryl Chessman, who waited 12 years on being sentenced to death in 1948 for kidnapping, and had a date for his execution set eight times followed by eight reprieves, received a ninth stay of execution just before he died in the gas chamber at San Quentin prison (Hibbert, 1966, pp. 437–9). Three years earlier, Burton Abbot was executed in the same gas chamber at the moment when the stay of his execution was telephoned through to the Governor of San Quentin (White, 1923, p. 13, quoted in Hibbert, 1966, p. 439).

Fifth, a sentence of execution which may have seemed appropriate at the time to those passing it may subsequently be deemed inappropriate. Such a view may develop in circumstances where the offender has been executed or where he or she has undergone a lengthy period of waiting. The wrong person may be identified as the murderer, found guilty and executed. The problems of identification are well-rehearsed. Since most murders are committed by a person known, and close, to the victim in Britain, the rate of detection by the police is relatively high. At the same time, many prosecutions rely on identification of the murderer by one or more witnesses. So, the fact that research confirms the unreliability of the processes of identification contributes to arguments against the death penalty (Tysoe, 1983, pp. 11–13). If the wrong person is executed, this cannot be redressed in retrospect. For example, Timothy Evans was hanged in 1949 and later John Christie, his fellow lodger in London, admitted committing this crime and also killing another six women, including his own wife. Evans was given a posthumous pardon. The Select Committee on Capital Punishment (1929–30) in England received from the Governor of Sing Sing prison a statement of many mistaken verdicts in the USA. Further,

Barbara Graham, executed in California in 1955, may not have been guilty; Wilbur Coffin, executed in Quebec, was also probably innocent; James Fulton Foster, condemned to death in Georgia in 1958, was released when a policeman confessed to his crime; in Massachusetts a Puerto Rican bus boy was also recently released after serving three years of a life sentence when the real murderer confessed.

(Hibbert, 1966, p. 433)

Moral arguments against

First, from Cesare Beccaria (1764) to the present day, there is the view that capital punishment is a form of murder. These opponents of capital punishment argue that if murder is wrong then it is equally wrong for the state to take a life in response. This argument represents opposition to the death penalty, which is very difficult to comment further upon, since it is based on a moral judgement.

Second, it can be argued that differential punishments imposed in different places, purely by virtue of different tariffs and for similar offences committed in similar circumstances, violate social justice. In the USA, for example, 38 states have the death penalty and 12 do not. Among states with the death penalty, the number executed in Texas since 1976 exceeded the total of executions in 21 of the remaining 25 states and was almost three times as high as the next highest total (see Table 7.2).

The number of executions in Southern states greatly exceeds those in other regions. Of the executions carried out during the period 1976 to 1995, two-thirds were in Southern states, 21 in the Midwest, 19 in the

Table 7.2   Number of Executions by State Since 1976

Texas	97	N. Carolina	7	Arizona	3
Florida	33	Delaware	5	California	2
Virginia	26	Nevada	5	Washington	2
Louisiana	22	Illinois	5	Idaho	1
Georgia	20	Mississippi	4	Maryland	1
Missouri	12	Oklahoma	4	Nebraska	1
Alabama	12	S. Carolina	4	Wyoming	1
Arkansas	10	Utah	4	Pennsylvania	1
Indiana	3	Montana	1		
Total	286				

Source: Death Penalty Information Center, 1995, *Facts About the Death Penalty*, 21 June, p. 1.

West, 97 in the state of Texas alone and only one in the Northeast (Death Penalty Information Center, 1995, *Facts About the Death Penalty*, 21 June, p. 3).

Third, execution reduces the humanity of the executions to the level of the murderer; it is an act which degrades society and humanity by association with it. Church leaders, such as Dr John Habgood, just before he became Archbishop of York in 1983, have tended to use moral arguments such as the dehumanising effect of executing offenders in cold blood: for instance, when speaking out against the reintroduction of capital punishment in advance of the parliamentary debate on the restoration of the death penalty (*Guardian*, 7 July 1983, p. 26). The General Synod of the Church of England voted overwhelmingly against capital punishment on 12 July 1983 (*The Times*, 13 July 1983, p. 2).

Fourth, if it is wrong to murder in the heat of the moment, then executing in cold blood is also wrong. Fifth, the death penalty is only justified if anyone is prepared to carry it out if called upon. Prison staff should not be asked to participate in what most of the public would not do. Sixth, the death penalty violates the human rights of the offender, during the period leading up to, and including, the execution (see below for the process of execution). Seventh, there is the lack of justification of protracted delays between the passing of the death sentence and carrying it out. A seven-member judicial committee of the Privy Council considered delays in executions in Jamaica (*Earl Pratt and Another* v. *The Attorney General of Jamaica and Another [1993] 3 WLR 995; The Times* law report, 4 November 1993). The committee made two observations. 'firstly, that there were "strong grounds for believing" that any delay of more than five years after sentence constitutes "inhuman and degrading punishment" ... and if such delay is attributable to the appellant system then it is the system that is at fault and not the prisoner for using it' (letter to *The Times*, 6 April 1995). Eighth, executions involve negative and harmful experiences: for offenders; for offenders' relatives and friends; for other participants, possibly including victims; and for other people in society. Ninth, executions violate progressive religious principles of reconciliation between offenders and society, though admittedly, one cannot impose on the friends and relatives of murder victims, for example, the necessity to forgive.

THE PROCESS OF CAPITAL PUNISHMENT

It is unsurprising that execution – so deeply embedded in many cultures – has become associated with highly ritualised procedures, many of which would need to be located in their social context in order for their significance to be appreciated. For example, condemned criminals in ancient Babylon were dressed up as kings before executing them, in a form of sacrifice (Frazer, 1913, pp. 354–5). The variety of official executions used in different countries is equalled in some cases by the diversity and complexity of regulatory procedures involved. Execution procedures frequently take on a ceremonial character, with elaborate rules, as though to emphasise in the detail some humanistic and reasonable features absent from the gross violence of the act of execution itself, notably the detailed regulation of execution by lethal injection in the USA. This section, however, does not consider the anthropological dimension of execution, but merely invites reflection on the phases of its staging and accomplishment, not least from the viewpoints of those on its receiving end, their families and friends.

Processes of execution may be routinised, partly perhaps to counteract the reality that their nature is anything but routine. The bureaucratic procedures evolved, for example, to sanitise procedures for execution by gas and lethal injection in the USA, may serve to neutralise the fact that a person is being killed by one or more officials: the segregation of the prisoner in the death chamber, the division of labour which distributes responsibilities for various tasks to several people – strapping the person in place, checking the equipment, pressing the buttons, pulling the switches. Throughout Kafka's fictional account of the execution process – death being achieved by transcribing an inscription with needles on the offender's body, over many hours – the commandant of the penal colony is never seen, a sign perhaps of his omnipotent omnipresence (Kafka, 1949, pp. 185–221).

STAGES IN THE EXECUTION PROCESS

The execution process involves a number of stages after the sentence is passed, directed towards fulfilling the functions of killing the offender, whilst meeting the interests of the major participants in the process. Typically, in the late twentieth century, executions involve participants having recourse to a number of aspects: terrorisation, mechanisation, sanctification or medicalisation (Linebaugh, 1995b, p. 3). Thus, the authorities may employ self-consciously methods of execution which contribute to the impact they desire to achieve, as in the use of the guillotine in the French Revolution, to confirm the ability of the new Republic to enforce terror through the ultimate infallibility of demonstrating power to achieve the imposition of instantaneous death by machine. Again, in the USA, the twentieth century has seen a shift towards medicalising execution in the total seclusion of quasi-quarantine, such as chambers, where offenders are offered tranquillising injections and religious intercessions before gas, poison or high voltage current is introduced to their bodies under the supervision of technical and medical experts. Computers are used to control the sequential injection of chemicals into the bodies of offenders, once the process has been activated by an official, from a supervisory position behind glass. Typical of these latter day methods is the emphasis on physically removing both operators and observers from the execution chamber. Further, the offender remains under scrutiny from many people, but alone in the total exclusion of the final sterilised environment – its routines as hygienised as the hospital operating theatre – for the killing to take place.

Permission and prohibition provide parameters for the management of the execution process, preserving the semblance of humaneness whilst ensuring the carrying out of the judicial killing of one person by others. Attempts by the authorities to manage the execution process by reducing the emotions associated with the event, and, by implication, distancing it from the fact that a State employee is paid to kill another person, tend to generate complex – sometimes idiosyncratic and local, even irrational to outside observers – rules and ceremonies about what the participants can and cannot do. Tranquillising medicine, for example, may be used, but no music or radio is allowed in the condemned cell (Linebaugh, 1995b, p. 1). In contrast, perhaps in the effort to divert attention and thereby stave off potential protests, others prisoners in the execution prison may be given pornographic films to watch (Linebaugh, 1995b, p. 19). Last-minute visits to the prisoner by relatives, friends, advocates and priests are provided, perhaps partly to ensure the compliance of the offender with the final stages of execution, which if physically resisted, cannot be cloaked in the deceit that it is just another complex manoeuvre in the ongoing interaction between officials and inmates in the penal process.

Officials concerned with execution may take courage from different sources. The executioner may be provided with a plethora of supports which technically break the rules, but, presumably, have a blind eye turned to them on the grounds that the end justifies this particular means. Thus, the hangman was invariably accompanied into the prison the evening before the execution by a crate of beer, to see him through that night (personal account to author by prison officer on duty at execution). Statutory observers such as the governor and chaplain, for example may be required to be present, but may distance themselves mentally, and in terms of direct actions, from what is going on.

In Utah since 1900, 39 out of 48 executions have been by firing squad, a method reportedly satisfying the requirement of the Mormon church for 'blood atonement' by murderers. Some hundreds of people volunteered to take part in the firing squad of five police which was to execute John Taylor in January 1996, convicted of murdering children, in the first execution by firing squad in Utah since Gary Gilmour in January 1977 (*The People*, 21 January 1996). Heads of law-enforcement agencies selected the members of the firing squad, each of whom was paid $300 in cash. Taylor was allowed to choose five witnesses in addition to the nine local reporters and five government representatives at his execution. He could also choose his last meal – pizza with extra vegetables and a Coke – but was not allowed to smoke with the meal since indoor smoking was banned under Utah's Clean Air Act, and he was allowed only to smoke while walking to the holding cell 24 hours before his execution (*Guardian*, 25 January 1996).

Waiting for Execution: Death Row

Dr Johnson commented that the thought of imminent death concentrates a criminal's mind like no amount of prolonged imprisonment. A great body of evidence exists about the mental and physical anguish experienced by the condemned person, relatives and friends, when awaiting execution (Amnesty International, 1989). The long period many prisoners spend before their execution is carried out raises the question as to whether such a lengthy delay makes a decision to carry out a sentence of death 'an inhuman and degrading punishment' (Hatchard, 1994, p. 928). There is a tendency for people to wait on death row for many years before suddenly being executed when appeals processes have run their course. In the USA, the lengthy procedures for appeals mean that prisoners commonly wait up to ten years on death row, before being executed, sometimes after many reversals and last-minute changes of the decision. The stressful impact of these on the offender, relatives and friends can be guessed at. In Japan, of more than 90 people on death row in 1995, 54 had exhausted all appeals and could be executed at any time; some had awaited execution in this situation for almost 30 years (Anon., 1995a, p. 13). One prisoner died in 1977 at the age of 95, having spent 25 years awaiting execution. At least two prisoners on death row in 1995 were over 70 years old (Anon., 1995a, p. 12). Japan is almost unique in executing very old prisoners. Executions in Japan 'are carried out at short notice and in secret. The prisoner's family and lawyer are not informed; the prisoner may be informed only a few hours before execution' (Anon., 1995a, p. 12)

In Japanese prisons, the rules governing all prisoners are strict. But prisoners under the death sentence are particularly targeted for harsh treatment:

> Prisoners under a death sentence must sit on the floor in the middle of the cell (in one of three designated positions). They cannot walk freely, lean against the wall or lie down outside sleeping time except with special permission. Visiting rights are generally restricted to a very few people – usually immediate family. Access has sometimes even been denied to adopted children or foster parents. Closed-circuit cameras are reportedly installed in the cells of prisoners appealing against their sentence. There are also severe limits on the number of letters a prisoner may write and on opportunities to mix with other prisoners. In Tokyo detention centre, death sentence prisoners can watch TV twice a month, and see a film and eat with other prisoners once every two months. In other centres, like Sapporo, no such facilities are available. In some, death sentence prisoners are not allowed to speak or meet with anyone in the prison other than guards and visitors.
>
> (Anon., 1995a, p. 14)

A series of vignettes may be drawn from Vogelman's research based on interviews with eight male ex-prisoners from death row in Pretoria central prison. The function of death row is to keep people alive until the authorities are ready to execute them. Brian Currin, Director of Lawyers for Human Rights comments: 'Death Row is like a factory … . It's a factory which produces corpses … . You go in live and you come out dead. To produce that product a system is developed. The whole place is serviced. They provide food. They make gardens. They give notice of execution. They hand. And they bury' (Black Sash Research Project, 1989, quoted in Vogelman, 1989, p. 195).

It may be claimed that the execution process degrades and adversely affects staff and prisoners close to the incident, as the son of a prison governor recalls:

> As a governor he dreaded the night of deeply intense silence that preceded the dawn hanging. As a child I recall one of those. Silence has gradations as does noise. The night before the hanging, there was a depth of silence that drowned sense. Then suddenly one inmate would

scream; others joined in; all began to smash tin plates against the walls of their cells, and the noise was frantic and terrifying. It went on for perhaps half-an-hour. Patently it was not a demonstration to attempt the impossible: prevention of the execution. It was a mass outburst of human emotion that was to leave the large prison society in emotional tatters for many months to come.

(letter to the *Guardian*, 7 July 1983).

Not all pre-execution experiences are this dramatic, as Lewin's description of a South African prison indicates:

The first thing you notice as you come into Central is the singing, the sound of the Condemneds. Up behind the huge sign in the hall saying Stilte/Silence, the Condemneds sing, chant, sing through the day and before an execution, through the night. At times the chant is quiet, a distant murmur of quiet humming softly. Then it swells: you can hear a more strident urgent note in the swell, sounding through the prison, singing the hymns that will take them through the double doors into the gallows ... . Condemneds, waiting their turn, singing their fellows through their last nights.

(Lewin, 1976, quoted in Vogelman, 1989, p. 184)

Whilst there are exceptions, new prisoners on death row tend to be welcomed, as they represent fresh stimulation, the possibility of new relationships and relief from the dominant activity, of reflection on the past (Vogelman, 1989, p. 184). Sadistic jokes may be played on newcomers.

One new inmate for example, was informed when he first arrived that during the night a rope would come from his cell's ceiling and throttle him. Consequently he did not sleep and remained vigilant all night. Then he was told by his fellow prisoners that even though he had arrived on the Friday, since there were too few people to hang on the Monday, he would have to make up the shortfall. That weekend he awaited his execution. Only late on Monday morning a prison warder who noticed his odd and extremely anxious behaviour informed him he need not worry about the rope or an early execution.

(Vogelman, 1989, p. 188)

Various strategies are adopted by prisoners facing execution. Some accept it, others deny it. Acceptance, after all appeals and other options have been exhausted, often is the point where the person realises that there will be no reprieve. 'Such news initially brings shock, then depression and finally the struggle of accepting death begins in earnest' (Vogelman, 1989, p. 191). When they receive their execution date, prisoners in Pretoria central prison are removed to a group of cells called 'The Pot', apparently because that is where prisoners 'stew before they die'. The speed of this move, apparently, is to minimise possible panic or resistance from the prisoners (Vogelman, 1989, p. 192). During their time in the Pot, prisoners have their heads, necks and weights measured, so as to calculate the correct strength of rope and length of drop required to kill them. It appears that Charles Duff, an English hangman, in his *Handbook on Hanging*, produced the formula that '412 divided by the square of the weight of the body in stones equals the length of drop in feet' (quoted in Vogelman, 1989, p. 192).

Families experience aspects of the punishment of the execution of a relative. Both the prisoner and relatives are likely to find visits in this final period very traumatic. 'The condemned are particularly concerned about the consequences of their death. They are upset about being unable to take emotional and financial care of family members and the sadness caused by their death. Family visits are often characterized by much crying by both the inmate and his family' (Vogelman, 1989, p. 193).

During this last wait, prisoners are able to talk as much as they wish. Often, they become manic, talking and making jokes all night long. Sometimes the jokes are about hanging – 'who had the largest neck and how much rope the hangman would need' (Vogelman, 1989, p. 192). At other times, prisoners may fantasise, perhaps wishing to marry the day before the execution, as though to symbolise a commitment to living and thereby preserve some aspect of life in spite of the execution (Vogelman, 1989, p. 193). Prisoners' responses reflect helplessness, and humour may reflect a growing acceptance of impending death. But feelings about dying are complex and often ambivalent. On the one hand there is terrible fear. On the other there is relief that the trauma is coming to an end' (Vogelman, 1989, p. 193).

The hearty meal offered to prisoners at Pretoria central prison the night before the execution comes close to the adage that the condemned prisoner ate a hearty breakfast. However, morning executions do not seem to be preceded by breakfast. After a brief prayer with the chaplain, the prisoner is led swiftly to the location of the execution. Resistance at this stage may be uncommon, but when it occurs, is met with equally determined force. 'In one incident teargas was used to get the prisoners out of their cells. In another case, a prisoner pleaded that he did not want to die and while being led to the gallows excreted in his pants' (Vogelman, 1989, p. 194).

The prisoner may be buoyed up in the final stages leading to execution by the hope of a last-minute reprieve, which may or may not be fulfilled.

During the Last Moments

During the last stages before the execution, the interaction between the guards and the prisoner tends either to the extreme of formalised, and minimal, interaction between the sentenced offender and the guards, or to extremes of *bonhomie* and informality. In the film of Norman Mailer's book about the circumstances, offence, apprehension, trial and execution of Gary Gilmour (Mailer, 1979), the party atmosphere of the gathering with him of officials just prior to his execution by firing squad in Utah, and then the shaking of hands and wishing him 'good luck' and goodbye, is bizarre, but serves to make the physical segregation of the offender prior to this, and subsequently in the journey to the execution shed, bearable. It underlines ironically the ultimate division of roles between killer and killed which is about to be accomplished.

The fact that many prisoners cannot face the reality of execution contributes to the creation of mythological beliefs and fantasies:

A popular myth that has been passed down over the years by death row prisoners is that one does not die on the day of 'the execution'. The myth is that instead of hanging and plummeting through the opening in the floor boards and dying, you are dropped into the pit alive. There below the floor boards, all those supposed to have been executed, live and work. According to the myth, they work in the government mint and the mountain that lies behind Pretoria prison is the soil that has been dug up in order to enlarge the mint and to accommodate the mint's extra residents and workers.

(Vogelman, 1989, pp. 189–90)

The fact that the prisoner's families do not see the body or take part in the burial feeds this myth.

The Killing

During the actual hanging, 'the rope is jerked with such force that it not only breaks the subject's neck but leaves a severe rope burn' (Vogelman, 1989, p. 194). Dr Chris Barnard notes:

The man's spinal cord will rupture at the point where it enters the skull, electrochemical discharges will send his limbs flailing in a grotesque dance, eyes and tongue will start from the facial apertures under the assault of the rope and his bowels and bladder may simultaneously void themselves to soil the legs and drip onto the floor.'

(*Rand Daily Mail*, 12 June 1978, quoted in Vogelman, 1989, p. 194)

In the absence of testimony, it is difficult to be certain, but Barnard maintains that such contortions seem to be the response to the massive trauma of the dislocation of the nervous system and do not indicate any feelings of pain (*ibid.*).

In the manner of their death, many prisoners appear to suffer. Subsequently, the denial of any right to attend a funeral, burial, or mourn at a grave, adds to the suffering of the relatives.

In Kafka's story, at the last minute the officer changes places with the condemned man, and is executed in his stead, despite the onlooking Explorer's attempt to stop the machine, 'for this was no exquisite torture such as the officer desired, this was plain murder' (Kafka, 1949, p. 218). Reality, however, is less indulgent. In Central Prison, North Carolina, David Lawson was executed by gas in the early morning of 15 June 1994. His attorney, Marshall Dayan described it:

[... medium pause; .. short pause]: He came in and he mouthed I'm okay ... within two or three minutes prison personnel put a mask over David's face .. the mask covered his eyes .. it left a hole for his nose and then there was an area round his mouth that had small holes to let the gas in ... then they strapped the mask to a post behind the chair so that his head was stationary ... and they strapped him to the chair .. legs and arms .. and then they left .. and we waited .. and before the process began David shouted out 'I'm human ... I'm human' .. and he did that about every fifteen seconds .. and then .. suddenly we heard a loud bang .. and then saw a big cloud of smoke rise up from the floor and we knew that was the gas .. and David took a breath and shook violently .. he really gasped very loudly ... and then he shouted again 'I'm human' .. and he was holding his breath .. and then he would gasp when he couldn't hold his breath any more and again he would shake violently and gasp loudly and then .. sort of release .. and again sort of try and cry out 'I'm human' and about two or three minutes into this process he couldn't say human any more and he said 'hum ... hum' ... and then two or three minutes later he couldn't say that but he continued to grunt again .. and then later his grunting was broken by his gasping .. taking in a breath. shaking .. and then settling back and then trying to call out again ... and that went on from 2.01 am to about 2.10.

(extract from *When the State Kills*, documentary from the Lethal Justice series, televised on Channel 4 in 1995, October Films production).

It took 18 minutes for David Lawson to die.

8 Evaluating Punishment

It is very hard to predict especially the future.
(J. P. Conrad (title of chapter in Ward and Schoen, 1981, pp. 15–24))

INTRODUCTION

The evaluation of the uses and abuses of punishment cannot be simplified without losing the force of many of the arguments deployed for and against it. There are two main reasons for this. First, the concept of punishment is inherently problematic. Major complicating factors are the different perspectives on criminology, criminal justice and penology which lead to different positions from which abuses of punishment may be defined and the evaluation of punishment undertaken. Second, the notion of evaluation is ambiguous. It could refer to evaluation of the idea of punishment, or to evaluation as an outcome of evaluative research. This chapter bridges these two, for reasons which will become clearer, but can be summarised here. Essentially, this chapter straddles rather awkwardly the schism between reviewing research on whether different punishments work and evaluating punishment from various moral and ethical vantage points, some of which – moral opposition to corporal and capital punishment, for example – render experimental research into their 'effectiveness' irrelevant. That is to say nothing about the difficulties of deciding how to judge effectiveness.

The full range of punishments considered in Chapters 3 to 7, from psychological, physically constraining, custodial, corporal to capital punishments, is not considered in this chapter, since this would not further the purpose of this book. Instead, a selection of forms of punishment is made for particular examination. The chapter also examines a number of ethical considerations which have a bearing on punishment.

EVALUATION: A PROBLEMATIC ENDEAVOUR

The central problem which preoccupies all evaluators of whatever activities is to try to predict which outcomes will follow from what sorts of actions in which specified sets of circumstances. The plain fact is that although quite a lot is known about the possible outcomes for certain proportions of people, following particular actions, it proves very difficult to predict precisely which people. In other words, it is almost impossible to translate general statistical trends and results into definite predictions that this person will act this way if that punishment is carried out.

Attempts to argue for or against punishment often ignore this core problematic and make assumptions about the effectiveness of particular measures. But what is meant by effectiveness? Unfortunately, there is no simple and easy answer to this question. In fact, such arguments often reflect the the results of assumptions and the moral and political stances of those using them, rather than being based on that unattainable goal – totally objective research. For example, those who oppose particular forms of punishment, *on principle*, may assert that corporal or capital punishment, for example, is ineffective as a deterrent. But this is to ignore the evidence that in particular circumstances punishing people in these ways may be effective, using the term effective in the strict sense of having an impact on their future behaviour. Thus, apprehending a person and then executing them makes it certain that they will never commit another crime; or, castrating a rapist reduces greatly the likelihood that he will continue to commit those particular sexual offences. Again, locking up a persistent housebreaker for natural life in conditions of maximum security effectively prevents further offences of that type. It is important, therefore, to acknowledge that at an immediate level the Draconian responses of execution, physical mutilation to remove the ability to act in a particular way, or physically incapacitating through isolation in a cell, may be effective. But these measures may be considered unacceptable for moral and political reasons, such as the degree of suffering they impose on the offender, perhaps considered to be out of all proportion to the seriousness of the offence.

The ambiguous nature of punishment, for example, uncertainties about its nature when employed through therapeutic or treatment regimes, may be interpreted as punitive. Behaviour modification, for example, may be experienced as punitive, but an indeterminate sentence in a treatment-oriented regime also may be experienced by its recipients as punitive.

Walters and Grusec argue that arguments against punishment on grounds of its ineffectiveness are misplaced and that it is effective under certain conditions (1977, p. 135). However, they admit that 'punishment, even when carefully and efficiently employed, can have undesirable and unintended consequences' (1977, p. 135).

Evaluation on one hand may focus on immediate outputs or longer-term outcomes. Alternatively, it may concentrate upon the quality of the process. Again, it may examine the situation from the point of view of more than one participant. A key question could be, what is the impact on the punisher? For example, the impact of flogging on the executioner may be judged by the account of John Shipp of the 87th Foot Regiment, reflecting on the many floggings he had carried out over eight years:

> it was my disgusting duty to flog men at least three times a week ... .
> When the infliction is ordered to commence, each drum-boy, in rota-
> tion, is obliged to strip, for the purpose of administering five-and-
> twenty lashes (slowly counted by the drum-major), with freedom and
> vigour. In this practice of stripping there always appeared to me some-
> thing so unnatural, inhuman, and butcher-like, that I have often felt
> most acutely my own degradation in being compelled to conform to it.
> After a poor fellow had received about a hundred lashes the blood
> would fly down his back in streams, and fly about in all directions with
> every additional blow of the instrument of torture; so that by the time
> he had received 300, I have found my clothes [covered with] blood
> from the knees to the crown of my head, and have looked as though I
> had just emerged from the slaughter-house. Horrified at my disgusting
> appearance, immediately after parade I have run into the barrack-room
> to escape from the observation of the soldiers, and to rid my clothes of
> my comrade's blood. Here I have picked and washed off my clothes
> pieces of skin and flesh that had been cut from the poor sufferer's
> back.
>
> (Shipp, 1831, quoted in Scott, 1938, pp. 181–2)

Again, the implications of the punishment for other immediate witnesses, and others in the offender's and the victim's networks, need to be
considered. This is complex. There may be an immediate emotional
impact on the person. But in cases where the offence and the sentence are
still contested, some participants may regard the offender as the victim of
the punishment and the authority as committing an injustice, itself requiring action through the due process of law. So, even the simple dichotomy
between offender and victim is inadequate as a conceptualisation for the
scenario of punishment, as has been noted by Newburn and Stanko
(Newburn and Stanko, 1994c, pp. 153–65).

Another form of evidence concerns the evaluation of unintended outcomes of punishment, that is, what was simply not anticipated. Another
may be consequences of something going wrong. For example, there is a
long history of executions going wrong. The following are a few more
recent illustrations. It took three attempts before John Evans was electro-

cuted on 22 April 1983, the first shock causing flames to jump from the electrode strapped to his leg. On 13 December 1988, the syringe injecting poison into Raymond Landry fell out of his vein after a couple of minutes and had to be reinserted; it was 40 minutes before he was declared dead. The electrocution of Wilbert Lee Evans on 17 October 1990 in Virginia was marked by the gruesome sight of blood spurting from the mask over his face, placed there to conceal the dying person's grimaces; he continued to moan after the first shock of electricity to his body. Billy Wayne White helped his executioners to find a vein into which to insert the lethal injection to kill him, after they had tried for 47 minutes, in Texas on 23 April 1992 (Jones, 1996, p. 16).

FINDINGS FROM RESEARCH

The Effectiveness of Punishment as a Deterrent

The two main targets of deterrent punishment are the offender and other people. It was noted above that, provided the offender is caught, found guilty and sentenced, execution has unrivalled effectiveness at ensuring the offender does not reoffend. Other Draconian penalties, such as amputating limbs, presumably warrant similar claims. But the purpose of this section is to review a range of other penalties and to assess the success of punishments, and the threat of punishments, in deterring other potential offenders.

There is no way of corroborating, or disproving, the assumption that particular punishments have a deterrent effect on the offender, since there is no body of systematic research which separates out the extent to which the impact on the individual is due to rehabilitative, or deterrent, factors. There is no research evidence conclusively supporting the assertion that convicting and/or sentencing offenders has a general deterrent effect on others (Martinson, 1974; Lipton, Martinson and Wilks, 1975 p. 610).

In order for punishment to act as a deterrent, the citizen needs to know what penalty follows a given offence. Radzinowicz and King (1977, p. 146) refer to a survey in California revealing that the average person knew the maximum penalty for less than three out of eleven listed offences.

The likelihood and immediacy of punishment have a great impact on its effectiveness. The relatively low rate of detection of the police and the relatively lengthy processes of remand and trial, for people charged and processed through the courts, do little to improve the deterrent effect of eventual sentencing disposals. The severity of punishment – often subject to public and mass-media calls for increases – is no necessary guarantee of the increased effectiveness of punishment. Not only is it questionable whether criminals balance the severity of punishment against the commission of more or less serious crimes, but also it is well known that possible disposals by sentencers operate on differential tariffs in which the element of individualised justice leads to a range of sentences from the maximum downwards.

At the same time, there are some circumstances in which deterrent effects are more obvious. For example, the professional criminal is more likely than the person who commits a violent offence in a fit of strong emotion, to calculate the possible chances of different outcomes, and the likely success of different bargaining strategies in attempting to avoid prison, for example, in the event of being caught.

At one extreme, mechanisms such as torture may be employed to maintain the rule of the people by the state on deterrence. Such repressive means as torture are not the prerogative of authoritarian dictatorships. McGuffin parallels the use of torture by the British government in Northern Ireland in the 1970s with similar practices by the French in Algeria, the Russians in Hungary and what was then Czechoslovakia, the Americans in Vietnam, Santo Domingo and parts of South America, as well as in Spain, Greece, Brazil and South Africa (McGuffin, 1973, p. 21).

It is difficult to sustain arguments justifying punishment which are based on the widespread, but anecdotal and untestable, assertion that 'when I was a child a good spanking by my father prevented me from going off the rails'. Even if memory was reliable, research based on extrapolation from the past to the present tends to neglect social changes which have taken place. The relatively close-knit circumstances of the traditional household, even if they were replicated in localities most prone to crime, are unlikely to be paralleled in the relatively depersonalised public environments – with the relatively remote likelihood of detection – in which crime rates are rising in many parts of the world.

> In a small, simple, and stable society there is at once more support for the law and less need of its deterrent sanctions. In a large, complicated, fragmented and changing society, where other restraints are loosened, where minorities of all kinds are emphasizing their differences and asserting their rights, where personal values are uncertain and conflicting, these sanctions are hard to enforce and even when enforced their impact is weakened.
>
> (Radzinowicz and King, 1977, p. 154).

The use of research on animals in the laboratory to evaluate the effectiveness of various methods of behavioural inducements and punishments (see Chapters 3 and 4) is even more suspect. Even if the ethical questions about the use of random controlled trials (RCTs) could be set aside, there are problems of the validity of the methodology:

> Their virtue lies precisely in the ability of the experimenter to exclude everything except the simple choice he wishes his rat to make, the reward which is to encourage a course of action, or the electric shock which is to discourage it. The complications of social life, with its manifold choices and pressures, the convolutions of human conscience and emotions, the uncertainties of human reward and punishment, are remote from all this. Whilst it is true that simplification is essential to answer certain basic questions, it is false to assume that the answers produced can be transposed direct to other and far more intricate organisms and environments.
>
> (Radzinowicz and King, 1977, p. 154)

Whilst introducing more severe penalties appears to have some impact at the lower end of the tariff, it seems to have least effect on the most serious offenders – sex offenders and violent offenders – on whom much of the debate about punishment and deterrence focuses.

Interest in research into deterrence in the 1970s (Zimring and Hawkins, 1973; Andenaes, 1974; Gibbs, 1975) experienced a revival partly through a growing disenchantment – especially from conservatives – with liberal approaches and partly because of the collapse of the rehabilitationist ideal. In his brief review of these arguments, Roshier suggests that 'most would agree with the general point that the existence of some kind of threat of some kind of punishment from some kind of criminal justice system does deter crime' (Roshier, 1989, p. 117). He quotes Andenaes's (1974) example of the considerable short-term increase in crime rates for some offences which followed the lack of a police force in Nazi-occupied Denmark. However, it is easy to argue that in such extraordinary social circumstances, fluctuations in crime rates may be explained in a variety of ways. The important thing would seem to be to hesitate before making premature judgements. For example, the seemingly homogeneous increase in looting during the 1981 urban riots in Britain apparently breaks down into remarkably discriminating activity – apparently involving larger stores, including chains and multiples, but not local 'corner' shops (Kettle and Hodges, 1982). Again, the destruction of apparently 'mindless' riots by Canadian prisoners was reported to have avoided damaging the education complex which many prisoners perceived as benefiting them (personal account to the author). Be that as it may, Roshier recognises that the use of more extreme corporal punishments – such as on-the-spot floggings for parking offences – 'tends to be restricted for moral and humane reasons, rather than those associated with effectiveness' (Roshier, 1989, p. 117).

The evaluation of the severity of deterrent sanctions tends not to support any firm conclusions. Anthony Storr observes that habitually violent offenders are far less likely than non-offenders to be deterred either by the disapproval of others, or by the threat of increasingly harsh punishments (Storr, 1991, p. 50). Yet Sir Samuel Romilly failed in 1814 to persuade Parliament to abolish the sentence of hanging, drawing partly on the grounds that removing this sanction for treason would lead to an increase in such crimes (Storr, 1991, p. 50).

Policing and Trial: Crime Control or Due Process?

Dilemmas in both criminal justice and trial processes betray different perspectives on their operation, which make their simple evaluation impossible. As far as criminal justice processes are concerned, the police play the central role in the operation of procedures which lead to a defendant appearing in court. Chapter 3 outlined aspects of this which may be experienced by the 'suspect' as punitive. The major dilemmas inherent in such circumstances arise from the choice facing police between crime control and due process (Packer, 1968). An undue emphasis on due process, on the other hand, may lead to perpetrators of violent crimes, for example, being perceived as 'getting off' and consequently the originally victims being punished further as a consequence. (Bottoms and McClean, 1976; McConville and Baldwin, 1981).

Different countries adopt different models, among which adversarial and inquisitorial approaches are the two prominent alternatives. Each has different strengths and weaknesses. Inquisitorial systems have the capacity to pursue the truth of a situation. But the adversarial system tends to provide more guarantees against the state abusing its investigative powers, and leads to the development of complex procedures for gathering evidence and trying to prove guilt. The contrasting trends occurring in different countries are an indication that no single system has a monopoly of advantages, just as no system is hopelessly flawed. In Italy and Germany there has been a shift towards an adversarial system and there have been proposals that France should follow suit. In Britain, there is ongoing debate about the merits of moving towards an inquisitorial system (Sanders and Young, 1994, pp. 18–20).

'Therapeutic' Punishments

This section acknowledges, but does not dissect further, the debates about whether particular treatments are essentially, or incidentally, punitive. Researchers tend to accept that treatment and therapy are not 'soft' (Foren and Bailey, 1968) and on the whole contain a punitive and/or deterrent component (Lösel, 1995, p. 88). Palmer's evaluation of the effectiveness of community-based corrections for young people (Palmer, 1974) was used to support the case for less custodial and more community-based approaches. Although research does not confront head-on the argument about whether a punitive element in the vast variety of different treatment programmes for offenders works or not, there is merit in posing, as do Fischer and Folkard and colleagues (Fischer, 1976; Folkard, Smith and Smith, 1972), the question as to whether these treatments in any case have been found to be effective. A comprehensive survey of studies evaluating the effectiveness of treatment programmes and methods was carried out in the mid-1970s (Lipton, Martinson and Wilks, 1975). This undertaking was made more complex by the task of taking into account the many variables in the circumstances of offenders and offences, taking due account of unanticipated or undesirable side effects and distinguishing the immediate from longer-term impact of treatment on offenders (Lipton, Martinson and Wilks, 1975, p. 20), as opposed to considering the perceptions of offenders (Allen and Treger, 1994). As they point out, 'the problem of crime is systemic; therefore, when one change is made other changes may occur, some of which may have negative consequences for the administrator interested in achieving economically the multiple goals of public safety, humane care of offenders and restoration of offenders to the community (Lipton, Martinson and Wilks, 1975, p. 515).

   Martinson's evaluation of available research on the treatment of offenders concludes that no clear pattern emerges which indicates that any particular method of treatment is effective (Lösel, 1995, p. 79). Research-based comparisons between different programmes are made more difficult by the heterogeneity of methods of intervention adopted and the difficulties of satisfying the requirements of traditional experimental research design (Lösel, 1995, pp. 99–101). The technique of meta-analysis is used to aggregate research studies and has allowed the collective analysis of the results of almost 400 studies of the effectiveness of treatment for delinquency. Some modest claims are made by Lipsey for 10 to 12 per cent improvements in terms of future recidivism, for those treatments involving at least two contacts with the offender per week and a minimum of 100 hours of contact overall over at least 26 weeks. As to the type of treatment, skills-based, behavioural and cognitive work are typical of those which are more efficacious (Lipsey, 1995, pp. 77–8).

Behaviour Modification

Evaluations of behaviour modification techniques from within the field tend to exclude wider critical questions about the lack of moral justification for its use, the questionability of basing techniques used on people on behavioural experiments carried out, in many cases, on animals, and the difficulty – within the short-run time-span of a typical behavioural programme – of estimating the long-term harmful impact on a person of imposing stresses or physical hurt on him or her. Further, the finding that most behavioural punishments will need reinforcing, in order to maintain the desired behaviour seems well established by research (Azrin, 1960; Lovaas, Schaeffer and Simmons, 1965), in contrast with the claims of some behaviourists that this is not so.

Difficulties arising also from the complexity of evaluating the effectiveness of punishment are increased by the need to take into account the stimulus and reinforcement variables which affect the maintenance of the response to punishment. The stimulus variables include the intensity, frequency, scheduling and immediacy of punishment after the undesired behaviour; the reinforcement variables include the frequency and scheduling of reinforcement and the opportunities given to the punished person of engaging in alternative forms of behaviour (Azrin and Holz, 1966, p. 442).

Brantner and Doherty point out that relatively few of the large number of studies carried out to examine the effectiveness of timeout satisfy methodological requirements (Brantner and Doherty, 1983, p. 93). However, even in cases where use of the technique achieved some modification of the undesirable behaviour, by definition, there is no necessary reason why any underlying problems would also have been addressed. In fact, there is a vast amount of research evidence that the side effects produced by punishment – hostility, emotional and physical withdrawal from the punisher, aggression and anxiety, and a tendency to imitate the punisher when the person punished subsequently comes into a situation of power – make it likely that punishment is in the longer term achieving the dubious end of reducing sensitivity to others and inducing violent acts, which may be endlessly replicated (Carroll, 1977).

'The child who is physically punished or who observes punishment of others may later utilize aggression as a behavior control technique'

(Newsom, Favell and Rincover, 1983, p. 292). Corporal punishment may teach aggressive behaviour (Newsom, Favell and Rincover, 1983) and can produce nightmares and other symptoms of post-traumatic stress syndrome. Newsom, Fowell and Rincover have detailed the consequences of punishment, other than on the behaviour of the person punished. Whilst many of these side-effects may appear inconsequential, others may be dramatic and significant, as when an in-patient disappears from the hospital (Newsom Favell and Rincover, 1983, p. 285). Other negative side-effects of punishment include the physical and emotional impact on the person punished – pain, trauma, distress, discomfort, loss of control (Newsom, Favell and Rincover, 1983, pp. 289–92), as well as disruptive social consequences for other people (Newsom, Favell and Rincover, 1983, p. 288), which may result from what onlookers may describe as 'non-functional' aggression or other disturbance displayed by the punished person (Azrin and Holz, 1966, p. 443). Patterson takes the view that whilst some kind of punishment may be necessary to curb anti-social behaviour, this runs counter to well-established findings in developmental psychology; these hold that more punitive persons model aggressive styles of behaviour similar to those they wish to discourage in others, and that the overall consequence of aggressive punishments is to produce more aggressive responses and still more use of punishment. It can be argued, for example, that the impact of punishment is superficial, in that it suppresses behaviour whilst not significantly weakening the underlying tendencies towards it (Azrin and Holz, 1966, pp. 436–7).

Aversive punishment may be applied to anyone, but in this discussion includes the use on infants, children or individuals with learning disabilities, of unpleasant and distorted sounds which could cause 'physiological damage to (the) subject's hearing' (Bailey, 1983, p. 261), smells, tastes, visual deprivation and 'novel aversive physical sensations' (Bailey, 1983, p. 247). The effects of these on modifying people's behaviour are very mixed. More concerning, however, is the nature of the punishments. For example, aversive smells consist among other things of ammonia capsules crushed under the noses of children, including a four-year-old girl with cerebral palsy, severe learning difficulties and affected by seizures (Bailey, 1983, pp. 252–3); the aversive taste punishments include sprinkling a pepper mixture, sometimes including Tabasco, on vomit which a boy with learning disability tended to reconsume when regurgitated. But·'the program was quickly discontinued and ruled unacceptable by the experimenter after its application resulted in some burns to the subject's mouth and lip' (Bailey, 1983, p. 255). In another experiment involving squirting shaving cream into the mouth of a child to stop her screaming, 'the authors caution that, although this particular child did not appear to swallow much of the cream, the possibility of harmful side effects caused by the ingestion of commercial shaving creams cannot be ignored' (Bailey, 1983, p. 261). Novel physical sensations included giving a soiling child five minutes in a cold bath (Bailey, 1983, p. 267), and in another case tugging the hair and giving electric shocks in order to stop a child screaming (Bailey, 1983, p. 271). It is necessary to pose the ethical question as to how adequate the advocacy and self-advocacy arrangements are in cases where such punishments are imposed on young children and children, and others, with learning disabilities.

Prison Custody

On the negative side, four points can be made. First, a vast body of evidence supports the view that prisons have unjust, inhumane and harmful consequences for offenders, their families and friends, as well as for staff working in them (Mathiesen, 1990). However, methodological limitations prevent most researchers from producing evaluations of prison custody which are valid, reliable and replicable across the wide range of settings which exist (Lösel, 1995, p. 95). Second, prison does not have a specific deterrent effect on offenders in general and white-collar criminals in particular – reputedly a highly rational group of offenders (Mathiesen, 1990, p. 40). Third, some research, notably into the experience of prisoners in special units, calls into question whether prison can do anything except reinforce problems of isolation and deprivation, inherent in imprisonment and removal from the family and the wider community (Cohen and Taylor, 1972). Cohen and Taylor draw on a wide range of studies examining the impact on people of dislocations and crises caused by the impositions and deprivations of migration and diaspora. More significant, their research challenged the dominance – and irrelevance, of much psychologically based research into the impact of imprisonment on prisoners, on the basis that it was too behaviourally based and too restricted in its definition of the impact on the person (Cohen and Taylor, 1972, pp. 204–5; Jupp, 1989, pp. 130–1, 140–2). Fourth, there is little or no evidence that laws introducing determinate sentencing rather than parole-style sentences affect the level of crime (Marvell and Moody, 1996a). Similarly, there is little evidence that legislation imposing mandatory minimum sentences or additions to sentences for crimes committed with guns has any impact on reducing crime or increasing prison populations (Marvell and Moody, 1996b).

Custody for Children and Young People

Typical of the wider problems attaching to research into the effectiveness of punitive institutional regimes in youth justice and criminal justice alike, is the controversial adoption of boot camps for young offenders. There is no evidence that punitive custodial sentences beneficially affect the future offending behaviour of the sentenced offender, or other offenders (McGuire, 1995, pp. 11–12) and preliminary indications are that boot camps may not be effective either (McGuire and Priestley, 1995, p. 26).

Thornton, Curran, Grayson and Holloway (1984) failed to find any grounds for optimism, when examining the very high reconviction rates of young offenders released from detention centres with a tougher regime than hitherto. Hagell and Newburn (1994) confirm the impossibility of distinguishing sufficiently clearly a group of persistent offenders and then developing a custodial regime which will offer any group of young offenders, let alone this group, an enhanced likelihood – over other sentencing options – of reduced future offending. In contrast, all the evidence points to the high failure rates of young offenders released from custody, which become even higher as they experience more custodial sanctions (Hagell and Newburn, 1994).

Corporal Punishment

Two kinds of evaluative research are considered here. First, research evidence points to three main conclusions: first, children on the receiving end of corporal punishment tend to imitate the person who administers that punishment and become more aggressive (Dollard, Doob, Miller, Mowrer and Sears, 1939; Bandura, 1973). Second, children living in households where for their parents corporal punishment is the norm, and where the parents act aggressively and display aggressive attitudes and words (Bandura and Walters, 1963), tend to be more delinquent than those who do not (Welsh, 1976). Third, children who receive corporal punishment tend to be more aggressive, anxious, tend to have more difficulty communicating with others, and tend to be more abusive towards other people, than those who do not receive corporal punishment. Punishment may lead to children displaying neurotic symptoms, chronic anxiety and deeply felt resentment towards the person who punishes them (Wright, 1973, pp. 33–44). They may feel doubly guilty, for having done something of which the punisher disapproves, and for their feelings of anger and resentment towards the punisher (Aronfreed, 1968). A significant proportion of sado-masochistic pornographic material relates to corporal punishment in schools and beating of children, and there may be associations between these (Livingstone, 1975).

Second, there is the impact of corporal punishment on future behaviour. There is no evidence that flogging an offender, whether adult or juvenile, is relatively more effective than other penal or rehabilitative measures, in deterring that person, or others, from committing further offences. Radzinowicz and King refer to long-term trends to substantiate their argument that corporal punishment has no discernible impact on the incidence of particular types of offence. The proportion of offenders convicted of robbery with violence subjected to corporal punishment declined from 11 per cent in 1898–1903 to 2.5 per cent in 1909–13. During this same period, the average numbers of convictions of this crime decreased from nearly 200 to 127. In contrast, between 1918 and 1939, when the use of corporal punishment more than doubled from 20 per cent to 45 per cent, crimes of robbery with violence actually increased (Radzinowicz and King, 1977, p. 158).

The Departmental Committee on Corporal Punishment in the 1940s, and subsequently the Advisory Council on the Treatment of Offenders, went through the records of all men flogged or birched between 1921 and 1947. In both cases,

> there was no evidence that offenders who were flogged as well as being sent to prison did any better than those who simply served terms of imprisonment or penal servitude. If anything, they did slightly worse. This was true whether their subsequent behaviour was gauged in terms of further convictions for robbery with violence, for other serious crime, or for lesser offences involving violence. It could not be explained away by the argument that the men flogged must have had worse previous records than the rest, and were therefore worse risks for the future: it still held good when comparisons were made between those with similar records. And even if it were accepted that, within each group, the courts had reserved corporal punishment for the very worst cases, there was no evidence that they had achieved anything in doing so.
>
> (Radzinowicz and King, 1977, pp. 158–9)

The effects of corporal punishment are likely to include encouraging crime, and causing physical injuries, rather than being able to effect psychological change, or ameliorating the social and environmental factors contributing to offending. Corporal punishment may cause medical or psychological problems to the offender and may also traumatise those involved in administering it. On the other hand, more insidiously, it may serve the sadistic purposes of the executioner and those witnessing the punishment. The misuse of corporal punishment may extend to sexual purposes. Scott documents the role of flagellation in sexual abuse and sadistic practices (Scott, 1938, pp. 194–239).

Cicely Craven, then Honorary Secretary of the Howard League, in a letter to the *Oxford Times* (30 July 1937), noted that a study over several years, of all cases in four towns where the birch was used for juvenile offenders, showed that 'of all the boys birched, over 25 per cent were re-convicted within one month, and over 76 per cent within two years. No other method had such a startling record of failure' (quoted in Scott, 1938, p. 189).

As Benthall, the anthropologist notes, whilst the immediate physical wounds of corporal punishment may heal, the 'symbolic wounds' on the psyche are often lifelong. The consequences for women of beatings of boys in all-male schools, for example, may be to increase the incidence of child abuse and violence against women: 'at an all male boarding school caning and birching had a great deal to do with feminization of deviant behaviour and implicitly downgrading of women, as well as with homosexuality' (Benthall, 1991, p. 386).

Capital Punishment

There are two fundamental paradoxes lie at the heart of the debate about the effectiveness of capital punishment. First, there is the obvious, but tautologous, statement that for the offender, capital punishment is 100 per cent successful in preventing further offences. As Stephen Spender implies, not just for prisoners facing execution, half a century ago, to all prisoners 'their Time is almost Death' (Spender, 1959, p. 41). Second, there is the tension between the superficially undeniable fact that the death of another offender is the most extreme, and therefore the strongest potential deterrent of other offenders, and the reality that invariably in countries retaining the death penalty, murder rates do not fall.

A number of features set statistics on the incidence of murders apart from those on other crimes. First, apart from the small proportion of murders committed in furtherance of another crime, for instance, of robbery, most murders are domestic, or what have been called '*crimes passionelles*': that is, the victim and the murderer knew each other well in at least two-thirds of cases and were involved in a longer history of dispute or conflict of some intensity. Second, about a third of all murderers commit suicide before they can be apprehended (Blom-Cooper and Morris, 1976). Third, the proportion of one-third non-domestic murders to two-thirds domestic murders remains fairly constant. Fourth, the proportion of murders committed in pursuit of another crime remains relatively constant. Between 1957 and 1977, the proportion varied between 5 per cent and 14 per cent of the total of murders (Blom-Cooper and Morris, 1976).

Behind attempts to use statistics to prove either the effectiveness or the ineffectiveness of the death penalty lies the intrinsically contested definition of murder itself. In some countries, for example, offenders may be executed for what in other countries are unambiguously non-capital offences. Radzinowicz and King speak with authority, as outstanding criminologists of the post-war years, the former as a member of the British *Royal Commission on Capital Punishment 1949–53*, on the difficulties of defining the capital offence of murder.

> The dividing line between murder and wilful homicide may be shifted. Distinctions may be introduced between murders that are capital and non-capital, or first and second degree. There have been examples of all these in England in the present century: infanticide ceased to be classed as murder; the concept of diminished responsibility allowed certain killings that would formerly have been classed as murder to count as homicide instead; and, prior to the abolition of capital punishment, murder was divided for a time into capital and non-capital categories ... . In the United States and elsewhere such calculations have been made even more difficult, since there has been a failure to distinguish, in statistical records, between capital murders, non-capital murders and homicides. Researchers have either ignored this or been compelled to assume, for comparative purposes, that capital murders remain a constant proportion of all homicides, or at least of all wilful homicides.
>
> (Radzinowicz and King, 1977, pp. 160)

The relatively low incidence of murder, in absolute terms, and in comparison with other crimes makes trends in murder rates vulnerable to large changes on the basis of fairly small numerical shifts. This makes much more problematic the interpretation of statistical evidence on the effectiveness or otherwise of capital punishment. Having said this, such data as exists suggests that fluctuations in the murder rate do not seem to be adversely affected, or in some cases appear not to be affected at all, either by the abolition of capital punishment, or its restoration some years after abolition. For example, the American Civil Liberties Union Foundation suggests that murder rates are at least the same, if not higher, in many countries with the death penalty as those without it. Again, the incidence of findings of murder in court rose soon after 1963 and dramatically in

1974, this latter purely as a result of murders associated with disturbances in Northern Ireland: 1961:38; 1961:38; 1963: 38; 1964: 47; 1970: 91; 1971: 85; 1972: 88; 1973: 82; 1974: 148 with 7 cases still pending (Radzinowicz and King, 1977, pp. 161). These statistics do not point to a sharp enough change of incidence of murder around 1965, the year in which capital punishment was suspended for five years in England before its abolition in 1969, to attribute to it any effect on the murder rate (Radzinowicz and King, 1977, pp. 161–2). In the USA, neither suspension nor abolition of the death penalty led to an increase in the murder rate. The abolition of capital punishment in Austria, Denmark, Germany, several Latin American countries, the Netherlands and Scandinavia did not lead to a significant increase in the murder rate; in Finland, the murder rate actually decreased after abolition (Radzinowicz and King, 1977, p. 162). This is not to say that there are not countries where the murder rate is rising. But the evidence suggests that in these – for example, France, Northern Ireland and the USA – the explanation for the increase lies in broader social factors (Radzinowicz and King, 1977, p. 162).

The American Civil Liberties Union Foundation estimates that murder rates are similar, if not higher, in countries retaining the death penalty than in those not using it. Thus, in the USA where in many states the death penalty is retained, there are ten people murdered per 100 000; in Russia 7.4, in Canada, where the death penalty is abolished for all except heinous crimes, it is 2.1 and in Britain 0.7 per 100 000 (Jones, 1996, p. 17).

Walker cautions against slipshod arguments either for or against the efficacy of capital punishment or long-term imprisonment as deterrents, though he concludes that, given the likelihood that murder is often intentional injury which goes too far, evaluation of all such violence suggests that both capital punishment and imprisonment deter future offending, more for the likelihood of punishment than the length of sentence' (Walker, 1991, p. 67).

Finally, as was indicated in Chapter 7, the death penalty is not very cost-effective, if the 1993 study at Duke University in North Carolina is typical of other localities. It indicates that on average the cost of a death penalty per execution, at about $2 million, is three times the cost of a sentence of life imprisonment (Death Penalty Information Center, 1995, p. 4).

Punishment in the Melting Pot: 'It All Depends ...'

It may seem unsatisfactory, but it is unavoidable that, depending on one's value position and perspective on criminology and criminal justice the kinds of research referred to in the foregoing discussion either can be accepted as the sole basis for a judgement about whether punishment is acceptable, or disregarded as irrelevant. Positivist methodologies are implicit in the administrative criminology which traditionally has dominated British criminology until the early 1970s. From that point, with the collapse of correctionalism (Adams, 1994, pp. 43–4), both left idealism and left realism provided increasingly strong alternative justifications for further action. The former tended to support abolitionism and the latter the reductivist and reformist positions (see Chapter 10). Left idealism broadly is compatible with a socialist view, whilst left realism incorporates those modifications to the socialist perspective consequent on the critical implications for idealist criminology brought about by the changing political and social conditions of the 1980s.

LEGAL AND ETHICAL CONSIDERATIONS

Controversy over the ethics of the use of therapeutic punishments illustrates the wider issues raised in the area of punishment more generally. Critics of therapeutic punishment tend to reject them on three main grounds: they are ineffective – or at any rate not proven more effective than their alternatives; they are dehumanising, both to the person punished and the punisher; and they are unethical. This section takes up the discussion of ethical issues. Griffith – who in principle does not oppose the use of punishment – argues that objections on the grounds that punishment is dehumanising or unethical may arise 'from clinical or philosophical bias, lack of exposure to punishment as a treatment option, or an unfortunate incident resulting in client injury' (Griffith, 1983, p. 317). The threat of litigation in Western countries, particularly in the USA (Griffith, 1983, pp. 318, 323–8), has increased the attention given to decision-making processes involving choices between punishment and alternative forms of therapy or judicial intervention. Campaigns for guidelines have been opposed by the argument that they are over-reactive, too time consuming and prescriptive (Griffith, 1983, p. 330). Lawyers and service users individually and through groups, pressuring for improved guidelines regulating the use of therapeutic punishment, also have been opposed by professionals such as the American Psychological Association, on the grounds that professional standards and ethics are sufficient to cover these circumstances (Griffith, 1983, pp. 329–30). Griffith questions this, partly on the grounds that therapeutic punishment is potentially risky (Griffith, 1983, p. 331), but especially given the contemporary trend towards interdisciplinary treatment: 'Adherence to professional standards would produce multidisciplinary conflict and inconsistency in methodology. Whose standards would prevail in a treatment program involving a psychiatrist, nurse, psychologist, social worker, and special educator?' (Griffith, 1983, p. 330).

Ethical issues arise where personal and professional values impinge on the principles and theories used to justify particular actions involving punishment. Often, arguments against punishment are based on ethical grounds, rather than on consideration of research into the effectiveness of its particular forms. However, some opposition to punishment rests on the argument that its side-effects cannot be predicted or controlled and may, in any case, be negative and undesirable (Griffith, 1983, p. 319). A further argument may be that some punishments are dangerous, intrusive, irreversible (Griffith, 1983, p. 320), 'mechanistic, gimmicky and devoid of human interpersonal elements' (Griffith, 1983, p. 221) .

Although certain forms of punishment may be technically effective, there may be arguments against their use, on legal or ethical grounds. Legal restrictions against some forms of punishment, such as the use of electric shocks (see Chapter 4), may be associated with advocacy of the rights of the person.

The development of procedural safeguards in the State of California and regular reviews, in the use of timeout, reflects a concern with protecting the rights of clients and – where the clients are children – their parents, guardians or other authorised persons (Brantner and Doherty, 1983, p. 122). Timeout may be regarded simply as providing a less reinforcing environment than timein. However, as Brantner and Doherty note, the less reinforcing environment may be in itself aversive (Brantner and Doherty, 1983, p. 92) and therefore is subject to the same reservations about its use as other aversive treatments. In short, although punishment is frequently used, it undoubtedly can produce undesirable emotional and physical consequences for the person punished and for those with whom he or she subsequently interacts (Azrin and Holz, 1966, pp. 439–40) .

CONCLUSIONS

The conclusion is unavoidable that the imposition of the most severe punishments is least likely to be effective precisely in those areas of criminality where deterrence is most sought by the public and by professionals. Psychological punishments, punishment by physical constraints, corporal and capital punishments perpetuate rather than challenge the violence of the crimes they aim to punish (Linebaugh, 1995b, p. 19). Psychological, sociological and historical research supports this view and points to a variety of negative outcomes from punishment. More insidiously, though, the element of punishment in routines, programmes, settings and institutions tends to be implicit and often goes under the label of treatment, therapy, education, discipline or control. Finally, responses to questions of effectiveness are shaped by moral and ethical considerations. The next two chapters deal respectively with campaigns and protests against aspects of punishment and strategies for overcoming the limitations of punishment.

9 Resistance to Punishment

A main basis for effective protest and struggle is that you contribute – and are inside and positive. But then an important main ground for the protest is simultaneously taken away. What you ought to wish to protest against is precisely the fact that the ones who do not contribute, *are resolutely expelled.* What you ought to wish to protest against, then, is the very basis of our type of society. But the main basis of our type of society is such that protest easily becomes effective only if it takes place on this basis. And thereby it is no longer really a protest.

(Mathiesen, 1974, pp. 197–8)

INTRODUCTION

This chapter considers two main types of resistance to punishment: by those subject to punishment themselves and by campaigns, the two selected for discussion here being those against corporal and capital punishment.

A WIDE SPAN OF RESISTANCE

Resistance to various forms of punishment has played a significant part in achieving changes in legislation and practice. It should be remembered that campaigns by groups -as well as protests by those subject to punishment – have contributed in their different ways to these changes. Also, in Britain the abolition of capital and corporal punishment on a broad front has been achieved only since 1948. Until 1957, for example, flogging was not abolished in the navy. Corporal punishment was only abolished in schools under the Education (No. 2) Act 1986, and then only in state schools and private schools where fees are paid wholly or in part by the state. The following were noted in a briefing from EPOCH: physical punishment is banned from children's homes under the Children's Homes Regulations 1991 (SI 1991 No. 1506) and in Scotland, in local authority and some other residential establishments under the Social Work (Residential Establishments – Child Care) (Scotland) Regulations 1987 (SI 1987 No. 2233); local authorities in England and Wales are obliged under the Foster Placement (Children) Regulations 1991 (SI 1991 No. 910) to obtain written agreement from prospective foster parents that they will not administer corporal punishment on any child placed with them; private foster parents are subject to similar regulations. Day-care settings, including childminding in England, Wales and Scotland are subject to the banning of corporal punishment (Children Act Guidance and Regulations vol. 2 para. 6.22; Scottish Office Children Act Guidance Annex A, para. 23); physical punishment – including smacking, slapping or shaking – of children in maintained schools such as hospital schools is illegal (Department of Health (HSG(91)1, The Welfare of Children and Young People in Hospital, para. 4.16; (EPOCH, 1993): However, it was in 1989 – a century after the first legislation against cruelty to children in 1889 – that physical punishment of children by parents was first challenged, during the passing of the Bill which became the Children Act 1989 (EPOCH, 1993). In the home, parents are still able to administer corporal punishment to their children with impunity.

Some complex questions in relation to arguments for and against punishment have been raised. It is clear from the conclusion to Chapter 8 that moral arguments about whether punishment is desirable cut across questions of effectiveness. The present chapter starts at this point, since opposition to different forms of punishment comes from a variety of sources. For example, apart from resistance from those punished, there may be opposition from families and friends, local, national – such as the Society of Teachers Opposed to Physical Punishment (STOPP) – and international groups – such as Amnesty International – and by the authorities, governments and international governmental organisations – such as the United Nations. Nicholas Nickleby's reaction against the tyrannical Squeers, the teacher at Dotheboys Hall, may be Dickens's way of protesting about excessive punishment in schools as a Victorian author with a social conscience (Dickens, 1971, p. 155).

Resistance by Those Subject to Punishment

First and most fundamental, is resistance which uses the self, or even directs the resistance against the self, in the case of the self-immolation or hunger strike, for example. Silent resistance in face of punishment preoccupies the main character in *Kes* (Hines, 1976) and *Papillon* (Charrière, 1981). In one sense, the continuum of resistance to punishment begins and ends with the personal – the harm inflicted on the individual, and the individual's struggle against this infliction.

Resistance may be regarded as a clue to the need of the person for protection from feelings of being influenced and controlled by other people.

Thus, the therapist works with the resistance rather than fighting it. So, resistance, far from being viewed as non-cooperation, is reframed as a route to the possibility of change. However, as documented elsewhere (Cohen and Taylor, 1972; Scraton, Sim and Skidmore, 1990; Adams, 1994), acts of resistance may be carried out by, or even – like self-mutilation or suicide – directed at, the self at one extreme, or collective, and directed at the authorities or the state at the other, or simultaneously at different points on this continuum. In wartime, soldiers who questioned orders were liable to be summarily court martialled and even executed (Allison and Fairley, 1979). In wartime also, some conscientious objectors refused to comply with prison rules, on the grounds that the state was wrongfully imprisoning them. The late Walter Perrin, a conscientious objector from the First World War, recalled refusing even to leave his cell for statutory periods of exercise and labour and having to be carried to the punishment block by prison officers for disobeying orders he refused to recognise (personal account to the author). The dirty protest in Northern Ireland during the 1980s involved prisoners who asserted political status and regarded the state as wrongfully treating them as criminals, smearing their cells with excrement (Adams, 1994, p. 149).

Cohen and Taylor note the contrast between the representation in novels of popular heroic characters and the portrayal of prisoners who resist:

> The long-term prisoner who fights back is not endowed with personal qualities such as nerve, bravery and 'character' nor is he allowed anything like an acceptable set of motives – let alone an ideology – through which his behaviour could be comprehended. When he tries to escape, goes on a hunger strike, makes a nuisance of himself by composing letters or petitions, smuggles information out or refuses to accept the rules of the system, he is a 'troublemaker' who 'can't take his medicine'.
>
> Cohen and Taylor (1972, p. 130)

Ellman has studied the use of resistance by the individual which employs bodily functions such as excretion, but particularly those to do with self-starvation. Her argument is that 'the notion of the self is founded on the regulation of the orifices. For it is at these thresholds that the other, in the form of food, is assumed into the body, and the body, in the form of waste, is expelled into the empery of otherness' (Ellmann, 1993, p. 105). She quotes Margaret Atwood's description of the maintenance of the economy of subjectivity through continual flux between inside and outside the body: 'taking things in, giving them out, chewing words, potato chips, burps, grease, hair, babies, milk, excrement, cookies, vomit, coffee, tomato-juice, blood, tea, sweat, liquor, tears, and garbage' (Atwood, 1980, p. 167 quoted in Ellmann, 1993, p. 105).

The Marxist argument that human history shapes human needs (Ellmann, 1993, p. 5) – through, for example, perpetuating poverty – rather than individual physiology and actions, is illustrated in the history of protest against punishment. Ellmann follows Gayatri Spivak's argument (Barr, 1989, quoted in Ellmann, 1993, p. 5) that

> even medical perceptions of the body are based upon a reading of its signs rather than a knowledge of its essence, for the same symptoms may be understood in different ways according to the pressures of the weltanschauung. Hunger, for example, may be read as 'starving, malnutrition, fasting, dieting, anorexia, and also political fact'. However, hunger has to be recoded 'as a sign of exploitation' in order to become a mobilizing force in politics.

Ellmann draws on the work on famine by Amartya Sen (Sen, 1982, p. 8)

> in which he shows that it is not the lack of food but the inability to purchase it that causes such catastrophes. People starve because they *have* no food, not because there *is* no food, and the problem, therefore, is 'entitlement' to food, rather than its notional availability. By interpreting famine as a fluke of nature rather than a symptom of political inequities, economic policies have often exacerbated the privations they purported to be trying to assuage.
>
> (Ellmann, 1993, p. 6)

Ellmann's insights compensate for Foucault's sometimes fragile link between ideas and events (Adams, 1994, p. 34), by bringing the powerful metaphors of eating and drinking to bear on the penal experience. She refers to Foucault's argument (Foucault, 1980, pp. 92–102) that 'the penitentiary is only the terminal form that power takes, for it inheres in all the bonds of knowledge, sexuality, or economics that intertwine the public and the private spheres. It is in torture, though, that power finds its deadliest hyperboles' (Ellmann, 1993, p. 98). In the dirty protest of the H-Blocks of Long Kesh in Northern Ireland, Ellman finds a powerful analogy between the penal experience and that of the body, since in Long Kesh

> the distinction between room and person virtually disappeared, because the inmates imprisoned themselves in their own substance by caking their cell walls with excrement. Although their world had been reduced

to four cramped walls, within that tiny compass self was everywhere. Through the dirty protest, they were striving to reclaim their cells, just as they reclaimed their bodies through the hunger strike, for they cocooned themselves into their excremental signatures.

(Ellmann, 1993, p. 100)

Mutiny and desertion traditionally have been capital offences in the British armed forces. Indian soldiers in barracks at Singapore mutinied during the 1914–18 war, in February 1915 (Gilbert, 1994, pp. 130–1); there was widespread desertion and mutiny among French troops in May 1917 (Gilbert, 1994, pp. 333–4); the execution of some mutineers among Austrian troops at Judenberg in Austria in May 1918 did not prevent the mutinies spreading to Ruthenian, Serbian and Czech troops (Gilbert, 1994, pp. 421–2). More than 200 British soldiers were executed during the 1914–18 war, but only three of these were publicly admitted as for the offence of mutiny (Allison and Fairley, 1979, p. 123), despite the fact that several executions were within days of the Étaples mutiny. Percy Toplis – shot by the Cumberland police in 1920 whilst on the run – played a key role in this five-day mutiny by British troops near Le Touquet, which began on 9 September 1917 and culminated in the raid by about 200 mutineers on a detention compound and the release of 50 or so prisoners (Allison and Fairley, 1979, p.).

Primo Levi points out the ignorance and insult of the question as to why the Jews did not revolt against being executed *en masse* in the Holocaust, given the brutality of the Nazis and the exhaustion induced in the Jews by being transported long distances in rail wagons with limited, if any, food and water (Levi, 1987, pp. 386–9). The significant levels of collective resistance by the Jews to the Holocaust documented by Martin Gilbert (Gilbert, 1986) are characterised not just by punishments such as setting prisoners to work hauling huge stone blocks in stone quarries, but also by executions (Gilbert, 1986, pp. 143–4).

The organisation Radical Alternatives to Prison published the first issue of its journal *The Abolitionist* in January 1979. The editorial of this made the explicit link between 'the economic and social crisis', 'the present law and order crisis' and the prison system. It distinguished between 'diversionary and cosmetic palliatives of action' such as addressing the grievances of prison staff, and the need for 'a radical re-appraisal of the penal and criminal justice systems', challenging 'the established logic which reflects and only serves to perpetuate an unequal and exploitive social system' not just by

emptying the prisons of their present occupants merely to replace them with another class of 'miscreants' but, ... to eradicate the concept of incarceration, and all that goes with it, from the thinking of our society. Thus it is not enough to consider changes of systems and administration but also our society's conception of these institutions and how they actually operate.

(The Abolitionist, editorial, January 1979)

It is difficult to make global comparisons about changing forms of punishment and resistance to punishment; in the developing countries with dictatorships rather than democratic governments there may be points of similarity with the situation in the USA; ironically, in those democracies in Western Europe with which politicians in the USA might more naturally align themselves, with the exception of the UK – with its problem of Northern Ireland, where conflict has produced particularly punitive responses by the state since the late 1960s, the comparison shows up the USA in a negative light. In the USA, one accompaniment to the increasing number of executions was that the new, high-tech means of capital punishment were cleaner, and therefore less horrific and messy than traditional, overtly violent methods.

Just as the history of religious thought – particularly in the Christian tradition – reflects a rationalisation of humanity's domination over the animal world which neutralises, or ignores, opposition to the exploitation and killing of animals by people (Singer, 1991, pp. 185–210), so the history of changing forms of execution of people has involved shifts towards methods which buttress the continuance of execution itself. For example, the invention and widespread adoption of the guillotine in France during the late eighteenth century attempted to provide a rationale for mechanistically extinguishing the lives of large numbers of people. Thus, 'by showing that the uniqueness of the individual could be mechanically destroyed, the guillotine also suggested that consciousness derived from the machine of the body. The existence of a "machine consciousness" was physically demonstrated by its annihilation' (Arasse, 1991, p. 48).

However, running alongside execution, and incorporated into the killing process, have often been beliefs and practices which, in effect, offer a route to transcending its purpose of annihilation of the self. Arasse, for example, describes how the historical moment of the widespread adoption of the guillotine in France was occupied also by the belief that the self survived execution. (Arasse, 1991, p. 45) The symbolic power of the guillotine in ending the life of the individual – and most notably the head of state, the monarch – by separating the head from the rest of the body, was undermined by the countervailing belief that all a person's intellectual and spiritual qualities resided not only in the head but in the nervous system which, analogous to democratic ideals, distributed power to the extremities of the body politic.

Within many so-called liberal, democratic countries, there are long-standing struggles between majority and minority groups. Sometimes these are associated with religious, territorial or political power. In the UK, for example, the conflict with the Republicans in Ireland extends back hundreds of years, with a consistent pattern of exploitation and imperialism by the English, at the expense of the Irish. In the twentieth century, there were several periods when the conflict reached the point of armed confrontation, notably up to the 1920s and from the 1970s. In contrast, there was a tradition of hunger strikes, in some cases to the death, as in the H Block hunger strike, as a dramatic form of protest against the denial by the courts and the British government of their claim to the status of political prisoners. This led in 1980 to the death of ten prisoners, including Bobby Sands (Adams 1994, p. 150). There is scarcely a family in Northern Ireland without a relative or friend killed, maimed, or otherwise emotionally scarred by the troubles of the last quarter of the twentieth century.

Formal punishment by the state relies invariably on a theory of the generation of fear and subjection, to justify its alleged outcomes – the production of conformity, or at any rate, acquiescence. But terror – whether through the guillotine during the French Revolution or in the electrocutions of African-Americans in the Southern States of the USA in the twentieth century – may fail. This may produce momentary rebellion (Adams, 1991; Linebaugh, 1995b, p. 17), or contribute to challenges against individual cases (sometimes long after the offender has been executed) or against forms of punishment (see, for example, the histories of organisations opposed to corporal punishment and the death penalty. Once the campaign against corporal punishment achieved some limited success – in state schools, its key supporters – notably Peter Newell – have gone on to found EPOCH to campaign on a national and international front for the abolition of physical punishment).

Resistance to corporal and capital punishment, particularly by offenders, punctures the attempts by the authorities to maintain a view of its 'rightness', inevitability and its contribution to sustaining stability in the community. Protests against aspects of punishment, whether by school pupils or by prisoners, are particularly prone to be either ignored, dismissed or their significance denied or defined as disruptiveness (Booth and Coulby, 1987), by the authorities. They represent not only a breach of social order and consensus about the so-called justice of the punishment, but also a contradiction of its logic – the attempt to present as unproblematic the inherently paradoxical equation between the maintenance of standards of law-abiding behaviour in the community, and acts involving constraining, beating or killing offenders. Central to this paradox at the personal level, is the fact that the prisoner – the offender – may become the victim, whether of penal custody or of some other form of punishment. Thus, the division between offender and offended against loses its sharpness, and may disappear, or even be reversed.

It is a mistake to perceive resistance as only real if it is visible. The small acts of solidarity and humanity in Solzhenitsyn's *A Day in the Life of Ivan Denisovitch* constitute resistance which is no less real than mass rioting (Solzhenitsyn, 1963). Denis Staunton's interview with 75-year-old Tadeusz Szymanscy on the eve of the fiftieth anniversary of the liberation of Auschwitz reveals how this man returned after the war to work in the museum at Auschwitz and, since he found talking to pilgrims about his experiences therapeutic, has stayed ever since. Szymanscy's simple and total concept of resistance in the concentration camp is illustrated through an anecdote of his arrival in Dachau:

> A few hours after he arrived, an inmate gave him a sheet of paper, an envelope and a stamp so that he could write home. Prisoners had to pay for stamps and envelopes, but the man told Szymanscy he could have them for nothing if he promised to do the same for another prisoner some time in the future. 'I understand this as an act of resistance. After all, what does resistance mean in Auschwitz? The intention of the SS was to kill us all, and everything we did against that seemed to me to be resistance,' he says.
>
> (Staunton, 1995, p. 15).

This profound insight positively correlates extreme repression in an equation balanced against total resistance.

Not surprisingly, perhaps, theorising about resistence and empowerment as it applies to prisoners remains outside popular and academic discourse in the West, to say nothing of the rest of the world.

Empowerment is a term largely circumscribed by a particular style of political ideology and democracy (Gurr, 1989, p. 113). It needs preserving from colonisation by the authorities (Adams, 1996b, pp. 181–2). In the same vein, Mathiesen's study of the Scandinavian prisoners' rights movement concludes that the only practicable way to outflank the authorities is to remain unpredictable, by retaining an unfinished agenda for radical action (Mathiesen, 1974, p. 202).

The conclusion of Gurr's historical research that peaceful protest has largely replaced political violence, hardly applies to the prison, which retains a concentration of high pressure, which is inherently macho, confrontational and violent, and for which, in some particularly constrained situations, violence offers one of the few outlets. This reflects the dominance of a particularly macho style of response to criminal justice processes. Protest has become routinised and legitimised in US civil society, according to Gurr (1989, p. 127) over the past century. It has lost its capacity to shock, as it has gained a deal of political influence and, thereby, attracts fewer crisis responses. The question is how relevant is this, first to communal protest in other countries such as the UK, and second, to settings such as institutions where punishment is practised. Whilst it is true that protesters may have learnt from feminism and Greenham (see Adams, 1991, p. 187) and that in the disability, self-help and self-advocacy movements a rich array of non-violent strategies for resistance and self and other empowerment have been developed (Adams, 1996b), it is also true that in Meadowell (Campbell, 1993) and Strangeways (Woolf and Tumin, 1991), violence was a feature of riots in the 1990s.

Gurr's research also poses the question as to what protesters have learned (Gurr, 1989, p. 125). This usefully raises the issue of the role of users, citizens, consumers, people punished or whatever, in the various sites of punishment considered in this book. On the whole, it would be true to say that the interests of those punished are not at the top of the authorities' agenda, just as the subject matter of this chapter, to the extent that the offenders are represented, will not be regarded as of prime relevance by all concerned.

Campaigns by Families, Friends and Others Associated With Those Punished

On the whole, families, friends and others associated with offenders are a dispersed, disparate and fragmented interest. In the case of an executed person, exceptionally, the death of the person may create a campaign which coalesces this dispersed interest group. The visibility of people does not lead necessarily to their being involved in active campaigning against punishment. Women who retain contact with men serving life sentences for murder tend to be regarded as subjects for journalistic portrayal (McGwire, 1994), whilst their needs and those of their families attract rather lower priority (Matthews, 1983; Light, 1992). Cassese reflects movingly on on his leadership of a group of international inspectors from 1989 to 1993, visiting places of detention in Western, Central and Eastern Europe, including prisons, detention centres for foreigners, police stations, barracks and psychiatric hospitals. He suggests that the lack of remedy for the violations of the human rights of detainees is explained partly because of the victims do not protest; the factors contributing to this include poor education, a lack of awareness – 90 per cent of them coming from under-privileged classes – fatalism, uneasy consciences – some may feel they have done something wrong – and fear of violent reprisals if they complain (Cassese, 1996, pp. 17–18).

Ruth Ellis, 28 when she was hanged in Holloway prison, London, on 13 July 1955 for shooting her lover, was the last woman to be executed in Britain. The night before her hanging, outside Holloway prison, 'for the first time this century, before an execution, police were unable to control the crowds. There were even attempts to storm the prison gates. Women wept as the shout went up: "Give her a reprieve"' (*Sunday Mirror*, 26 June 1983). Subsequently, it was argued by Lord Denning, former Master of the Rolls, that Ruth Ellis should not have been executed, and that in later years she would have served ten years or less in prison (*Sunday Mirror*, 26 June 1983). Technological changes since the commercialisation of electricity from the late nineteenth century in the USA and the introduction of pharmacological prescriptions in the twentieth century have reduced the uncertainties attached to administering death by gassing and lethal injection. Executors, other participants, witnesses and victims take part in a drama with the formal purpose of excluding any possible ambiguity of interpretation, apart from that of lawful killing by the state following sentence for a crime committed. Yet the reality is that the execution often does not dispel controversy over the finding of guilt. In the meantime, the punishment cannot be reversed. Just as the weals on the flogged person's back can be healed but never made not to have happened, so the life of an executed person can never be brought back. And such an execution may have excited rather than extinguished controversy about the justice of a sentence, in a case which, may have become a *cause célèbre*. The very irreversibility of sentences of lengthy terms of imprisonment on the IRA prisoners known as the Guildford Four and the Birmingham Six had a similar effect on campaigns, eventually successful, for their release, on the grounds of flawed evidence.

Part of the function of particular methods of carrying out punishment – especially in its more overtly physically violent forms such as corporal and capital punishment – consists in anticipating, and where possible neutralising or overcoming, opposition to its use. The development in the USA of heavily technology-based methods of execution – by electrocution, lethal gas and lethal injection – could be interpreted as an attempt to render sanitary, hygienic and depersonalised, or at any rate disperse responsibility for, the state-sanctioned, intrinsically violent act of one person killing another. A further association could be made between medical practice and the execution chamber, which in the late twentieth century resembled more and more the operating theatre, with the patient strapped down, priests in attendance to sanctify the act, anaesthetising drugs being injected prior to doctors certifying the propriety of the process and the appropriateness of its end result. The achievement of the new methods of execution in the USA lay in their, perhaps serendipitous, convergence with debates about, and the increasing use of, euthenasia, by consent of the relatives and sometimes of the person killed. In this respect, Gary Gilmour's request to be executed opened not only the door to his killing, but provided an opportunity for such a link to be made (see Chapter 1). Such a request also took the initiative, and the power to impose the sentence, away from the authorities, albeit temporarily. It was on a par with the suicide in prison in 1994 of Frederick West of Gloucester, then awaiting trial for multiple murders.

Campaigns by Local, National and International Groups

A great number and range of groups have been involved in resistance to various forms of punishment. The most notable have operated in the fields of international abuses of human rights – such as Amnesty International – and the campaigns against corporal and capital punishment discussed below.

Campaigns by the Authorities: Governments and Intergovernmental Organisations

The history of efforts to bring about collective action by governments and international organisations coordinating governments is complex and outside the scope of this chapter and this book. It is extremely important, however, to recognise the role of organisations such as the United Nations in formulating and publishing standards of treatment of people and concerning human rights.

CAMPAIGNS IN BRITAIN TO ABOLISH PARTICULAR FORMS OF PUNISHMENT

This section considers briefly two areas of particular controversy, in which campaigns have been fought to abolish corporal and capital punishment respectively.

Campaigns against Corporal Punishment

Campaigns against corporal punishment have been conducted intermittently in Britain over the past 300 years, leading to its abolition in the criminal justice system since 1948 and in state schools since 1986.

The Children's Petition, a 70-page document subtitled 'A modest remonstrance of that intolerable grievance our youth lie under, in the accustomed severities of the school-discipline of this Nation' (1669) and a similar petition of 1698–99, are surviving evidence of formal action taken by children to protest against corporal punishment. The 1669 Petition was more a publication intended for circulation among Members of Parliament than in itself a petition (Freeman, 1979, p. 43). The 1699 Petition appears to have been similarly targeted and was subtitled '...a sensible address to the Parliament, for an Act to remedy the foule abuse of children at schools, especially in the great schools of this nation ...' (Freeman, 1979, p. 44). The general consensus of support for corporal punishment in the nineteenth century was evidenced by the fact that the Corporal Punishment in Schools Bill introduced by Viscount Raynham and Mr Dunlop in 1863 failed to survive to a second reading. Also, of three Bills against corporal punishment – for the Better Protection of Children, Servants and Apprentices – introduced by the Marquess of Townshend in 1867–68, 1868–69 and 1870, two were withdrawn and the third did not get a second reading (Freeman, 1979, p. 48).

Campaigns led in the 1880s to the ending of flogging in the army and navy and the Prison Act 1898 restricted corporal punishment to the offences of mutiny, incitement to mutiny and gross personal violence to an officer. But there was more ambivalence over whether juveniles should receive corporal punishment; the Howard League did not adopt abolition as its policy till after the retirement in 1901 of its secretary William Tallack, who all his life remained steadfastly committed to deterrent punishments, including birching (Rose, 1961, pp. 66, 208).

Despite some attempts to achieve the abolition of corporal punishment in the early twentieth century, notably by the Humanitarian League, the campaigns suffered from the lack of a single organisation devoted to this cause (Rose, 1961, pp. 208–9). In the 1930s, there were attempts to use the legal system to protest against corporal punishment. Among occasional cases brought by parents against the use of corporal punishment in schools, there is an account of a girl of 13 being awarded £20 damages, after her parents took legal action, when her teacher struck her on the hand with a stick because she was not able to answer a question on the meaning of coal (*Daily Mail*, 10 March 1938, quoted in Van Yelyr, 1941, p. 236).

In 1937, pressure by reformers led to the setting-up of the Departmental Committee on Corporal Punishment headed by the Hon. Edward Cadogan MP. Research carried out for the Committee by the Home Office supported the case for abolition (see Chapter 8). The Report of the Committee (Home Office 1938) recommended abolition, but the Second World War intervened and the Criminal Justice Bill 1938, which included the proposal to abolish corporal punishment – except for grave offences in prisons – was not reintroduced until 1947 (Rose, 1961, p. 213).

The campaign against corporal punishment in schools became more influential when the Society of Teachers Opposed to Physical Punishment (STOPP) was founded in September 1968 by Gene Adams and a group of colleagues at a public meeting in Caxton Hall, Westminster (Newell, 1989, p. 113) and took on a full-time worker as education secretary in 1979. STOPP was a pressure group with a small membership never exceeding 1000. Its finances were always limited and its organisation dependent on voluntary effort, since charitable grants could not be given directly. However, organisations such as the Joseph Rowntree Charitable Trust were able to fund research which provided evidence strengthening the campaigns of STOPP (Newell, 1989, p. 114). Tom Scott, its education secretary from 1979 to 1985, set out to use publicity to build a climate of opinion against corporal punishment. STOPP based its campaign on individual cases which were used to counter the defence of existing practices. This strategy also had the effect of strengthening positive links between STOPP and the media.

Nevertheless, it was 1980 before the Labour Party adopted the abolition of corporal punishment in schools as its policy. As the Education Bill went through its parliamentary stages, the arguments for abolition were strengthened. Tory MPs joined the opposition to corporal punishment, as evidence against its appropriateness accumulated. The final spur to abolition was the ruling by the European court in Strasbourg that the failure of schools to respect the right of parents to object to corporal punishment in schools was contrary to the European Convention on Human Rights. But the abolition of corporal punishment in state schools in Britain, which became operational in law from August 1987, only served to highlight the wider cause ·of banning corporal punishment of children in other settings, notably private schools and households. In April 1989, the organisation End Physical Punishment of Children (EPOCH) was founded and in 1990, an international informal network with the same aim was launched under the banner of EPOCH Worldwide.

Campaigns against Capital Punishment

In Britain, whilst campaigners against capital punishment gained ground with professionals and in Parliament steadily from the early nineteenth century until the abolition of capital punishment in the 1960s, a majority of the general public have remained firmly retentionist.

Samuel Romilly in 1808 initiated a broad-based attack on capital punishment when he introduced a Bill to have it abolished as a punishment for in excess of some 200 offences. From the early nineteenth century in Britain, campaigns to reduce, or abolish capital punishment can be traced. The Society for the Diffusion of Knowledge upon the Punishment of Death and the Improvement of Prison Discipline, founded in all probability in 1808 by a Quaker, William Allen (Rose, 1961, p. 26), was reportedly the first organisation in Britain concerned with the abolition of capital punishment. In 1828, the Society for the Diffusion of Information on the Subject of Capital Punishment was founded. William Allen was its chairman in London and its members included Sir Thomas Fowell Buxton, who campaigned against slavery. William Allen became chairman of the London Anti-Capital Punishment Society, which was active in the 1840s, but seemingly was defunct by 1860 (Rose, 1961, p. 26). In 1866, the Howard Association was formed, which later became the Howard League for Penal Reform, leading the very active campaign against capital punishment in unsucceful attempts to present Bills for its abolition in 1869, 1872, 1973, 1878 and 1881 (Rose, 1961, p. 28). But the Royal Commission on Capital Punishment in 1866 only abolished public executions. The Society for the Abolition of Capital Punishment was still active in the early twentieth century (Rose, 1961, p. 75). But execution itself was not abolished for another century, in the Murder (Abolition of the Death Penalty) Act 1965, and even then for treason, piracy and such offences as arson in Her Majesty's dockyards, it remained on the statute books.

In the UK, the opposition of the Church of England to the reintroduction of capital punishment was asserted by the Archbishop of Canterbury just before the vote in the British Parliament on 13 July 1983 on the reintroduction of the death penalty for certain crimes. At the same time, Amnesty reported that in the previous five years, Spain, France and the Netherlands had abolished the death penalty, 13 of the 21 member states of the Council of Europe had signed a protocol calling for its removal from domestic legislation, whilst 11 countries, including Guatemala, Iran, Iraq, Mozambique and Pakistan, had reintroduced it (*Guardian*, 8 July 1983).

The Royal College of Psychiatrists in the past has taken its opposition to capital punishment to the extent of advising its members not to cooperate with the Government in assessing any prisoners condemned to death, in the event of a restoration of the death penalty (*Guardian*, 7 July 1983, p. 26).

The Howard League for Penal Reform led the abolitionist campaign from the 1920s, alongside the National Council for the Abolition of the Death Penalty, which collapsed in 1948. The campaign against capital punishment continued in Britain for decades after its partial abolition in the Homicide Act 1957 which distinguished capital from non-capital murders, the experimental abolition of the death penalty for all murders in 1965, permanent abolition being confirmed by Parliament in December 1969 (Rose, 1961, p. 222). This was occasioned largely because of repeated attempts to reintroduce the death penalty for particular types of offences, notably the murder of police officers, children and pensioners.

There is a question about whether it is consistent with the Hippocratic oath for doctors to be involved directly in an execution, for example, in supervising a paramedic in administering the fatal injection.

The consistent opposition to capital punishment by such groups as the prison governors' branch of the Society of Civil and Public Servants (for instance, as reported in the *Guardian*, 11 July 1983, p. 2), throughout the second half of the twentieth century contrasts with the view of the person in the street. Public opinion, along with the significantly lower middle- and working-class membership of the Police Federation and Prison Officers' Association, remains more than four-fifths in favour of retaining the death penalty (Blom-Cooper, 1983, p. 15). A poll by Public Opinion Surveys of more than 1000 people, published in the *Sunday People* on 19 June 1983, showed that more than 90 per cent wanted terrorist killers and child killers executed automatically, but only 30 per cent wanted capital punishment given to all murderers (*Guardian*, 20 June 1983).

Whilst it is tempting to opt for the argument that punishment simply reflects the class struggle, this does not do justice to the complexity and variety of forms of punishment identified in Chapters 3 to 7. Class divisions are not sufficient to describe these. Linebaugh asserts that it is not sufficient for campaigns against the death penalty to develop strategies bringing together in association relatives or murderers and relatives of murder victims. This is an issue of social class and discrimination, racism. 'Its abolition must be situated among the struggles against other types of socially induced morbidity. Otherwise, as history teaches, slavery will follow for all, and not just for the most desperate, who already must sell their body parts, and blood (Linebaugh, 1995b, pp. 32–3).

CONCLUSIONS

Controversies about punishment create conditions which exacerbate uncertainties over what is to be done about law and order, social control, discipline in schools, and bringing up children to be responsible citizens. It is noteworthy that whilst Britain was in the forefront of spreading forms of corporal and capital punishment round the world in the heyday of the Empire, it has lagged behind many other Western European countries in responding to campaigns to abolish these practices. Whilst organisations have played a part in these campaigns, a lengthy history of protests by children – particularly pupils – and prisoners themselves, attests to the significant, if often underestimated, contribution made to such campaigns by people subject to punishment.

The next chapter considers some of the major implications arising from the survey of punishments undertaken in this book and examines possible future strategies.

10 Transcending Punishment

The founders of a new colony, whatever Utopia of human virtue and happiness they might originally project, have invariably recognised it among their earliest practical necessities to allot a portion of the virgin soil as a cemetery, and another portion as the site of a prison.

(Hawthorne, 1906, p. 59)

INTRODUCTION

Punishment is becoming more central as a means of social control and response to crime. Longer sentences and tougher regimes – including increased use by some states of capital punishment – mean that in Britain and the USA at any rate, institutions such as the prison are also becoming more punitive. Debates about whether parents should be allowed to smack children and whether corporal punishment should be reintroduced in schools are additional complicating factors. The key factors here are how these debates are being shaped and by whom. On the whole, the shift of the political centre-ground to the Right since the 1970s has contributed to the sterility of debates about alternatives to punishment in the mid-1990s-reductivism and abolitionism, as opposed to strengthening punishments – rigorism. With the publication on 26 October 1996 of the Crime Bill in Britain, Michael Howard, Home Secretary, set out to follow the USA and the authoritarian policies of south-east Asian countries such as Malaysia and Thailand, towards lengthy minimum sentences for repeat offenders and at least 12 more private prisons each holding almost 1000 inmates, which double the available prison space since 1979 (Alan Travis, 'Jailhouse Britain', *Guardian*, 26 October 1996, p. 1).

The foregoing chapters have demonstrated that the best one could say of punishment is that its rationale is imperfectly articulated and at worst it is abused, through excessive and inconsistent application. This concluding chapter argues that although in Britain, the grossest abuses of punishment in schools and by professionals and state and state registered/licensed employees formally have been abandoned, many forms of punishment continue, not least informally, in domestic settings; it considers likely future trends in use of corporal and capital punishment in particular; it examines the prospects for change, in different forms of punishment in

217

different parts of the world, in the light of contemporary debates about criminal violence in the home, especially male violence against partners, abuse – especially child and elder abuse, the use of dietary and corporal punishment to control children and young people; finally, it considers the viability of developing strategies in the home, in criminal justice and in society at large, which will transcend punishment. It considers which punishments should be abandoned as totally unjustified and under what conditions some should be retained.

DRAWING THE THREADS TOGETHER

It is difficult to avoid two conclusions from the foregoing chapters: that in practice, the use of punishment is all too commonly corrupted; and that the methods of punishment commonly employed intrinsically deprave those who administer them, notably exemplifying a dominant masculinity which reinforces, and is reinforced by other authoritarian and right-wing tendencies in some societies; these trends dehumanise people involved, and others by association, and degrade the settings in which they take place. In Britain, the systematic beatings and abuse to which children and young people have been subjected for centuries until curtailed to an extent by the banning of corporal punishment in state schools, should be understood in the context of the devaluation of childhood and children. At the same time, there have been trends in the second half of the twentieth century in some Western countries towards less severe formal punishments, notably the declining use of corporal and capital punishment. Apart from the general observation that punishment increases in more authoritarian societies, there is no obvious explanation as to why people in civilised societies physically constrain, cane, beat, torture and execute children and adults. To transcend punishment is to transcend the discourse of the restraining chain, isolation 'room', restricted diet, medication, custodial institution, cane, whip, executioner's axe, the noose, the electric chair, the bullet and the cyanide pellet.

How can society move beyond the widespread abuses of punishment discussed in previous chapters? There is a noteworthy tendency for the uses of punishment to become abuses. Transcending punishment is by no means achieved through ignoring, underrating, misinterpreting, or bypassing it. The institutional and cultural context of crime, dissent and conflict in which punishment is delivered could be interpreted as a social fact, or simply as happenstance, beyond human intervention or understanding. The array of punishments surveyed in Chapters 3 to 7, therefore, could be taken for granted as responses to misbehaviour, naughtiness, deviance, criminality, delinquency, intransigence, hostility or violence. But punishment needs recoding as an act of aggression and a sign of oppression, in order for effective challenges to it to be mobilised. The argument goes thus: people are punished as a consequence of a situation in which they have acted in a particular way, rather than because they *are* bad. The problem, therefore, is how to address the situation which has led to their punishment, rather than their individual badness. By defining the problem as a misdemeanour which confirms badness, rather than as evidence of the outcome of a combination of personal, social and political factors, penal policies have often contributed to the very behaviour they have claimed to be trying to reduce.

Transcending dominant masculine values

The punishments surveyed in this book have two things in common: first, their capacity to be abused and to inflict harm on people in the process; second, their likeness with a particular version of masculinity which is pretty well dominant in many settings where authority is exercised by professionals over people – prisons, schools, the armed forces are exemplars, but there are other settings too. Among these are the family (Olivier, 1989), particularly the family where one member is subjected to abusive punishment by another (Pringle, 1995). However, not all masculine attitudes and actions are outlawed here, but only those versions of masculinity associated with criminal violence, oppressiveness, authoritarian activities and abusive punishment. Newburn and Stanko have noted the need to go beyond 'the simply association of masculinity with, say, machismo' (Newburn and Stanko 1994b, p. 2). Not all forms of punishment display that crude positive correlation between toughness and violence which is the preserve of the abusive punishment, although, of course, it is argued here that *all* of the corporal punishments and capital punishments considered in Chapters 6 and 7 and *most* of those discussed in Chapters 3, 4 and 5 are inherently abusive.

Children and young people are particularly prone to be affected by such features of society. A report by Swedish Save the Children (Brett and McCallan, 1996) estimates that among some 250 000 children serving in armed forces in 26 countries round the world, many had been used in executions:

> children were often given drugs and alcohol before fighting ... .
> Children carried out executions in Burma, Colombia, Honduras, Liberia,
> Mozambique, Peru and Uganda ... children in Peru were induced to cut

the throats of those found guilty by people's courts and to eat the entrails and drink the blood of executed rebels. In Colombia, boys and girls aged 12 and 13 were executed in front of their peers, who were then forced to drink their blood. Brutalisation of recruits was standard, often involving the torture or death of relatives in front of them... . In Uganda, most child soldiers had been ordered to torture, main or kill children or adults attempting to escape.

(Victoria Brittain, 'Army of Children Fight Adult Wars', *Guardian*, 1 November 1996, p. 16)

Such research renders problematic simplistic analyses of punishment, such as the dichotomy between punisher and punished – offender and victim – since the children who are required to execute others are, in a real sense, also victims of oppressive circumstances. Theoretical as well as practical issues need to be addressed rather than avoided. In feminist criminology, a neighbouring field to penality, postmodern ideas have focused attention on correctional penology, state power and penal relations, which Howe maintains have suffered from a lack of theorisation (Howe, 1994, p. 165), and to which Newburn and Stanko have given impetus through the innovative collection of essays pulling masculinity and criminology together (Newburn and Stanko, 1994). These publications confirm the need to open up the territory of contemporary criminology to critical debates about such issues as the impact of feminism and the relationships between masculinities and criminology/criminal justice, let alone arriving at a consensus on the concept of punishment, which remains essentially contested (Sack, 1995, p. 49).

Arguments against punishment
The arguments against punishment referred to in Chapter 1 are firstly, moral, as for example, may be put forward by opponents of corporal and capital punishment, regardless of any research evidence of their so-called efficacy; secondly, they are pragmatic, that is, humane punishments are in the best interests of the authorities (Weschler, 1991, p. 11); thirdly, there are financial reasons to reduce the costs of imprisonment, at the start of the 1990s running annually in the USA at more than $20 000 per prisoner (Weschler, 1991, p. 7) and in Britain totally hundreds of millions of pounds per year.

Equal doubts can be raised about the effectiveness of approaches to rehabilitation as more overtly punitive methods of responding to offenders (Chapter 8). Further, rehabilitation methods themselves can be viewed as punitive, in their impact on offenders, if not in intent. Again, within penal sanctions themselves, despite the increasing interest in rational choice, neo-classical approaches to criminal justice since the early 1970s (Roshier, 1989, p. 117), there is doubt about whether more severe punishments constitute effective deterrents (Walker, 1980, p. 71).

Whether the activities of officials with various responsibilities in criminal justice systems can be rendered more accountable without simultaneously compromising their independence and ability to refuse to carry out cruel and unusual punishments, is doubtful. The tension between these will continue to be difficult to manage.

It is further possible to use reform of the law or campaigns for human rights (Gostin, 1988) as a means of pressuring for changes in punitive practices. Thus, the campaign against the use of torture in Israel included proposals in 1992 for a bill prohibiting its use, in the form of amendments to Israeli penal law (Gordon and Marton, 1995, p. 175). More radical changes may involve challenging the established political regime with the purpose of replacing it.

In few fields so much as punishment do policies and informal as well as formal practices taken so little account of research into effectiveness. Perhaps the overlap between penal theories and practice and the personal and professional values of participants in the field contribute to this. There are few people who can claim that they have no intellectual or emotional responses to questions about whether corporal or capital punishments, for example, should be used.

Treatment: attractions of so-called less punitive options?

The question is whether welfare-based approaches to dealing with offenders are less punitive and are, therefore, preferable to other more obviously punitive options. The early 1970s saw youth justice policies, in Britain, at any rate, receding from the high-water mark of social democratic consensus, about the appropriateness of developing treatment and community-based alternatives to custody. At the same time, radical non-intervention was viewed as not only attractive, but practicable, since liberals argued that most young people grew out of offending, provided professional intervention was minimised (Schur, 1963). Delinquency management (Thorpe, Smith, Green and Paley, 1980) tended to focus also on ensuring that youth justice systems were as diversionary as possible – from custody, from court and from professional involvement altogether. Such approaches attracted not only radicals, but agencies concerned to cut costs, since maintaining the boundaries of official intervention took the emphasis off the necessity to devise and implement ways of working with delinquents. In some ways, the vital necessity for positive interaction between young people and professionals was neglected at the expense of the argument that professionals were best taken out of the situation as far as possible.

In contrast, other radical, and conservative, ideologies concerning criminal and youth justice have converged, focusing on ways to make the punishment fit the crime, rather than the criminal (Adams, Allard, Baldwin and Thomas, 1981). The radical argument is that welfare approaches may act to the detriment of the offender – treatment can actually be more punitive and lead to more rapid progress up the tariff of sanctions, than straightforward sanctions matched to the offence. Also, behavioural and cognitive approaches to working with offenders have developed since the 1970s, some based on a correctional curriculum (McGuire and Priestley, 1985). The correctional curriculum for working with young offenders is one example.

A future for positive community-based initiatives?

A further strand of debate, from the late 1970s, concerns the potential for developing more innovative community-based strategies for crime prevention rather than crime control – Adams, Allard, Baldwin and Thomas, 1981). In the 1990s, Charles Leadbetter argues for strategies based on creativity rather than confrontation (Leadbetter, 1996a). These are based on self-policing, and policing practices which complement informal means of social control, rather than overriding them. The role of the police is perceived as narrower and targeted more on the specific problems the public perceives as requiring police intervention. Leadbetter joins a widespread and long-standing professional and – outside a hard core of conservatives – widespread consensus that custody, in the form of prison, is sterile and wasteful. This converges with the argument that the development of alternatives, in the form of enhanced probation supervision and community-based programmes, tends not to lead to higher reconviction rates than the continued use of prison. Leadbetter illustrates from Japan his argument that most of the work of working with offenders in the community could be carried out by volunteers. In Japan,

> reliance on non-custodial forms of punishment is possible because it has a large volunteer probation service. In the late 1980s the prison system in Japan was accommodating 69,000 inmates a year at an annual cost of 137 billion yen, while the non-custodial system was dealing with 83,000 offenders at a cost of 12 billion yen ... . In 1989 there were 900 probation officers in Japan dealing with those 83,000 offenders. however, most of the face-to-face contact was handled by 48,547 volunteers. The occupational background of these volunteers is varied, but 72 per cent

are more than 50 years old, 25 per cent are unemployed and 12 per cent are from religious groups.

(Leadbetter, 1996b, p. 17).

However, Adam Crawford of the Centre for Criminal Justice Studies, University of Leeds points out that Leadbetter's argument that communities should learn to police themselves more effectively does not take account of the facts that different communities vary in the nature of crimes committed and in their ability to organise themselves to respond to them. Crawford notes that the social polarisation and geographical concentrations of poverty and inequality in Britain contrast with Japan, where unemployment and poverty are low and relative deprivation is less extreme. Hence,

> there are dangers that the politics of community could become a by-word for social exclusion. Shifting responsibility, and hence blame for failure to prevent crime onto the public may simply mean that those who can afford to will retreat behind gated communities while those who cannot will be forced to live in increasingly dangerous places, as crime is displaced onto the least powerful sections of society.

(*Guardian*, 9 September 1996)

Returning to the spectacle of punishment in the community?
The tendency since the mid-nineteenth century for various forms of public punishment to be removed from the town square to the relatively private territory of the execution shed or prison cell, could be viewed as a civilising trend. However, it could also be seen as a functional means of discouraging the informal use of, for example, hangings by lynch mobs. Marquart, Ekland-Olson and Sorensen have argued that after 1918 the replacement of public hangings in Texas by electrocutions in execution chambers of prisons had the purpose of reducing mob violence rather than effecting more fundamental criminal justice reforms. Notably, there was no attempt made to reduce the targeting of black African descendants by such sanctions (Marquart, Ekland-Olson and Sorensen, 1994). One argument for bringing the spectacle of punishment back into the public domain is that it enables more people, through their witness, to take collective responsibility for the act of punishing.

Punishments which involve the public in showing disapproval of offenders may be regarded as a radical option for the future or as a return to a historical era when criminal justice was less professionally, and justly, managed. Thus, Leadbetter's suggestion that 'men who commit acts of violence against women could be required to make public apologies, in addiction to other forms of punishment' (Leadbetter, 1996b, p. 17), is a matter for debate. The wealth of evidence on the range of uses by the state of physical and psychological force and terror as sanctions makes it difficult to foresee any significant substitution in future for these, by informal rituals and processes, through which societies traditionally have settled disputes and grievances. In this latter category is E. P. Thompson's description of 'rough music' rituals in English villages from the sixteenth century, in which men who beat their wives and couples who married out of their age cohort were shamed out of the local community (Thompson, 1971).

STRATEGIES

We can apply more generally to punishments Hawkins's four main approaches to prison policy: the abolitionist, the rigorist, the reformist and the reductivist. One group of abolitionists, he claimed, make their claim dependent 'upon the prior achievement of other changes in social organization, changes so universal in scope and radical in nature that by comparison the abolition of prisons seems a relatively minor adjustment. (Hawkins, 1976, p. 5) Another group may seem abolitionist, but in practice are not. Rigorists generally argue for a policy of deterrence: 'a sternly repressive, vigorously disciplined, punitive regimen for the prison' (Hawkins, 1976, p. 12). Reformists argue for a more full-blooded implementation than hitherto of regimes based on correctional reforms (Hawkins, 1976, p. 16) and adequate funding, staffing, administration and community support to ensure these regimes' effectiveness (Hawkins, 1976, p. 26). Reductivists challenge the reformists' commitment to correctional treatment regimes and programmes and argue that their scope should be drastically curtailed (Hawkins, 1976, pp. 21–2). Cross, for example, expresses profound scepticism about the reformative power of prisons (Mathiesen, 1990, p. 137).

Rigorist

Approaches aiming to increase the deterrent power of sentences are well illustrated in the thinking and proposals of Michael Howard, Home Secretary in the Conservative government as this book is being written in the autumn of 1996. The foregoing chapters have offered nothing to support rigorist arguments.

One obvious means by which to strengthen punishment is to increase the risk to offenders of being caught, either whilst committing the offence, or soon afterwards. Realistically, 100 per cent certainty cannot be achieved; but there is merit in examining, for example, how policing strategies and individual responses to the risk of being the victim of crime, can be enhanced. However, the issue is complicated. Increased policing in a locality can have unintended consequences. Operation Swamp – involving a more proactive police presence on the streets of Brixton – was a major contributory factor to ill-feeling between the black community and the police, before the outbreak of the Brixton riot in 1981 (Scarman, 1981). Increased policing may also increase rather than decrease the reporting of certain, perhaps targeted, categories of offences. This may not mean offending rates have increased, so much as reflecting changed patterns of reporting by the public and recording by the police.

The introduction of security cameras and video recorders in some shopping precincts have been held responsible for decreases in recorded offences of damage and theft. But such measures may simply shift criminal activity to areas where surveillance is less continuous and effective.

The postscript to this section is a reminder of what could happen in a rigorist world. Whilst the horrors of punishment in non-Western, Second- or Third-World countries tend to be reported in detail, those of, for example, executions by electrocution in the USA tend to be largely taken for granted or ignored. The representation of fundamentalist Islam serves to highlight its severity, in contrast with the so-called civilisation of other Western countries. Although fundamentalist methods of punishment are undeniably severe, it is necessary to set the following accounts alongside accounts of executions in the USA, for example.

In Iraq, on 4 June 1994, following a decree signed by Saddam Hussein introducing the punishment of amputating a hand below the wrist for theft and for a second offence the amputation of a foot below the ankle, there were television reports of the amputation of hands and ears of thousands of offenders, targeting men who evade military call-up and army deserters. Amputees sometimes died as a result, since aftercare was forbidden by surgeons and doctors, to prevent bleeding or infection. Other punishments included the families of amputees losing part of their rations and being forced to live in special areas allocated by the government to 'cowards'. The television reports in Iraq, designed to shock people into compliance, included video footage of a man before and after his hand was amputated, allegedly for stealing a television. Offenders also had an X branded on their foreheads. The amputations appeared to be widespread, with one army deserter who had part of his·ear amputated reportedly seeing 300 people in a detention camp similarly punished (*Independent*, 13 January 1995).

In another incident from Somalia, the headline in the *Observer* over an account of 'how fast and brutal justice can be for a three-time petty thief' was 'Issa pays Islam's bloody price for stealing a shawl worth 90p' (*Observer*, 12 February 1995 p. 15). The account is beneath an article occupying the rest of the page, under the headline 'Somalia braced for new dark age', describing how the different factions are preparing to fight for power when the UN has left. It reduces to a laconic description the devastating hurt of public amputation and the additional humiliation of separation afterwards from the amputated limbs, left for the public to inspect and reflect on.

It did not matter that the prosecutor never produced the knife the young man had used to threaten Amina, before stealing her shawl and running off into the night ... . In the rising heat, Issa sat cross-legged on the courtroom's tiled floor. Witnesses were called; three men who had chased Issa through the ruins of Mogadishu ... . No knife was produced, but Issa eventually admitted that he had one ... . The judge asked the audience of 40 or 50 people how much they thought the shawl was worth: they settled on $1.50 or 90p. ... At 3pm, the court reconvened. Judge Dere flicked the copy of the Koran lying on the table in front of him. Both criminals were asked if they believed in the Koran, and whether their punishments should be those advocated within it. Yes, they both said. Judge Dere eyed the pages as he told Hussein that his punishment would fit the crime. Then Hussein was taken from the courtroom into the sandy square ... . A white plaster statue of two Aryan revolutionaries bearing a flag once stood in the square as a symbol of Somalia's past under its former dictator, Mohemed Siad Barre. When *sharia* was introduced last August, it, like all statues, was torn down for being un-Islamic. Since then there have been eight hand and foot amputations, five hand amputations, and three executions – one by stoning and two by firing squad. Beside its plaster remains, court officials took turns to whip Hussein 39 times on the shoulders, back and chest. Hussein fell to the ground and was taken to prison ... . Issa was bound with rope in a yard behind the court ... . Issa was led into a dingy room. He stared without speaking. He didn't even struggle where he lay on the floor. A man wearing a plastic apron and a while turban that covered his face, then bound his right wrist and left ankle. There was no sound. Another man joined the man with the turban in the room. Both men took 6in knives, one gripped Issa's arm and the other his leg, and both began sawing. Blood spurted from Issa's wrist, but still he said nothing. The hand came away, leaving a bloody stump, and was laid on the doorstep in its last living grip. But the foot would not come off. The man sawed for two minutes, then three, four, five, six. He had started on the top of the foot. Issa looked down to see how far the man had got. Still he was silent. The man picked up a sharper knife from the grimy floor, and sawed and pushed in the blade. Eventually only the tendon was left, and he sliced through it. Issa was carried out still conscious, put in the back of a pick-up truck and taken to hospital. His hand and foot were laid on the pedestal of the destroyed statue in the square, where people milled around and took a look. Everybody agreed that, if Somalia's anarchy was ever to be ended, people should be punished for their crimes.

Reformist

Reformist strategies, whether applied in the home, the school or the criminal justice system, tend to adjust components of situations rather than set out fundamentally to change them. In home and school, for example, the aim could be to displace punishment as the sanction for loss of good order and discipline, with mutual respect between people.

Reforming criminal justice processes
Martin Wright, until 1981 Director of the Howard League for Penal Reform, correlates the excessive emphasis on punishment in the penal system with the tendency towards an elaborate adversarial – professionally dominated and resource-hungry – court system. This leads the alleged offender to be defended whilst the victim of the crime is aggressively cross-examined, both subsequently feeling 'that they have not had a proper chance to tell their side of the story' (Wright, 1981, p. 444). Wright notes the lack of contact between offender and victim in this process and advocates the extension of schemes bringing them together in programmes of reparation, mediation or conflict resolution. Two principles of this include first, offering the offender and the victim the opportunity to feel that their respective cases have been adequately and fairly heard and an acceptable resolution reached; second, focusing not on the past but on the future (Wright, 1981, p. 445).

Relational justice
The relational justice approach seeks to emphasise the importance of relationships between people, in understanding the origins of offending and addressing the consequences of this, in terms of how they should be treated, in which kinds of institutional and community contexts; it has the

weakness that it does not proceed from a single theoretical perspective, but seeks to draw on an eclectic variety of disciplines and professions, to work at the level of relationships between individuals and groups, thereby possibly to empower victims and offenders, among others, to work together (Burnside and Baker, 1994).

In Eric Lomax's autobiographical account, this former prisoner of war finds a personal way of addressing his unresolved feelings of hatred towards his Japanese jailers on the Burmese railway a quarter of a century previously; he gets in touch with, and meets one of his Japanese torturers and challenges this man about what he did. He refuses to accept the man's rebuttal that he was simply an agent for the will of the Emperor. He asserts thereby that moral responsibility is shared by those who actually carry out punishments. A similar conceptual unity binds the activities of executioners at one extreme and the great variety of professionals in criminal justice at the other – from prison guards to chaplains and probation officers.

Reductivist

Reductivism depends on the notion of not challenging punishment *per se*, but confining existing strategies for punishment.

Typical of reductivist strategies are examples from domestic settings, such as child-rearing, where parents are persuaded to adopt non-physical and other non-oppressive ways of punishing children. This challenging task may involve parents unlearning and relearning the values and skills of parenting. A similar strategy involves declaring certain domains of society free of physical punishment, such as public areas, work areas, institutions and schools.

Given that punishment is least effective in those circumstances where more serious offences make it likely that punitive sanctions will be more severe, the need to invest in alternative, less punitive strategies becomes greater. The fact that reductivism does not aim for abolition across the board leads to some exchanges of methods without considering the fundamental rationale for the penalty as a generality. In the USA, for example, the development of high-tech executions has taken place in the twentieth century, on the claimed grounds of efficiency, reducing the pain to the offender and the horror to the spectators.

In the household, it may be more difficult to identify what should *not* be done to children; that is, abuses are more readily recognisable than the appropriate uses of punishment. Nevertheless, the effort may be made to develop a culture where non-violent responses to misbehaviour are the norm and problems are addressed and violence, on the part of adults, is not tolerated as an acceptable 'short-cut' solution.

Reducing categories of people subject to punishment
The prevalence, but the pointlessness, of the excessive use of punitive sanctions, in the face of research evidence indicating their general in-effectiveness (see Chapter 8), indicates the need to look beyond the status quo. One option is to develop a positive rationale for the use of formal and informal sanctions, not dependent on punishment. An example of this

> could involve bringing together the quartet of interests with a stake in the enterprise of criminal justice – the victims of crime, the families of prisoners, offenders and the staff working with them – to work out how contractual relationships in criminal justice could be better deployed than currently, in order for all parties to realise at least some of their claims for benefit and/or compensation. In the process, the issue of advocacy for these different interests – at present not very well articu-lated in criminal justice – would also need to be addressed.
>
> (Adams, 1996a, p. 190)

In education, there are adherents to the methods which found expression in movements for free and progressive education. A. S. Neill, founder of Summerhill school in Suffolk, has come to epitomise the values embodied in progressive schooling. John Holt, the renowned educationalist, expresses sympathy for Neill's Summerhill school, where children are treated with respect and love and offered freedom and responsibility, rather than repression and harsh discipline (Holt, 1970, pp. 85–97). Nathan Ackerman, the international authority on family therapy, expresses sympa-thy with Neill's commitment to putting love and respect for children first (Ackerman, 1970, pp. 225–49). One approach to discipline in schools, for example, is based on developing home–school contracts between teachers, pupils and their parents (Bastiani, 1996).

The progressive school movement had roots in the same utopian tradition as the therapeutic communities movement (Armytage, 1961). Dr Maxwell Jones of the Henderson hospital, London, wrote (Jones, 1968, pp. 86–116) convincingly of the theory and practice of operating a psychiatric unit along rehabilitative rather than custodial and segregative lines.

The empowerment of people who formerly would have been coerced or punished is at best a fragile enterprise in a hierarchical society, where punitive practice goes hand in hand with abusive treatment. Neill's

Summerhill and Maxwell Jones's therapeutic hospital wards remain significantly peripheral in their respective systems and isolated against the mainstream of dominant values in schooling and mental health respectively.

Abolitionist

It is acknowledged that punishments are difficult to abolish without the existence of effective substitutes, often in the face of a large retentionist majority. In Britain, a Gallup Poll in 1996 found more than two-thirds of people questioned wanted corporal punishment reintroduced to schools (*Sunday Telegraph*, 3 November, p. 1). This section, however, considers various abolitionist strategies.

Abolishing harmful forms of punishment
These include, for example, outlawing inhumane punishments such as torture, and corporal and capital punishment, which contravene human rights, inflict physical and/or psychological harm, or deprive people of having their basic needs met.

Developing alternatives to punishment
Alternative approaches, rather than punishment, include positive approaches to discipline and modelling, rather than negative, other forms of punishment. It is preferable to set clear limits to behaviour considered acceptable, rather than simply to attempt to control behaviour by punishing it.

It was noted in Chapter 2 that criminological ideas are influential beyond Foucault's focus on power and knowledge; they extend to 'the cultural and intellectual life of the societies in which they become established' (Garland, 1992, p. 412). The argument of Singer that violating animals' rights dehumanises not just the perpetrator but also the society in which the violation takes place, is paralleled by the analogy this makes possible with circumstances in which physical, corporal and capital punishment are inflicted upon a person. It follows that the study of punishment, as the history of criminology, needs to develop intellectual, institutional, social and cultural, power and knowledge dimensions, as well as encompassing its nature as cultural discourse (see Garland, 1992, pp. 412–21).

In examining the relationship between criminology and utopian thinking, Peter Young observes that much of the radical work of the 1960s and 1970s has converged with the more modest, middle ground of what is immediately attainable (Young, 1992, p. 423). He instances the shift of Jock Young from self-proclaimed 'left idealism' to 'left' or 'radical' realism (Young, 1992, p. 424).

Young's article, which amounts to a defence of radicalism nearly two decades after the publication of the first major Marxist criminological statement (Taylor, Walton and Young 1973), locates criminology in the UK in the late 1980s as at a crossroads, in the light of the success of radical criminology in the 1970s and 'the particular flair of the State-centred administrative criminology' (Young, 1988, p. 159). This set of circumstances, he suggests, has produced 'much influence of ideas despite little meld of paradigms' (Young, 1988, p. 165).

Young asserts that crime in society arises not from the defects of individuals but from 'inequality, avarice and fascism'. It is impossible, he asserts,

> to solve a moral problem in the long run without a moral solution. In the last analysis administrative criminology, Fabian positivism and conservative approaches to crime all have this failing in common. Whereas the first ignores justice, the second negates it and the third turns immorality into its own form of justice. It is only radical criminology which views justice as the core of the cause, its measurement and the control of crime and by searching for the roots of crime holds the promise of its solution.
>
> (Young, 1988, p. 180)

At its weakest, the radical tradition is still long on rhetoric and short of detailed exegesis. Thus, Quinney (1995) explores a number of dimensions of what he terms a socialist humanist approach to criminology and responses to crime. His radical response to crime is predicated on the existence of a crime-free world, 'as we act peacefully towards ourselves and one another' (Quinney, 1995, p. 148). He argues that

> punishment is not the way of peace. Responses to crime that are fueled by hate, rather than generated by love, are necessarily punitive. Such responses are a form of violence, a violence that can only beget further violence. Much of what is called 'criminal justice' is a violent reaction to, or anticipation of, crime. The criminal justice system, with all of its procedures, is a form of *negative peace*, the purpose being to deter or process acts of crime through the threat and application of force. *Positive peace* on the other hand, is something other than the deterrence or punishment of crime ... . Positive peace is the attention given to all

those things, most of them structured in the society, that cause crime, that happen before crime occurs. Positive peace exists when the sources of crime – including poverty, inequality, racism and alienation – are not present. There can be no peace – no positive peace – without social justice. Without social justice and without peace (personal and social), there is crime. And there is, as well the violence of criminal justice. The negative peacemaking of criminal justice keeps things as they are. Social policies and programs that are positive in nature – that focus on positive peacemaking – create something new. They eliminate the structural sources of violence and crime. A critical peacemaking criminology is engaged in the work of positive peace. Thus our socialist humanism, the attention given to every day existence, love and compassion, and social justice. [*sic*] Our efforts not so much out of resistance as they are an affirmation of what we know about human existence. The way is simply that of peace in everyday life.

(Quinney, 1995, pp. 154–5)

Young asserts, however, that left realism has a distinctive contribution to make, as a practicable alternative both to the Draconian scenario of increasingly punitive community penalties and ever-expanding custodial facilities to cope with longer sentences, and to left-idealism which argues for the causes of offending to be addressed.

BEYOND PUNISHMENT: ELIMINATING THE ABUSES

We need to review what is left from Chapters 3 to 7. The first question is whether some forms of punishment should be ruled out, probably largely on moral and ethical grounds, as inappropriate, inhumane or whatever. The response to this is that certain aspects of punishment *should* be eliminated, notably those which inflict irreversible and major physical and psychological harm or injury on the offender. This includes torture, aversive and punitive behavioural programmes, punitive physical constraints, corporal and capital punishments.

What does this leave? It leaves a range of activities which are non-punitive and can be considered as alternatives to punishment. It also leaves some punishments for further consideration. Prison and youth custody, for example, have crucial roles to play, if used minimally, in circumstances where, as Lea and Young put it, 'there is extreme danger to the community' (Lea and Young, 1984, p. 267). In other words, there are situations where the incapacitation of a dangerous offender is necessary. But 'where full-term imprisonment is necessary it should restrict itself to civilized forms of containment' (Lea and Young, 1984, p. 267). Lea and Young are referring here to the use of full-term prison custody only in circumstances where the dangerousness of the offender warrants it. This excludes sentencing offenders to custody as a demonstration of the anger of the community, or whatever.

The term 'civilised' needs retaining in any reshaping of the nature of prison. For those few offenders who warrant it – and they should only be few – it should be a human, humanising custodial experience. In contrast, three-quarters of the current prison population should be sentenced to non-full term imprisonment – weekend prison, or similar schemes in the community – or non-prison altogether.

But this does not address those negative features of total institutions which Goffman implies are intrinsic to their culture – such as, isolation from the community, batch living, social distance between staff and inmates, subversion of the primary goals of the institution (Goffman, 1967). Can these features be modified or are they inevitable? Would increased resources and smaller institutions contribute to a humanizing process? According to the exponents of relational justice, because such settings comprise relationships between people, some significant reforms could be achieved by improving those relationships (Coyle, 1994, pp. 122–30). But it is questionable whether the relational approach could address features embedded in the totality of the culture of the institution. The only solution might be to close down and start again with different staff, somewhere else.

Corporal Punishment

In the household, it is arguable that corporal punishment satisfies adults' feelings, for instance those of frustration, rather than achieving objective of curbing undesirable behaviour (Carey, 1994, p. 1007). This can lock adults into a spiral of self-reinforcing activity. 'As well as the parents being directly reinforced, the family system is being maintained, which in itself is reinforcing' (Carey, 1994, p. 1008). As Chapter 7 demonstrates, research does not justify punishment, either as a means of reducing undesirable behaviour, or as a method of inducing alternative behaviour. Even without considering these adverse long-term effects, children may grow up feeling that they deserved the punishments they received and this implies that when they become parents they are likely to use similar punitive strategies to those employed by their own parents, and so on *ad infinitum* (Carey, 1994, p. 1008).

A way of addressing this is to examine societies, such as Scandinavian countries, where corporal punishment has been banned by law. In such circumstances, in the school and in the family, the onus is on people to seek alternatives to violent, physical means of curbing children's unwanted behaviour. One approach is to reframe the problem and avoid targeting the behaviour of an individual, but to locate the task at the level of the family system. Thus, the emphasis shifts to developing goals by asking family members, and the family group as a whole, 'in an ideal world, what would you like to happen?' This enables family members to examine what they need to do – and what skills they may need to develop – in order to achieve this desired state. Carey refers to several examples of programmes designed to enable parents, for example, to enhance their skills and develop positive methods (Carey, 1994, p. 1008). Another approach may be to focus on empowering the person – in this case, the child – to take responsibility.

> Techniques such as reasoning, restitution, problem solving, relaxation, self-monitoring, self-evaluation, self-reward, and the application of natural and logical consequences, are all designed to shift responsibility for the behaviour from the parent to the child ... . The long-term effect of these kinds of strategies is that the child learns some measure of self-control by being allowed to take responsibility for behaviors in a positive way. Thus, the mental facilities and moral character of the child are being shaped, refined, and corrected in socially constructive ways.
>
> (Carey, 1994, p. 1008)

Penelope Leach has published guidelines for parents on what she calls 'positive discipline' without violence. This is based on the principle that cooperation and rewards are a more effective basis for learning than coercion and punishments (Leach, n.d., p. 11).

Capital Punishment

Although this book has set the parameters for an examination of forms of punishment much wider than corporal and capital punishment, these can be used as a barometer of the larger-scale incidence of punishment. In one sense, decisions by some countries to pass legislation restricting or banning the use of corporal or capital punishment offers the prospect of its more restricted use. Judicial decisions may reinforce this trend, as in South Africa, where on 6 June 1995 the Constitutional Court ruled that the death penalty contravenes the new constitution of South Africa. Until

1990, when the use of the death penalty in South Africa was suspended, that country had one of the highest judicial execution rates in the world. More than 1200 offenders were executed there during the 1980s and 453 sentenced prisoners still await execution (*Amnesty*, July/August 1995, p. 8).

ISSUES

This chapter is broader than much of the current debate about punishment, in Britain at any rate. But that is largely a reflection of the unhealthy state of that debate, at least as conducted in the mass media, with its focus on such questions as whether corporal punishment should be reintroduced in state schools. This is to deflect attention from the key questions, which should not be about whether to return to the era of corporal punishment, or capital punishment, but should focus on how to reduce the overall presence of abusive punishments still further. In doing this, three particular issues will probably need to be addressed.

First, how can we reduce punishments while curbing serious crime? Pardoxically, the reduction of the scope and level of punishments in some domains of society, such as the school, may increase demands for more punishments elsewhere, such as through punitive sanctions, including custody, for children and young people. Some teachers, for example, are likely to insist that if they no longer have physical sanctions, then more pupils whom they cannot control will need to be excluded from school and sent elsewhere as a corrective sanction. There is clearly a tension here between reducing the profile of punishments for the vast majority of the population, whilst retaining a punitive resource for a small minority.

Punishment is an ultimate act of oppression. In principle, sheer logic may define its core and set its boundaries so as to make it acceptable. In practice, the scope for corruption is broad. This brings us to the second issue.

Second, *quis custodes custodiet*? Who will guard the guards? This question is a reminder of the persistence and pervasiveness of those informal punitive practices associated with institutions processing people which are negative in character and harmful as a consequence. It is difficult to make a simple prescription capable of producing automatic improvements in this area. Whilst quality may be controlled at a minimal level, this question can best be addressed through an approach to quality maximisation, involving the empowerment of all stakeholders in a particular setting (Adams, forthcoming).

Third, there is the revaluation of people's rights. Debates about the justice or injustice of punishment take place at varying positions along the continuum between people's – whether victims or offenders – rights and responsibilities. The question is how to achieve societal situations which are likely to reduce the demands for more and more punishment. Associated with this is the need to develop policies which are less authoritarian, militaristic and less in keeping with dominant macho conceptualisations of masculinity. This is far easier to state than to spell out how it should be achieved, particularly in Britain and the USA, which, on this issue at any rate, seem to be moving away from other more liberal countries in Western Europe, notably in Scandinavia.

CONCLUSIONS

One inescapable implication of the sociological siting of analysis of punishment, is that its rationale lies beyond its more limited justification based on penal purposes.

The use of orders to deter low-risk offenders through community service and detain them through home-detention and in safe-houses may be presented as a positive option (Leadbetter, 1996b, p. 17) or as a symptom of the expansion of formal social control mechanisms into the community. Certainly, measures to outlaw psychological punishments may be termed rubber paragraphs, because of the difficulty of producing unambiguous definitions of their non-physical forms. In such circumstances, the only practicable approach is to reframe each setting so that punishment itself is outlawed from it. This is on the assumption that it is unreliable to permit punishment in a setting at all, since abuses will inevitably creep in. Ultimately, the only safe way is to exclude it. A more modest goal may be to develop versions of punishment which are reframed so as to be non-aggressive and non-harmful to people. For example, the redefinition of the identity of prison custody should involve its detachment from the traditional principles of less eligibility. If we follow the classic statement that offenders go to prison as and not for punishment, then prison custody should be no different from any other form of residential accommodation.

In any discussion of theory, the purpose should be to link in with the practice of changing penal arrangements in society. Whilst prisons are the most obvious, and iconic feature on the landscape of punishment, the foregoing chapters have considered many aspects of punishment which lie outside them. So, any project concerned with theorising the practice of penal reform will inevitably be concerned with social change in other societal institutions, such as the workplace and the family. Significant change towards reducing or abolishing punishment in one of these domains will have knock-on consequences for the others, as the history of reductions in the scope of corporal punishment in Britain since the late nineteenth century shows.

Perhaps Nathaniel Hawthorne is correct to indicate in his Boston-based novel quoted at the start of this chapter, that punishment is an inevitable feature of any society. Thus, the best we can hope to do is to minimise its harm and expense, eliminate its grossest psychological and physical abuses and thereby reduce its dehumanising consequences for all – victims, offenders, punishers and other members of society. Until the position improves, Britain and the USA will continue among world leaders in the abusive punishment of people of all ages, and regrettably, since we are collectively implicated in its continuance, of children and young people in particular.

Bibliography

Note: Place of publication is London unless stated otherwise.

Ackerman, N. (1970) 'Nathan W. Ackerman', in Hart (ed.), pp. 224–49
Adams, R. (1988) 'Finding a Way In: Youth Workers and Juvenile Justice', in
  J. Jeffs and M. Smith (eds) *Welfare and Youth Work Practice*, Macmillan,
  pp. 171–86
Adams, R. (1996a) *The Personal Social Services: Clients, consumers or citizens?*
  Addison Wesley Longman
Adams, R. (1996b) *Social Work and Empowerment*, Macmillan
Adams, R. (1991) *Protests by Pupils: Empowerment, schooling and the state*,
  Falmer Press, Basingstoke
Adams, R. (1994) *Prison Riots in Britain and the USA*, Macmillan
Adams, R. (forthcoming) *Quality Social Work*, Macmillan
Adams, R., Allard, S., Baldwin, J. and Thomas, J. (1981) *A Measure of Diversion?*
  Case studies in intermediate treatment, National Youth Bureau, Leicester
Adelson, A. and Lapides, R. (1989) (eds) *Lodz Ghetto: Inside a community under*
  siege, Viking
Albrecht, H-J. (1984) 'Recidivism after fines, suspended sentences, and im-
  prisonment', *International Journal of Comparative and Applied Criminal*
  Justice, Vol. 8, No. 2, Winter, pp. 199–207
Allen, G. F. and Treger, H. (1994) 'Fines and restitution orders – probationers'
  perceptions', *Federal Probation*, Vol. 58, Part, 2, June, pp. 34–40
Allison, W. and Fairley, J. (1979) *The Monocled Mutineer*, Quartet Books
Amnesty International (1978) *Report of a Mission to Northern Ireland,* Amnesty
  International
Amnesty International (1984) *Torture in the Eighties,* Martin Robertson, Oxford
Amnesty International (1989) *When the State Kills*, Amnesty International
Amnesty International (1992) *Repression Trade (UK) Ltd: How the United*
  Kingdom makes torture and death its business, Amnesty International
Amnesty International (1994) *Prisoners Without a Voice: Asylum-seekers detained*
  in the United Kingdom, Amnesty International
Andenaes, J. (1974) *Punishment and Deterrence*, University of Michigan Press,
  Ann Arbor
Andrews, W. (1890) *Bygone Punishments*
Anon. (1981) 'New publication: "A quarter of a million beatings"', *STOPP News*,
  August/September
Anon. (1983) 'Three quarters of a million beatings in United States', *STOPP*
  News, October/November, p. 9
Anon. (1984) '12,369 secondary school beatings in Cleveland in less than three
  years', *STOPP News*, February/March, p. 5
Anon. (1995a) 'A fate worse than death', *Amnesty International*, July/August,
  pp. 12–14
Anon. (1995b) 'Stop the deadly trade', *Amnesty*, 72, March/April, p. 9
Arasse, D. (1991) *The Guillotine and the Terror*, Penguin, Harmondsworth

Arkin, J. (1980) 'Discrimination and arbitrariness in capital punishment: an analysis of post-*Furman* muder cases in Dade County, Florida, 1973–1976', *Stanford Law Review*, 33, pp. 75–101

Armytage, W. H. G. (1961) *Heavens Below: Utopian experiments in England 1560–1960*, Routledge & Kegan Paul

Arnold, M. and Laskey, H. (1985) *Children of the Poor Clares: The story of an Irish orphanage*, Appletree Press, Belfast

Aronfreed, J. (1968) 'Aversive control of socialization', in W. J. Arnold (ed.) *Nebraska Symposium on Motivation*, Vol. 16, University of Nebraska Press, Lincoln, pp. 271–320

Arthur, J. A. and Marenin, O. (1995) 'Explaining crime in developing countries: the need for a case study approach', *Crime, Law and Social Change* 23, pp. 191–214

Atwood, M. (1980) *The Edible Woman*, Virago

Atwood, M. (1996) *Alias Grace*, Bloomsbury

Axelrod, S. and Apsche, J. (eds) (1983) *The Effects of Punishment on Human Behaviour*, Academic Press, New York

Azrin, N. H. (1960) 'Effects of punishment intensity during variable interval reinforcement', *Journal of the Experimental Analysis of Behaviour*, 3, pp. 123–42

Azrin, N. H. and Holz, W. C. (1966) 'Punishment' in W. K. Honig (ed.) *Operant Behaviour: Areas of research and application*, Appleton-Century-Crofts, New York, pp. 380–447

Bailey, S. L. (1983) 'Extraneous aversives', in Axelrod and Apsche (eds), pp. 247–83

Baldus, D. C., Pulaki, G. and Woodworth, C. (1990) *Equal Justice and the Death Penalty*, Northeastern University Press, Boston

Bamford, S. (1984) [1884] *Passages in the Life of a Radical*, Oxford University Press, Oxford

Bandura, A. (1973) *Aggression: A social learning analysis*, Prentice-Hall, Englewood Cliffs

Bandura, A. and Walters, R. H. (1963) *Social Learning and Personality Development*, Holt, Rinehart & Winston, New York

Barr, L. (1989) 'An interview with Gayatri Chakravorty Spivak', *BLAST unLtd* (Summer) p. 12 (*sic*)

Bastiani, J. (1996) *Home-School Contracts and Agreements – Opportunity or Threat?* Royal Society for the Encouragements of Arts, Manufactures and Commerce

Bean, P. and Mounser, P. (1993) *Discharged from Mental Hospitals*, Macmillan/ MIND

Beccaria, C., trans. (1769) [1764] *An Essay on Crimes and Punishments*

Behan, B. (1958) *Borstal Boy*, Hutchinson

Benenson, P. (1959) *Gangrene*, John Calder

Benthall, J. (1991) 'Invisible wounds: corporal punishment in British schools as a form of ritual', *Child Abuse and Neglect*, Vol. 15, Part 4, pp. 377–88

Bercé, Y-M. (1990) *History of Peasant Revolts: The social origins of rebellion in early modern France*, trans. A. Whitmore, Cornell University Press, Ithaca

Berkman, R. (1979) *Opening the Gates: The rise of the prisoners' movement* D. C. Heath, Lexington

240   *Bibliography*

Best, G. (1983) *Humanity in Warfare: The modern history of the international law of armed conflicts*, Methuen

Bettelheim, B. (1970) *The Informed Heart: The human condition in mass society*, Paladin

Bienen, L. B., Wiener, N. A., Denno, D. W., Allison, P. D. and Hills, D. L. (1988) 'The reimposition of capital punishment in New Jersey: the role of prosecutorial discretion', *Rutgers Law Review*, 41, pp. 327–72

Black Sash Research Project (1989) *Inside South Africa's Death Factory*, 53, publisher unknown, quoted in Vogelman, p. 195

Blom-Cooper, L. (1983) 'How abolitionists have not moved the masses', *Guardian,* 14 July, p. 15

Blom-Cooper, L. and Morris, T. (1976) 'Where hanging is no deterrent for the "crime apart"', *Guardian*, 9 April

Booth, T. and Coulby, D. (1987) *Producing and Reducing Disaffection*, Open University Press, Milton Keynes

Borges, J. L. (1970) *Labyrinths*, Penguin, Harmondsworth

Borges, J. L. (1975) *A Universal History of Infamy*, Penguin, Harmondsworth

Bose, P. (1995) 'Regulatory errors, optimal fines and the level of compliance', *Journal of Public Economics*, Vol. 56, Part 3, March, pp. 475–84

Bottoms, A. E. (1980), *The Suspended Sentence after Ten Years,* Centre for Social Work and Applied Social Studies, University of Leeds

Bottoms, A. E. (1983) 'Neglected Features of Contemporary Penal Systems' in Garland and Young (eds), pp. 166–202

Bottoms, A. E. and McClean, J. D. (1976) *Defendants in the Criminal Process* Routledge & Kegan Paul

Bottoms, A. E. and McWilliams, W. (1979), 'A non-treatment paradigm for probation practice', *British Journal of Social Work,* Vol. 9, No.2

Boyle, J. (1977) *A Taste of Freedom*, Pan

Boyle, J. (1985) *The Pain of Confinement: Prison diaries*, Pan

Boynton, Sir J. (1980) Rampton Hospital Review: Department of Health and Social Security, *Report of the Review of Rampton Hospital* (Chairman Sir John Boynton), Cmnd. 8073, HMSO

Bradley, A. (1993) 'Smacking kids', *Living Marxism*, October, p. 12

Bradley, A. G., Champneys, A. C. and Baines, J. W. with Taylor, J. R., Brentnall, H. C. and Turner, G. C. (1927) [1893] *A History of Marlborough College,* John Murray

Brantner, J. P. and Doherty, M. A. (1983) 'A Review of Timeout: A Conceptual and Methodological Analysis', in Axelrod and Apsche, pp. 87–132

Brassard, M. R., Gramain, R. and Hart, S. N. (eds) *Psychological Maltreatment of Children and Youth*, Pergamon, Oxford

Braye, S. and Preston-Shoot, M. (1992) *Practising Social Work Law,* Macmillan

Brett, R. and McCallan, M. (1996) *Children: The invisible soldiers*, A Report for Swedish Save the Children (Rädda Barnen), Sweden

Brittain, V. (1996) 'Army of children fight adult wars', *Guardian*, 1 November, p. 16

Brody, S. (1976) *The Effectiveness of Sentencing: A review of the literature*, Home Office Research Report No. 35, HMSO

Bryant, M., Coker, J., Estlea, B., Himmel, S. and Knapp, T. (1978), 'Sentenced to social work', *Probation Journal,* Vol. 25, No. 4, pp. 110–14

Burchell, G. (1981), 'Putting the child in its place', *Ideology and Consciousness*, Spring, No. 8, pp. 73–95

Burnham, J. W. (1981), 'The new orthodoxy', *Probation Journal*, Vol. 28, No. 4

Burnside, J. and Baker, N. (eds) (1994) *Relational Justice: Repairing the breach*, Waterside Press, Winchester

Byrne, R. (1992) *Prisons and Punishments of London*, Grafton

Campbell, B. (1993) *Goliath: Britain's dangerous places*, Methuen

Campbell, D. (1996) 'Howard approves "safe" CS sprays', *Guardian*, 22 August, p. 3

Camus, A. (1961) 'Reflections on the Guillotine', in *Resistance, Rebellion and Death*, New York

Camus, A. (1973) *The Plague*, Penguin, Harmondsworth

Caputi, J. (1987) *The Age of Sex Crime*, The Women's Press

Carey, T. A. (1994) 'Spare the rod and spoil the child. Is this a sensible justification for the use of punishment in child rearing?', *Child Abuse and Neglect*, Vol. 18, No. 12, pp. 1005–10

Carlen, P. (1976), *Magistrates' Justice*, Martin Robertson

Carpenter, M. 1968 [1851] *Reformatory Schools for the Children of the Perishing and Dangerous Classes and for Juvenile Offenders*

Carr, E. G. and Lovaas, O. I. (1983) 'Contingent Electric Shock as a Treatment for Severe Behavior Problems', in Axelrod and Apsche (eds), pp. 221–45

Carroll, J. C., 'The intergenerational transmission of family violence: the long-term effects of aggressive behaviour', *Aggressive Behaviour*, 3, pp. 289–99

Casale, S. and Plotnikoff, J. (1989) *Minimum Standards in Prisons: A programme of change*, NACRO

Cassese, A. (1996) *Inhuman States: Imprisonment, detention and torture in Europe today*, Polity Press, Cambridge

Catholic Institute for International Relations (CIIR) (1989) *States of Terror: Death squads or development?* Proceedings of CIIR conference on 'Death Squads and Vigilantes – Block to Third World Development', London, May 1988, CIIR

Charrière, H. (1981) *Papillon*, Granada

Chesshyre, R. (1983) 'The Texan way of death', *Observer Magazine*, 16 January, pp. 7–10

Chibnall, S. (1977) *Law-and-order News: An analysis of crime reporting in the British press*, Tavistock

Children's Legal Centre (1983) *Children in Care – The Need for Change*, Evidence and Recommendations submitted by the Children's Legal Centre to the Inquiry into Children in Care by the Social Services Committee of the House of Commons, Children's Legal Centre

Christie, N. (1977) 'Conflicts as property', *British Journal of Criminology*, Vol. 17, No. 1

Christie, N. (1982) *Limits to Pain*, Martin Robertson

Chu, C. Y. C. and Jiang, N. (1993) 'Are fines more efficient than imprisonment?', *Journal of Public Economics*, Vol. 51, pp. 391–413

Clavell, J. (1975) *King Rat*, Coronet Books

Clough, R. (1981) *Old Age Homes*, Allen & Unwin

Cobbett, W. (1957) *Rural Rides*, Vol. 1, J. M. Dent

Coetzee, J. M. (1990) *The Life and Times of Michael K.*, Martin Secker & Warburg

Cohen, J. M. and Cohen, M. J. (1992) *The New Penguin Dictionary of Quotations*, Penguin, Harmondsworth

Cohen, S. (1977) 'Prisons and the Future of Control Systems: From Concentration to Dispersal', in M. Fitzgerald *et al.* (eds) *Welfare in Action*, Routledge & Kegan Paul/ Open University Press, pp. 217–27

Cohen, S. (1985) *Visions of Social Control: Crime, punishment and classification*, Polity Press, Cambridge

Cohen, S. and Taylor, L. (1972) *Psychological Survival: The experience of long-term imprisonment*, Penguin, Harmondsworth

Compton, D. G. (1994) *Justice City*, Gollancz

Contamine, P. (1990) *War in the Middle Ages*, trans. M. Jones, Blackwell, Oxford

Cooke, J. (1995) *Light Through Prison Bars*, Kingsway Publications, Eastbourne

Cooper, W. M. (1869) *Flagellation and the Flagellants: A history of the rod*, John Camden

Coutts, J. A. (1994) 'Suspended sentences after 1991', *Journal of Criminal Law*, Vol. 58, Part 1, February, pp. 50–1

Coyle, A. (1994) 'My Brother's Keeper: Relationships in Prison' in Burnside, A. and Baker, N. (eds), pp. 122–30

Cretney, A. and Davis, G. (1995) *Punishing Violence*, Routledge

Crighton, N., Favell, J. E. and Rincover, A. (1983) 'The Side Effects of Punishment' in Axelrod and Apsche (eds) pp. 284–317

Crow I., Pease, K. and Hillary, M. (1989), *The Manchester and Wiltshire Multifacility Schemes,* NACRO

Davie, M. (ed.) (1976) *The Diaries of Evelyn Waugh*, Weidenfeld & Nicolson

Davies, M. (1979), 'Through the eyes of the probationer', *Probation Journal,* Vol. 26, No. 4, pp. 84–8

Day, P. (1983), 'Consumer and supervisor perspectives on probation', *Probation Journal,* Vol. 30, No. 2, pp. 61–3

Death Penalty Information Center (1995) *Facts About the Death Penalty*, Death Penalty Information Center, Washington, DC

Departmental Committee (1895) *Report from the Departmental Committee on Prisons*, Cmnd 7702 (Gladstone Report), Parliamentary Papers (1895), Vol. 56

Department of Health (1995) *Child Protection: messages from research*, HMSO

DHSS (1974), *Report of the Committee of Inquiry into the Care and Supervision Provided in Relation to Maria Colwell,* HMSO

DHSS (1981) *Control and Discipline in Community Homes: The report of a working party*, DHSS

Dickens, C. (1953) *Great Expectations*, Oxford University Press

Dickens, C. (1956) *Bleak House*, Oxford University Press

Dickens, C. (1971) *Nicholas Nickleby*, Oxford University Press

Dinsmoor, J. A. (1954) 'Punishment: I. The avoidance hypothesis', *Psychological Review*, 61, pp. 34–46

Docking, J. W. (1980) *Control and Discipline in Schools: Perspectives and approaches*, Harper & Row

Dodgson, C. L. (Lewis Carroll) (1993) *Alice's Adventures in Wonderland*, Ann Arbor, Ardis

Dollard, J., Doob, C. W., Miller, N. E., Mowrer, O. H. and Sears, R. R. (1939) *Frustration and Aggression*, Yale University Press, New Haven

Donaldson, Lord (1995) 'Beware this Abuse', *Guardian*, 1 December, p. 21

Donzelot, J. (1979) *The Policing of Families*, Hutchinson

Doré, G. and Jerrold, B. (1872) *London. A pilgrimage*, Grant & Co.

Dostoyevsky, F. (1965) *Crime and Punishment*, Penguin, Harmondsworth

Douglas, M. (1966) *Purity and Danger: An analysis of the concepts of pollution and taboo*, Routledge

Drakeford, M. (1983) 'Probation: containment or liberty?, *Probation Journal*, Vol. 30, No. 1, pp. 7–10

Duff, R. A. and Garland, D. (1994) *A Reader on Punishment: Socio-legal Readings*, Oxford University Press

Duodo, C. (1995) 'Hanged activists were starved', *Observer*, World, 19 November, p. 24

Durkheim, E. (1933) [1895] *The Division of Labour in Society*, trans. G. Simpson, Macmillan, New York

Durkheim, E. (1973) *Moral Education*, Macmillan, New York

Durkheim, E. (1983) [1902] 'The Evolution of Punishment', in S. Lukes and A. Scull (eds) *Durkheim and the Law*, Blackwell, Oxford

Dyer, C. (1996) 'Parents could face new restrictions on smacking children', *Guardian*, 10 September

Eliot, T. S. (1968) *The Waste Land*, Arnold

Elliot, K. W. and King, R. D. (1978) *Albany: Birth of a prison, end of an era*, Routledge & Kegan Paul

Ellmann, M. (1993) *The Hunger Artists: Starving, writing and imprisonment*, Virago

EPOCH (1993) *The Law and Physical Punishment* Briefing, December, Association for the Protection of All Children (APPROACH) Ltd

EPOCH Worldwide and Rädda Barnen (1996) *Hitting People is Wrong* and *Children are People Too*, Association for the Protection of All Children (APPROACH) Ltd

Everett, S. (1991) *History of Slavery*, Bison Books

Ewing, A. C. (1929) *The Morality of Punishment*, Kegan Paul, Trench, Trubner & Co.

Ezorsky, G. (1972) *Philosophical Perspectives on Punishment,* State University of New York Press, Albany

Farrell, W. (1994) *The Myth of Male Power: Why men are the disposable sex*, Fourth Estate

Faulkner, W. (1960) [1948] *Intruder in the Dust*, Penguin, Harmondsworth

Ferri, E. 1917 [1881] ed. W. W. Smithers, trans. J. I. Kelly and J. Lisle, *Criminal Sociology*, Little, Brown, Boston

Fischer, J. (1976) *The Effectiveness of Social Casework*, Charles C. Thomas

Fitzgerald, M. (1977) *Prisoners in Revolt*, Penguin, Harmondsworth

Fitzgerald, M. and Sim, J. (1979) *British Prisons*, Blackwell, Oxford

Flew A. (1973), *Crime or Disease?*, Macmillan

Foley, C. (1995) *Human Rights, Human Wrongs*, The Alternative Report to the United Nations Human Rights Committee, Rivers Oram Press

Folkard, M. S., Smith, D. E. and Smith, D. D. (1972) *IMPACT Vol II: The results of the experiment,* HMSO

Foot, P. (1996) 'Sir, the sadist', *Guardian*, Guardian Society, 4 September, pp. 2–3

Foote, P. and Wilson, D. M. (1979) *The Viking Achievement*, Book Club Associates

Foren, R. and Bailey, R. (1968) *Authority in Social Casework,* Pergamon Press

Foucault, M. (1980) *The History of Sexuality, Vol. 1: An introduction*, Vintage, New York

Foucault, M. (1982) *Discipline and Punish: The birth of the prison*, Allen Lane

Franke, H. (1992) 'The rise and decline of solitary confinement: socio-historical explanations of long-term penal changes', *British Journal of Criminology*, Vol. 32, No. 2, Spring, pp. 125–43

Frazer, J. G. (1913) *The Scapegoat*, Part 6 of *The Golden Bough*, Macmillan

Freeman, C. B. (1979) 'The Children's Petition of 1669', in Hyman, I. A. and Wise, J. H. (eds) *Corporal Punishment in American Education*, Temple University Press, Philadelphia, pp. 41–9

French, A. (1994) *Billy*, Minerva

Fuller, R. (1959) *The Ruined Boys*, André Deutsch

Garlan, Y. (1988) *Slavery in Ancient Greece*, trans. J. Lloyd, Cornell University Press, Ithaca

Garland, D. (1981) 'The birth of the welfare sanction', *British Journal of Law and Society*, Vol. 8, Summer, pp. 292–45

Garland, D. (1985a) 'The criminal and his science: a critical account of the formation of criminology at the end of the nineteenth century', *British Journal of Criminology*, Vol. 25, No. 2, April, pp. 109–37

Garland, D. (1985b) *Punishment and Welfare: A history of penal strategies*, Gower, Aldershot

Garland, D. (1992) 'Criminological knowledge and its relation to power: Foucault's genealogy and criminology today', *British Journal of Criminology*, Vol. 32, No. 4, Autumn, pp. 403–22

Garland, D. (1995) *Punishment and Modern Society: A study in social theory*, Clarendon Press, Oxford

Garland, D. and Young, P. (eds) (1983) *The Power to Punish: Contemporary penality and social analysis*, Heinemann

Gathorne-Hardy, J. (1977) *The Public School Phenomenon 1597–1977*, Hodder & Stoughton

Gatrell, V. A. C. (1994a) *The Hanging Tree: Execution and the English people 1770–1868*, Oxford University Press, Oxford

Gatrell, V. (1994b) 'A cruel justice', *Times Higher Education Supplement*, 23 September, p. 17

Genefke, I. (1995) ' Evidence of the Use of Torture', in Gordon and Marton (eds), pp. 97–103

Ghazi, P. (1995) 'Shell refused to help Saro-Wiwa unless protest was called off', *Observer*, 19 November, p. 1

Gibbs, J. (1975) *Crime, Punishment and Deterrence*, Elsevier, New York

Gibson, I. (1978) *The English Vice: Beating, sex and shame in Victorian England and after*, Duckworth

Gilbert, M. (1986) *The Holocaust: The Jewish tragedy*, Collins

Gilbert, M. (1994) *First World War*, Weidenfeld & Nicolson

Giller, H., and Morris, A. (1981) *Care and Discretion: social workers' decisions with delinquents*, Burnett Books

Goethe, J. W. von (1904) *The Early Life of Goethe. Books I–IX of the Autobiography*, trans. John Oxenford, Hutchinson & Co.

Goffman, E. (1967) *Asylums: Essays on the social situation of mental patients and other inmates*, Penguin, Harmondsworth

Goodstein, L. and Mackenzie, D. (eds) (1989) *The American Prison: Issues in research and policy*, Plenum Press, New York

Gordon, H. (1995) 'Political Evil: Legalized and Concealed Sadism', in Gordon and Marton (eds), pp. 11–19

Gordon, N. and Marton, R. (1995) (eds) *Torture: Human rights, medical ethics and the case for Israel*, Zed Books

Gordonstoun School (n. d.) *Gordonstoun School* (Prospectus) Gordonstoun, Elgin

Gostin, L. (1977), *A Human Condition*, MIND

Gostin, L. (ed.) (1988) *Civil Liberties in Conflict*, Routledge

Grace, J. (1975) *Domestic Slavery in West Africa*, Frederick Muller Ltd

Griffith, R. G. (1983) 'The Administrative Issues: An Ethical and Legal Perspective', in Axelrod and Apsche (eds), pp. 317–38

Griffiths, A. (1991) *In Spanish Prisons: The Inquisition at home and abroad, prisons past and present*, Dorset Press, New York

Griffiths, W. A. (1982), 'Supervision in the community', *Justice of the Peace*, 21 August

Grunsell, R. (1980) *Beyond Control? Schools and suspension*, Writers and Readers

Grupp, S. E. (ed.) (1971) *Theories of Punishment*, Indiana University Press, Bloomington

Gulbenkian Foundation (1993) *One Scandal Too Many – The case for comprehensive protection for children in all settings*, Report of a Working Group convened by the Gulbenkian Foundation, Calouste Gulbenkian Foundation

Gurr, T. R. (ed.) *Violence in America, Vol. 2: Protest, rebellion, reform*, Sage, Newbury Park

Gurvitch, G. (1945) 'Social Control' in G. Gurvitch and W. Moore (eds) *Twentieth Century Sociology*, New York

Hagell, A. and Newburn, T. (1994) *Persistent Young Offenders*, Policy Studies Institute

Hall, S., Clarke, J., Critcher, C., Jefferson, T. and Roberts, B. (1978), *Policing the Crisis*, Macmillan

Handler, J. (1973), *The Coercive Social Worker,* Academic Press

Harding, A. (1996) 'Prisoners of war for sale', *Guardian*, 28 February, p. 10

Harding, J. (1982), *Victims and Offenders,* Bedford Square Press

Harris, R. J. (1977), 'A changing service: the case for separating care and control in probation practice', *British Journal of Social Work*, Vol. 10, No. 2, pp. 433–42

Harris, R. J. (1982), 'The probation officer as social worker', *British Journal of Social Work,* Vol. 7, No. 4, pp. 163–84

Harris, R. J. and Timms, N. (1993) *Secure Accommodation in Child Care: Between hospital and prison or thereabouts?*, Routledge

Hart, H. H. (ed.) (1970) *Summerhill: For and against,* Hart Publishing Co., New York

Hartley, L. P. (1972) *The Go-Between*, Penguin, Hardmondsworth

Hatchard, J. (1994) 'Capital punishment in southern Africa: some recent developments', *International and Comparative Law Quarterly*, Vol. 43, October, pp. 923–34

Hawkins, G. (1976) *The Prison: Policy and practice*, University of Chicago Press, Chicago

Hawthorne, N. (1906) *The Scarlet Letter: A romance*, J. M. Dent

Haxby, D. (1978), *Probation: A changing service,* Constable

Heartfield, J. (1993) 'Why children's rights are wrong', *Living Marxism*, October, pp. 13–14

Heath, J. (1963) *Eighteenth Century Penal Theory*, Oxford University Press, Oxford

Hecht, S. B. (1994) 'Love and death in Brazil', *New Left Review*, No. 204, March/April

Her Majesty's Inspectorate (1978) *Behavioural Units: A survey of special units for pupils with behavioural problems*, DES

Hibbert, C. (1966) *The Roots of Evil: A social history of crime and punishment*, Penguin, Harmondsworth

Hill, P. (1991) *Stolen Years: Before and after Guildford*, Corgi Books

Hilton, J. (1938) *To You Mr Chips*, Hodder & Stoughton

Hine, J., McWilliams, W. and Pease, K. (1978), 'Recommendations, social information and sentencing', *Howard Journal,* Vol. 17, No. 2, pp. 91–100

Hines, B. (1976) *A Kestrel for a Knave* (film title: *Kes*), Penguin, Harmondsworth

Hinton, N. (1976), 'Developments in the probation service', *Probation Journal,* Vol. 23, No. 3, pp. 90–3

HM Inspector of Prisons (1994) *Report of an Inspection of Preston Prison,* Home Office

Hobbes, T. (1909) [1651] *Leviathan,* Clarendon Press, Oxford

Hobsbawm, E. (1995) *The Age of Empire 1875–1914*, Weidenfeld & Nicolson

Hodgkin, R. (1986) 'Parents and corporal punishment', *Adoption and Fostering*, Vol. 10, No. 3, pp. 47–9

Hoggett, B. (4th edn 1993) *Parents and Children*, Sweet & Maxwell

Holt, J. (1970), 'John Holt', in R. Hart (ed.) *Summerhill: For and against*, Hart Publishing Co., New York, pp. 84–97

Home Office (1938) *Report of Departmental Committee on Corporal Punishment* (chaired by the Rt Hon. Edward Cadogan), HMSO

Home Office (1968), *Children in Trouble*, Cmnd 3601, HMSO

Home Office (1969), *The Sentence of the Court,* HMSO

Home Office (1976a) *Working Party on Judicial Training and Information: Consultative working paper*, First Report of the Bridge Working Party, Home Office

Home Office (1976b) *Judicial Studies and Information: Report of the working party*, Final Report of the Bridge Working Party, Home Office

Home Office (1980), *Young Offenders,* Cmnd 8045, HMSO

Home Office (1983), *The British Crime Survey: First report* (by M. Hough and P. Mayhew), HMSO

Home Office (1984), *Probation Service in England and Wales: Statement of national objectives and priorities*, HMSO

Home Office (1988) *Punishment, Custody and the Community*, Cm 424, HMSO

Home Office (1990) *Crime, Justice and Protecting the Public*, Cm 965, HMSO

Home Office Prison Department (1964) *The Borstal Rules*, Home Office

Honderich, T. (revised edn 1976) *Punishment: The supposed justifications*, Penguin, Harmondsworth

Honig, W. K. (ed.) (1966) *Operant Behaviour: Areas of research and application*, Appleton-Century-Crofts, New York

Hood, R. (1965) *Borstal Re-assessed*, Heinemann

Hood, R. and Sparks, R. (1970) *Key Issues in Criminology*, Weidenfeld & Nicolson

House of Commons (1996) *Select Committee on Home Affairs Report on Judicial Appointments*, HMSO

House of Lords debate in the House of Lords, 5 April 1995 and November/ December 1995, about probation training, *Hansard*

Howe, A. (1994) *Punishment and Critique: Towards a feminist analysis of penality*, Routledge

Hoyles, M. (ed.) (1979) *Changing Childhood*, Writers and Readers

Hudson, B. and Macdonald, G. (1986) *Behavioural Social Work. An introduction*, Macmillan, Basingstoke

Hughes, T. (1939) *Tom Brown's Schooldays*, Collins

Hugman, R. (1991) *Power in Caring Professions*, Macmillan

Hulsman, L. (1983) 'Civilising criminal justice', address to the Annual Conference of the Howard League, unpublished

Human Rights Watch (1993) *Global Report on Prisons*, Human Rights Watch

Hume, D. (1740), *A Treatise of Human Nature*, Book III, Thomas Longman

Hunt, A. W. (1964), 'Enforcement in probation casework', *British Journal of Criminology*, Vol. 4, No. 3

Hutcheon, L. (1990) *The Politics of Postmodernism*, Routledge

Huxley, A. L. (1952) *The Devils of Loudun*, Chatto & Windus

Hyman, I. A. (1979) 'Psychological Correlates of Corporal Punishment', in Brassard, Gramain and Hart (eds)

Ibsen, H. (1960) *John Gabriel Borkman*, Hart-Davies

Ignatieff, M. (1978) *A Just Measure of Pain: The penitentiary in the industrial revolution*, Macmillan

Ignatieff, M. (1981) 'State, Civil Society and Total Institutions: A Critique of Recent Social Histories of Punishment', in M. Tonry and N. Morris (eds) *Crime and Justice, Vol. 3*, University of Chicago Press, Chicago, pp. 153–92

Ignatieff, M. (1983) 'Hanging women', *Observer: Sunday Plus*, 10 July, p. 25

Irwin, J. (1980) *Prisons in Turmoil*, Little, Brown, Boston

Irwin, J. (1985) *The Jail: Managing the underclass in American society*, University of California Press, Berkeley

Jacobs, J. (1968) [1892] *Celtic Fairy Tales*, Dover Publications, New York

Jenkins, P. (1994) *Using Murder: The social construction of serial homicide*, Aldine de Gruyter, Hawthorne

Jones, A. (1996) 'Sentenced to death', *Cosmopolitan*, March, pp. 14–18

Jones, A. H. M. (1990) *The Decline of the Ancient World*, Longman

Jones, H. (1967) *Crime in a Changing Society*, Penguin, Harmondsworth

Jones, K. and Fowles, A. J. (1984) *Ideas on Institutions*, Routledge & Kegan Paul

Jones, M. (1968) *Social Psychiatry in Practice*, Penguin, Harmondsworth

Jones, S. (1993) *London ... The sinister side*, Wicked Publications, Nottingham

Joyce, J. (1936) [1916] *A Portrait of the Artist as a Young Man*, Jonathan Cape

Jupp, V. (1989) *Methods of Criminological Research*, Unwin Hyman

Kadish, S. (ed.) (1983) 'Comparative Criminal Law and Enforcement', in *Encyclopaedia of Crime and Justice*, I, pp. 182–214

Kafka, F. (1949) 'In the Penal Settlement' in *In the Penal Settlement: Tales and short prose works*, trans. W. and E. Muir, Secker & Warburg, pp. 185–221

Kafka, F. (1966) *The Trial*, Penguin, Harmondsworth

Keith, M. (1993) *Race, Riots and Policing: Lore and disorder in a multi-racist society*, UCL

Keller, F. S. and Schoenfeld, W. N. (1950) *Principles of Psychology*, Appleton-Century-Crofts, New York

Kent Probation and After-Care Service (1981), 'Probation Control Unit: a community based experiment in intensive supervision', *Annual Report of the Work of the Medway Centre*, Kent Probation and After-Care Service

Kent Probation Service (1982), *The Kent Probation and After-Care Control Unit: the first year of operation,* Development, Information and Training Unit, Kent Probation Service

Kesey, K. (1977) *One Flew Over the Cuckoo's Nest*, Penguin, Harmondsworth

Kettle, M. and Hodges, L. (1982) *Uprising: The police, the people and the riots in Britain's cities*, Pan

Killingray, D. (1994) 'The "Rod of Empire": the debate over corporal punishment in the British African Colonial Forces, 1888–1946', *Journal of African History*, Vol. 35, Part 2, pp. 201–16

King, J. F. S. (1979) (ed.) *Pressures and Change in the Probation Service,* Cambridge Institute of Criminology, Cambridge

King, R. D. and Morgan, R. (1976) *A Taste of Prison: Custodial conditions for trial and remand prisoners*, Routledge & Kegan Paul

Korbin, J. E. (ed.) (1987) *Child Maltreatment in Cross Cultural Perspective*, Aldin de Gruyter, New York

Lamb, D. (1996) 'Prisons bring boom times to rural areas', *Guardian*, 15 October, p. 14

Lane, B. (1993) *The Encyclopedia of Cruel and Unusual Punishment*, Virgin

Lane, B. (1994) *The Butchers: A casebook of macabre crimes and forensic detection*, True Crime

Larzelere, R. E. (1993) 'Response to Oosterhuis: empirically justified uses of spanking: toward a discriminating view of corporal punishment', *Journal of Psychology and Theology*, Vol. 21, No. 2, Summer, pp. 142–7

Larzelere, R. E. and Schneider, W. N. (1991a) 'The association of parental discipline responses with the subsequent probability of a recurrence of the misbehaviour in toddlers.' Paper presented at the biennial conference of the Society for research in Child Development, Seattle

Larzelere, R. E. and Schneider, W. N. (1991b) 'Does parental punishment reduce misbehavior in toddlers? Testing predictions from behavioural vs. survey research.' Paper presented at the annual meeting of the American Psychological Association, San Francisco

Lea, J. and Young, J. (1984) *What is to be Done About Law and Order? Crisis in the eighties*, Penguin, Harmondsworth

Leach, P. (n.d.) *Smacking – A short cut to nowhere*, EPOCH

Leadbetter, C. (1996a) *The Self-Policing Society*, Demos

Leadbetter, C. (1996b) 'Get fear off the streets', *Guardian*, 6 September, p. 17

Leech, M. (1993) *A Product of the System: My life in and out of prison*, Gollancz

Lemert, E. (1967) *Human Deviance, Social Problems and Social Control,* Prentice-Hall, Englewood Cliffs

Levi, P. (1984) *The Periodic Table*, Sphere Books

Levi, P. (1985) *If Not Now, When?*, Sphere Books

Levi, P. (1987) *If this is a Man* and *The Truce*, Sphere Books

Levy, A. and Kahan, B. (1990) *The Pindown Experience and the Protection of Children: the report of the Staffordshire Child Care Inquiry*, Staffordshire County Council, Stafford

Lewin, H. (1976) *Bandiet: Seven years in a South African prison*, quoted in Vogelman, p. 184

Life in Care Conference (1981)

Light, R. (ed.) (1992) *Prisoners' Families: Keeping in touch*, Bristol Centre for Criminal Justice, Bristol

Lindesmith, A. R. (1968) 'Punishment', *International Enclyclopedia of the Social Sciences,* Vol. 13, ed. D. L. Stills, Macmillan/ Free Press, New York, pp. 217–22

Linebaugh, P. (1991) *The London Hanged: Crime and civil society in the eighteenth century*, Penguin, Harmondsworth

Linebaugh, P. (1995a) 'A current of fear to scare the poor', *Guardian*, 8 April, p. 29

Linebaugh, P. (1995b) 'Gruesome Gertie at the buckle of the Bible Belt', *New Left Review*, No. 209, January/February, pp. 15–33

Lipsey, M. (1995) 'What Do We Learn from 400 Research Studies on the Effectiveness of Treatment with Juvenile Delinquents?', in McGuire (ed.), pp. 63–78

Lipton, D., Martinson, R. and Wilks, J. (1975) *The Effectiveness of Correctional Treatment: A survey of treatment evaluation studies*, Praeger Publishers, New York

Livingstone, S. (1975) 'Implications of corporal punishment', *New Behaviour*, 25 September, pp. 490–2

Lomax, E. (1995) *The Railway Man*, Vintage Books

Lombroso, C. (1918) *Crime: Its causes and remedies*, trans. H. P. Horton, Little, Brown

London Armagh Group, The (1984) *Strip Searches in Armagh Jail*, Women Behind the Wire, No. 2, London Armagh Group

London, J. (1957) [1907] *The Iron Heel*, Sagamore Press, New York

Lösel, F. (1995) 'The Efficacy of Correctional Treatment: A Review and Synthesis of Meta-evaluations', in McGuire (ed.), pp. 79–111

Lovaas, O. I. (1987) 'Behavioural treatment and normal educational and intellectual functioning in young autistic children', *Journal of Consulting and Clinical Psychology*, Vol. 55, pp. 3–9

Lovaas, O. I. and Newsom, C. D. (1976) 'Behaviour modification with psychotic children', in H. Leitenberg (ed.) *Handbook of Behavior Modification and Behavior Therapy*, Prentice-Hall, Englewood Cliffs

Lovaas, O. I., Schaeffer, B., and Simmons, J. Q. (1965) 'Experimental studies in childhood schizophrenia: building social behaviour in autistic children by use of electric shock', *Journal of Experimental Research in Personality*, 1, pp. 99–109

Lovaas, O. I., and Simmons, J. Q. (1969) 'Manipulation of self-destruction in three retarded children', *Journal of Applied Behaviour Analysis*, 2, pp. 143–57

Lytton, Lady C. (1976) [1914] *Prisons and Prisoners: Experiences of a suffragette*, E. P. Publishing, Wakefield

MacKenzie, D. L. (1989) 'Prison Classification: The Management and Psychological Perspectives', in Goodstein and MacKenzie (eds), pp. 163–206

Maguire, M. (1980), 'The impact of burglary upon victims', *British Journal of Criminology,* Vol. 20, No. 3

Mailer, N. (1979) *The Executioner's Song: The story of Gary Gilmore*, Hutchinson

Marquart, J. W., Ekland-Olson, S. and Sorensen, J. R. (1994) *The Rope, the Chair, and the Needle. Capital punishment in Texas 1923–1990*, University of Texas Press, Austin

Martinson, R. (1974), 'What works?', *The Public Interest,* New York, March

Marvell, T. B. and Moody, C. E. (1996a) 'Determinate sentencing and abolishing parole: the long-term impacts on prisons and crime', *Criminology*, Vol. 34, No. 1, pp. 107–28

Marvell, T. B. and Moody, C. E. (1996b) 'The impact of enhanced prison terms for felonies committed with guns', *Criminology*, Vol. 33, No. 2, pp. 247–81

Marx, K. (1959) 'Capital Punishment', in *Marx and Engels: Basic writings on politics and philosophy,* ed. L. Feuer, Anchor Books, Garden City, pp. 487–89; also in Ezorsky, pp. 358–9

Mathiesen, T. (1965) *The Defences of the Weak: A sociological study of a Norwegian correctional institution*, Tavistock

Mathiesen, T. (1974), *The Politics of Abolition,* Martin Robertson

Mathiesen, T. (1990) *Prison on Trial*, Sage

Matthews, J. (1983) *Forgotten Victims*, NACRO

Matthews, J. (ed.) (1991) *Choirs of the God: Revisioning masculinity*, Grafton Books

Matthews, R. (1979) 'Decarceration and the Fiscal Crisis', in B. Fine *et al.* (eds) *Capitalism and the Rule of Law: From deviancy theory to Marxism*, Hutchinson, pp. 100–17

Maxwell, J. (1968) *Social Psychiatry in Practice: The idea of the therapeutic community*, Penguin, Harmondsworth

May, Justice (1979) *Report of the Committee of Inquiry into the United Kingdom Prison Service*, Cmnd 7673 (The May Committee), HMSO

Mayhew , H. and Binney, J. (1862) *The Criminal Prisons of London and Scenes of Prison Life,* Griffin, Bohn & Co.

McCleery, R. H. (1961) 'The Governmental Process and Informal Social Control', in D. R. Cressey (ed.) *The Prison: Studies in institutional organization and change*, Holt, Rinehart & Winston, New York, pp. 149–88

McConville, M. and Baldwin, J. (1981) *Courts, Prosecution and Conviction*, Oxford University Press, Oxford

McFarland, R. B. (1995) 'Beating the devil out of them – corporal punishment in American families', *Journal of Psychohistory*, Vol. 22, Part, 3, Winter, pp. 366–9

McGuffin, J. (1973) *Internment*, Anvil Books

McGuire, J. (ed.) (1995) *What Works? Reducing reoffending: guidelines from research and practice*, John Wiley & Sons, Chichester

McGuire, J. and Priestley, P. (1985) *Offending Behaviour: Skills and stratagems for going straight*, Batsford

McGuire, J. and Priestley, P. (1995) 'Reviewing "What Works": Past, Present and Future', in McGuire (ed.), pp. 3–34

McGwire, S. (1994) *Women Who Love Men Who Kill*, Virgin Books

McKelvey, B. (1968) *American Prisons: A study in American social history prior to 1915*, Patterson Smith, Montclair

Melossi, D. and Pavarini, M. (1981) *The Prison and the Factory: Origins of the penitentiary system*, Macmillan

Miedzian, M. (1992) *Boys will be Boys: Breaking the link between masculinity and violence*, Virago

Milgram, S. (1963) 'Behavioural study of obedience', *Journal of Abnormal and Social Psychology*, 67, pp. 371–8

Milgram, S. (1974) *Obedience to Authority*, Harper & Row, New York

Mill, J. S. (1982) [1859] *On Liberty*, Penguin, Harmondsworth

Miller, E. J. and Gwynne, G. V. (1972) *A Life Apart*, Tavistock

Millham, S., Bullock, R. and Hosie, K. (1978) *Locking Up Children*, Saxon House, Farnborough

Milner, A. (1969) *African Penal Systems*, Routledge & Kegan Paul

Mitford, J. (1977) *The American Prison Business*, Penguin, Harmondsworth

Mixon, D. (1989) *Obedience and Civilization: Authorized crime and the normality of evil*, Pluto Press

Morris, A. H., Szwed, E. and Geach, H. (1980) *Justice for Children*, Macmillan

Morris, D. (1967) *The Naked Ape: A zoologist's study of the human animal*, Jonathan Cape

Morris, N. (1974) *The Future of Imprisonment*, University of Chicago Press, Chicago

Morris, N. and Rothman, D. J. (eds) (1995) *The Oxford History of the Prison*, Oxford University Press, Oxford

Morris, T. and Morris, P. (1963) *Pentonville: A sociological study of an English prison*, Routledge & Kegan Paul

Morrissey, O. and Pease, K. (1982), 'The black criminal justice system in West Belfast', *Howard Journal*, Vol. 21, No. 3, pp. 159–77

Nabokov, V. (1959) [1935] *Invitation to a Beheading*, Penguin, Harmondsworth

NACRO Race Issues Advisory Committee (1986) *Black People and the Criminal Justice System*, Report of the NACRO Race Issues Advisory Committee, NACRO

NAPO (1981) *The Provision of Alternatives to Custody and the Use of the Probation Order*, National Association of Probation Officers

National Association of Young People in Care (NAYPIC) (1983) *Sharing Care*, Report to the Select Committee for Social Services of the House of Commons for its Inquiry into Children in Care, February, NAYPIC, Bradford

National Institute for Social Work (1988a) *Residential Care. A positive choice report of the Independent Review of Residential Care*, Vol. 1 (the Wagner Report), HMSO

National Institute for Social Work (1988b) *The research reviewed. Report of the Independent Review of Residential Care*, Vol. 2 (the Wagner Report), HMSO

NAVSS (1984) *Fourth Annual Report*, National Association of Victims' Support Schemes

Neill, A. S. (1960) *Summerhill: A radical approach to child rearing*, Penguin, Harmondsworth

Nellen, D. (ed.) (1994) *The Futures of Criminology*, Sage

Newburn, T. and Stanko, E. A. (eds) (1994a) *Just Boys Doing Business? Men, masculinities and crime*, Routledge

Newburn, T. and Stanko, E. (1994b) 'Men, Masculinity and Crime', in Newburn and Stanko (eds), pp. 2–9

Newburn, T. and Stanko, E. (1994c) 'When Men are Victims: The Failure of Victimology', in Newburn and Stanko (eds), pp. 153–65

Newell, P. (1972) *A Last Resort: Corporal punishment in schooling*, Penguin, Harmondsworth

Newell, P. (1989) *Children are People Too: The case against physical punishment*, Bedford Square Press of the NCVO

Newell, P. and Lynn, R. (1996) 'I won't tell you again', *Guardian*, 14 September, p. 4

Newsom, C., Favell, J. and Rincover, A. (1983) 'The Side Effects of Punishment', in Axelrod and Asche (eds), pp. 285–316

Newson, J. and Newson, E. (1970) *Four Year Olds in the Urban Community*, Penguin, Harmondsworth

Newson, J. and Newson, E. (1976) *Seven Year Olds in the Home Environment*, Allen & Unwin

Nokes, P. (1967) *The Professional Task in Welfare Practice*, Routledge & Kegan Paul

Northern Ireland (Emergency Provisions) Act (1973)

Nottinghamshire Probation Service (1984), *Observations on Whatton Detention Centre Discharges (Juveniles) 1983*, Nottingham

Oatham, E. and Simon, F. (1972) 'Are suspended sentences working?', *New Society*, Vol. 21, pp. 233–5

Olivier, C. (1989) trans. G. Craig, *Jocasta's Children: The imprint of the mother*, Routledge

Oosterhuis, A. (1993) 'Abolishing the rod', *Journal of Psychology and Theology*, Vol. 21, No. 2, pp. 127–33

Orr, D. (1995) 'Hutus held in worst prison in world', *Independent on Sunday*, 16 July

Oxford English Dictionary (compact edn 1979), Book Club Associates

Packer, H. L. (1968) *The Limits of the Criminal Sanction*, Stanford University Press, Stanford

Pallister, D. (1996) 'British firms still offering "shock batons" abroad', *Guardian*, 13 March, p. 4

Palmer, T. (1974), 'The youth authority's community treatment project', *Federal Probation*, Vol. 38, No. 1, pp. 3–14

Papanek, E. (1970) 'Ernest Papanek', pp. 156–173 in Hart (ed.)

Parke, R. E. (1974) 'Rules, Roles and Resistance to Deviation: Recent Advances in Punishment, Discipline, and Self-control', in A. D. Pick (ed.) *Minnesota Symposia on Child Psychology*, Vol. 8, University of Minnesota, Minnesota

Parkinson, L. (1983), 'Conciliation', *British Journal of Social Work*, Vol. 13, No. 1, pp. 19–37

Paternoster, R. (1984) 'Prosecutorial discretion in requesting the death penalty: a case of victim-based discretion', *Law and Society Review*, 18, pp. 437–78

Patterson, G. R. (1982) *A Social Learning Approach, Vol. 3: Coercive Family Process*, Castalia Publishing Co., Eugene

Payne, M. A. (1989) 'Use and abuse of corporal punishment: a Caribbean view' *Child Abuse and Neglect*, Vol. 13, pp. 389–401

Pease, K. and McWilliams, W. (1980), *Community Service by Order*, Scottish Academic Press

Phillips, B. (1994) 'The case for corporal punishment in the United Kingdom. Beaten into submission in Europe?', *International and Comparative Law Quarterly*, Vol. 43, January, pp. 153–63

Pietroni, P. (1991) *The Greening of Medicine*, Gollancz

Plato (1961) *Gorgias*, in *The Collected Dialogues of Plato*, ed. E. Hamilton and H. Cairns, Princeton University Press, Princeton, pp. 162–3

Platt, A. M. (1969) *The Child Savers: The invention of delinquency*, University of Chicago Press, Chicago and London

Potter, H. (1993) *Hanging in Judgement: Religion and the death penalty in England from the Bloody Code to abolition*, SCM Press

Powers, E. and Witmer, H. (1951), *An Experiment in the Treatment of Delinquency*, Columbia University Press, New York

Pringle, Keith (1995) *Men, Masculinities and Social Welfare*, UCL Press

Pringle, Kelmet (1974) *The Needs of Children*, Hutchinson

Prison Reform Trust (1984) *Beyond Restraint: The use of body belts, special, stripped and padded cells in Britain's prisons*, Prison Reform Trust

Quinney, R. (1995) 'Socialist humanism and the problem of crime: thinking about Eric Fromm in the development of critical peacemaking criminology', *Crime, Law and Social Change*, 23, pp. 147–56

Radelet, M. L. and Pierce, G. L. 1985 'Race and prosecutorial discretion in homicide cases', *Law and Society Review*, 19, pp. 587–621

Radzinowicz, L. (1958) *The Results of Probation*, Macmillan

Radzinowicz, L. and Hood, R. (1986) 'A History of English Criminal Law and its Administration from 1750', *The Emergence of Penal Policy*, Vol. 5, Stevens, pp. 689ff.

Radzinowicz, Sir L. and King, J. (1977) *The Growth of Crime: The international experience*, Penguin, Harmondsworth

Reed, C. (1996) 'Women put to work in US chain gang', *Guardian*, 20 September, p. 10

Regan, G. (1994) *The Guinness Book of Historical Blunders*, Guinness Publishing, Enfield

Report of the Commission to Consider Legal Procedures to Deal with Terrorist Activities in Northern Ireland (1972) (the Diplock Report), Cmnd 5185, HMSO

Report of the Committee of Inquiry into Police Interrogation Procedures in Northern Ireland (1979) (the Bennett Report), Cmnd 7479, HMSO

Report to the Government of the UK on the Visit Carried Out by the European Committee for the Prevention of Torture and Inhuman or Degrading Treatment or Punishment (1994), CPT/Inf (94) 17, Brussels

Reyes, H. (1995) 'The Conflict between Medical Ethics and Security Measures', in Gordon and Marton (eds), pp. 41–7

Richards, B. (1977) 'Psychology, prisons and ideology: the prison psychological service', *Ideology and Consciousness*, Autumn, No. 2, pp. 9–25

Rigby, R. (1965) *The Hill*, Mayflower Paperbacks

Ritchie, J. and Ritchie, J. (1981) *Spare the Rod*, Allen & Unwin, Sydney

Roberts, K. and White, G. (1972) 'The impact of character-training courses upon young people: an empirical investigation', *British Journal of Social Work*, Vol. 2, No. 3, pp. 337–54

Roberts, S. (1979), *Order and Dispute: An introduction to legal anthropology*, Penguin, Harmondsworth

Romig, D. A. (1978), *Justice for Our Children: An examination of juvenile delinquent rehabilitation programs*, Lexington, New York

Rose, G. (1961) *The Struggle for Penal Reform*, Stevens

Rose, M. E. (2nd edn 1986) *The Relief of Poverty 1834–1914*, Macmillan

Roshier, B. (1989) *Controlling Crime: The classical perspective in criminology*, Open University Press, Milton Keynes

Rossi, J. (1989) *The Gulag Handbook*, Paragon House, New York

Rothman, D. (1971) *The Discovery of the Asylum: Social order and disorder in the new republic*, Little, Brown, Boston

Royal Commission on Capital Punishment 1949–1953, Report, Cmnd 8932, HMSO

Rusche, G. (1978) 'Labour market and penal sanction: thoughts on the sociology of criminal justice', *Crime and Social Justice*, 10, pp. 2–8

Rusche, G. and Kirchheimer, O. (1968) *Punishment and Social Structure*, Russell & Russell, New York

Rutherford, A. (1986) *Prisons and the Process of Justice*, Oxford University Press, Oxford

Rutherford, A. (1989) 'The mood and temper of penal policy. Curious happenings in England during the 1980s', *Youth and Policy*, 27, pp. 27–31

Sack, F. (1995) 'Socio-political change and crime: a discourse on theory and method in relation to the new face of crime in Germany', *Crime, Law and Social Change*, 24, pp. 49–63

Sanders, A. and Young, R. (1994) *Criminal Justice*, Butterworths

Saunders, P. (1980), *Urban Politics*, Penguin, Harmondsworth

Scarman, Lord (1981) *The Brixton Disorders 10–12 April 1981: Report of an Inquiry by the Rt Hon. The Lord Scarman OBE*, Cmnd 8427, HMSO

Schama, S. (1995) *Landscape and Memory*, Harper Collins,

Scheff, T. J. (1966), *Being Mentally Ill*, Aldine

Schur, E. (1963) *Radical Non-intervention: Rethinking the delinquency problem*, Prentice-Hall, Englewood Cliffs

Scott, G. R. (1974) *The History of Corporal Punishment: A survey of flagellation in its historical, anthropological and sociological aspects*, Gale Research Co., Detroit

Scottish Home and Health Department (1985) *Report of the Review of Suicide Precautions at H.M. Detention Centre and H.M. Young Offenders Institution, Glenochil*, HMSO, Edinburgh

Scraton, P., Sim, J. and Skidmore, P. (1990) *Prisons under Protest*, Open University Press, Milton Keynes

Scruton, R. (1995) 'Why do we in Britain flinch from the ultimate act of retribution?', *Daily Mail*, 6 April

Scull, A. (1977) *Decarceration: Community treatment and the deviant*, Prentice-Hall, Englewood Cliffs

Scull, A. (ed.) (1991) [1837] *The Asylum as Utopia: W. A. F. Browne and the mid-nineteenth century consolidation of psychiatry*, Tavistock/Routledge

Sen, A. (1982) *Poverty and Famine: An essay on entitlement and deprivation*, Clarendon Press, Oxford

Serge, V. (1969), *Men in Prison*, Doubleday, New York

Shapland, J. (1982), 'The victim in the criminal justice system', *Home Office Research Bulletin*, 14

Shaw, G. B. (1922) 'Imprisonment', preface to S. J. and B. Webb, *English Prisons Under Local Government*, Longmans Green

Shaw, M. (1974), *Social Work in Prison*, HMSO

Shaw, R. (1978) 'The persistent sexual offender – control and rehabilitation', *Probation Journal*, Vol. 25, No. 1, pp. 9–13

Sheldon, B. (1982) *Behaviour Modification*, Tavistock
Sheldon, B. (1995) *Cognitive-Behavioural Therapy*, Routledge
Shipp, J. (1831) *Flogging and its Substitute*
Sillitoe, A. (1959) *The Loneliness of the Long-distance Runner*, W. H. Allen
Sindall, R. (1990) *Street Violence in the Nineteenth Century: Media panic or real danger?*, Leicester University Press/Pinter Publishers, Leicester
Singer, P. (2nd edn 1991) *Animal Liberation*, Thorsons
Skinner, B. F. (1953) *Science and Human Behaviour*, Macmillan, New York
Smith, David (ed.) (1979) *Life Sentence Prisoners*, Home Office Research Study No. 51, HMSO
Smith, D., Sheppard, B., Mair, G. and Williams, K. (1984), *Reducing the Prison Population,* Home Office Research and Planning Unit Paper 23, HMSO
Smith, G. (1980), *Social Need,* Routledge & Kegan Paul
Socolar, R. S. and Stein, R. E. K. (1995) 'Spanking infants and toddlers – maternal belief and practice', *Pediatrics*, Vol. 95, Part 1, January, pp. 105–11
Solzhenitsyn, A. (1963) *One Day in the Life of Ivan Denisovich*, Penguin, Harmondsworth
Solzhenitsyn, A. (1984) *The Gulag Archipelago 1918–1956*, Collins
Somerville, A. (1951) [1848] ed. J. P. Carswell, *Autobiography of a Working Man*, Turnstile
Sontag, S. (1991) *Illness as Metaphor and AIDS and its Metaphors*, Penguin, Harmondsworth
Sorensen, J. R. and Wallace, D. H. (1995) 'Capital punishment in Missouri: examining the issue of racial disparity', *Behavioral Sciences and the Law*, Vol. 13, Part 1, pp. 61–80
Sparks, R., Bottoms, A. and Hay, W. (1996) *Prisons and the Problem of Order*, Clarendon Press, Oxford
Spender, S. (1959) *Collected Poems 1928–1953*, Faber & Faber
Spender, S. (1959) *The Prisoners,* in Spender (1959), pp. 41–2
Staunton, D. (1995) 'A prisoner who went to live among the ghosts of Auschwitz', *Observer*, 22 January, p. 15
Stedman Jones, G. (1976) *Outcast London: a study in the relationship between people and classes,* Penguin, Harmondsworth
Stevenson, R. L. (1909) *The Weir of Hermiston*, Chatto & Windus, Edinburgh
Stewart, G. and Tutt, N. (1987) *Children in Custody*, Avebury, Aldershot
Stone, N. (1994) 'The suspended sentence since the Criminal Justice Act 1991', *Criminal Law Review*, June, pp. 399–408
STOPP (n.d.) *Corporal Punishment in Schools – Submission by the Society of Teachers Opposed to Physical Punishment (STOPP)*, STOPP, Croydon
STOPP (1980) *Review of Corporal Punishment Cases 1979*, press release issued in January, STOPP, Croydon
STOPP (1982) *The Case Against Judicial Beating: A STOPP Paper*, March, STOPP, Croydon
Storr, A. (2nd edn 1991) *Human Destructiveness: The roots of genocide and human cruelty,* Routledge
Straus, M. A. and Donnelly, D. A. (1993) 'Corporal punishment of adolescents by American parents', *Youth and Society*, Vol. 34, Part 4, June, pp. 419–42
Straus, M. A. and Donnelly, D. A. (1994) *Beating the Devil Out of Them: Corporal punishment in American families*, Lexington/Macmillan, New York

256 *Bibliography*

Straus, M. A. and Gimpel, H. (1992) *Corporal Punishment by Parents and Economic Achievement: A theoretical model and some preliminary empirical data*, University of New Hampshire, Family Research Laboratory, Durham, NH, USA

Straus, M. A. and Kantor, G. K. (1994) 'Corporal punishment of adolescents by parents: a risk factor in the epidemiology of depression, suicide, alcohol abuse, child abuse, and wife beating', *Adolescence*, Vol. 29, No. 115, pp. 543–61

Strawson, P. F. (1968), 'Freedom and Resentment', in Strawson (ed.) *Studies in the Philosophy of Thought and Action*, Oxford University Press

Summary Record of 92nd Meeting of UN Committee on Torture (1991) November, United Nations

Sumner, D. (ed.) (1990) *Censure, Politics and Criminal Justice*, Open University Press, Milton Keynes

Sutherland, A. (1898) *The Origin and Growth of the Moral Instinct*, Longmans

Sylvester, S. F. (1977), 'The dilemma of the correctional idea', *Federal Probation*, Vol. 41, No. 2

Taft, D. R. (1956) *Criminology*, Macmillan, New York

Taylor, C. G., Norman, D. K., Murphy, J. M., Jellinek, M., Quinn, D., Poitrast, F. G. and Gosho, M. (1991) 'Diagnosed intellectual and emotional impairment among parents who seriously mistreat their children: prevalence, type and outcome in a court sample', *Child Abuse and Neglect*, Vol. 15, Part 4, pp. 389–401

Taylor, I., Walton, P. and Young, J. (1973) *The New Criminology*, Routledge and Kegan Paul London

Taylor, J. and Chandler, T. (1995) *Lesbians Talk Violent Relationships*, Scarlet Press

Taylor, L., Lacey, R. and Bracken, D. (1979) *In Whose Best Interests?*, Cobden Trust/MIND

Taylor, L., Morris, A. and Downes, D. (1977) *Signs of Trouble*, BBC

Thackeray, W. M. (1898) 'Going to See a Man Hanged', in *The Book of Snobs and Sketches and Travels in London*, Vol. xiv, Smith, Elder & Co., pp. 382–96

Thompson, E. P. (1971) 'The moral economy of the English crowd in the eighteenth century', *Past and Present*, 50, February, pp. 76–136

Thornton, D., Curran, L., Grayson, D. and Holloway, V. (1984) *Tougher Regimes in Detention Centres*, report of an evaluation by the Young Offenders Psychology Unit, Home Office, HMSO

Thorpe, D. H., Smith, D., Green, C. J. and Paley, J. (1980), *Out of Care: The community support of juvenile offenders,* Allen & Unwin

Tolstoy, L. N. (1900) *Resurrection,* trans. E. Halpérine-Kaminsky, Flammarion

Travis, A. (1995) 'Bodybelt restraint "routine in jails"', *Guardian*, 16 November, p. 12

Travis, A. (1996) 'Jailhouse Britain', *Guardian,* 26 October, p. 1

Travis, A. and Dyer, C. (1995) 'Howard backs off in row with judges', *Guardian*, 2 December, p. 5

Treggiari, S. (1993) *Roman Marriage: Iusti coniuges from the time of Cicero to the time of Ulpian*, Clarendon Press, Oxford

Turner, B. (ed.) (1973) *Discipline in Schools*, Ward Lock Educational

Twain, M. (1942) [1884] *The Adventures of Huckleberry Finn*, Thomas Nelson

Tysoe, M. (1983) 'And if we hanged the wrong man?', *New Society*, Vol. 65, No. 1077, 7 July, pp. 11–13

Vakkalanka, R. (1996) 'Management of Female Offenders'. Paper presented to *Crisis in the Human Services* conference, University of Cambridge, September 1996, unpublished paper from Osmania University, Hyderabad, India

Van Yelyr, R. G. (1941) *The Whip and the Rod: An account of corporal punishment among all nations and for all purposes*, Gerald G. Swan

Vansittart, P. (ed.) (1989) *Voices of the Revolution*, Collins

Veitch, A. (1977) 'Do Britain's prisons use drugs as a means of control?', *Guardian*, 3 December, p. 11

Vogelman, L. (1989) 'The living dead: living on death row', *South African Journal on Human Rights*, Vol. 5, pp. 183–95

Vogt, J. (1993) *The Decline of Rome*, Weidenfeld & Nicolson

Voltaire, F. M. A. de (1988) [1759] *Candide*, trans. J. Butt, Penguin, Harmondsworth

Walker, N. (1980) *Punishment, Danger and Stigma: The morality of criminal justice*, Blackwell, Oxford

Walker, N. (1985) *Sentencing Theory, Law and Practice,* Butterworths

Walker, N. (1991), *Why Punish?*, Oxford University Press, Oxford

Walter, J. (1978) *Sent Away: A study of young offenders in care*, Saxon House, Farnborough

Walters, G. C. and Grusec, J. E. (1977) *Punishment*, W. H. Freeman & Co., San Francisco

Ward, D. A. and Schoen, K. F. (1981) *Confinement in Maximum Custody: New last-resort prisons in the United States and Western Europe*, D. C. Heath, Lexington

Wardle, D. (1974) *The Rise of the Schooled Society: The history of formal schooling in England*, Routledge & Kegan Paul

Wasserstrom, R. (1972) [1964] 'Why punish the guilty?', *Princeton University Magazine,* 20, pp. 14–19, reprinted in Ezorsky, pp. 328–41

Watch Report, Human Rights Watch, New York

Wells, H. G. (1933) *The Shape of Things to Come: The ultimate revolution*, Hutchinson

Welsh, D. (1969) *Capital Punishment in South Africa*, in A. Milner, *African Penal Systems*, Routledge & Kegan Paul, pp. 397–427

Welsh, R. S. (1976) 'Severe parental punishment and delinquency: a developmental theory', *Journal of Clinical Child Psychology,* Vol. 5, No. 1, pp. 17–21

Weschler, J. (1991) *Prison Conditions in the United States*, Human Rights

White, W. A. (1923) *Insanity and the Criminal Law*, New York

Wilkinson, G. T. (1991) [1828] *The Newgate Calendar*, Cardinal Books

Wilks, M. (1921) *History of the Persecutions of the Protestants* (quoted in Van Yelyr)

Williams, B. (ed.) (1995) *Probation Values*, Venture Press, Birmingham

Wilson, J. Q. (1975) *Thinking About Crime*, Basic Books, New York.

Wilson, P. S. (1971) *Interest and Disipline in Education*, Routledge & Kegan Paul

Wolfensberger, W. (1972) *The Principle of Normalisation in Human Services*, National Institute on Mental Retardation, Toronto

Wolfensberger, W. (1994) 'A personal interpretation of the mental retardation scene in light of (sic) "Signs of the Times"', *Mental Retardation*, Vol. 32, No. 1, February, pp. 19–33

Woolf, the Rt Hon. Lord Justice and Tumin, His Hon. Judge S. (1991) *Prison Disturbances April 1990: Report of an Inquiry*, Cm 1456, HMSO

Wright, D. (1973) 'The Punishment of Children', in Turner (ed.)

Wright, G. (1983) *Between the Guillotine and Liberty: Two centuries of the crime problem in France*, Oxford University Press, Oxford

Wright, K. N. and Goodstein, L. (1989) 'Correctional Environments', in Goodstein and MacKenzie, pp. 253–70

Wright, M. (1981) 'Crime and reparation: breaking the penal logjam', *New Society*, Vol. 58, No. 995, 10 December, pp. 444–6

Wright, M. (1982a) *Making Good: Prisons, punishment and beyond*, Burnett Books

Wright, M. (1982b) *Victim/Offender Reparation Agreements: A feasibility study in Coventry,* West Midlands Probation Service

Wu, B. (1988) 'Suspended sentence for torture and illegal detention', *Chinese Law and Government*, Vol. 21, Part 3, pp. 85–6

Xianliang, Z. (1994) *Grass Soup*, Secker & Warburg

Xui, X. (1995) 'The impact of Western forms of social control on China: a preliminary evaluation', *Crime, Law and Social Change*, 23, pp. 67–87

Young, J. (1971), *The Drugtakers,* Paladin

Young, J. (1988) 'Radical criminology in Britain: the emergence of a competing paradigm', *British Journal of Criminology*, Vol. 28, No. 2, Spring, pp. 159–83

Young, P. (1983) *Sociology, the State and Penal Relations,* in Garland and Young (eds), pp. 84–100

Young, P. (1992) 'The importance of utopias in criminological thinking', *British Journal of Criminology*, Vol. 32, No. 4, Autumn, pp. 423–37

Zimring, F. and Hawkins, G. (1973) *Deterrence: The legal threat in crime control*, University of Chicago Press, Chicago

Index